Theology, Religion, and Dystopia

THEOLOGY, RELIGION, AND POP CULTURE

Series Editor: Matthew Brake

The *Theology, Religion, and Pop Culture* series examines the intersection of theology, religion, and popular culture, including, but not limited to television, movies, sequential art, and genre fiction. In a world plagued by rampant polarization of every kind and the decline of religious literacy in the public square, *Theology, Religion, and Pop Culture* is uniquely poised to educate and entertain a diverse audience utilizing one of the few things society at large still holds in common: love for popular culture.

Titles in the Series

Theology, Religion, and Dystopia, edited by Scott Donahue-Martens and Brandon Simonson

Theology and H.P. Lovecraft, edited by Austin M. Freeman

Theology and Breaking Bad, edited by David K. Goodin and George Tsakiridis

Theology and the Star Wars Universe, edited by Benjamin D. Espinoza

Theology and Black Mirror, edited by Amber Bowen and John Anthony Dunne

Dread and Hope: Christian Eschatology and Pop Culture, by Joshua Wise

Theology and the Game of Thrones, edited by Matthew Brake

Theology and Spider-Man, edited by George Tsakiridis

René Girard, Theology, and Pop Culture, edited by Ryan G. Duns and T. Derrick Witherington

Theology and Horror: Explorations of the Dark Religious Imagination, edited by Brandon R. Grafius and John W. Morehead

Sports and Play in Christian Theology, edited by Philip Halstead and John Tucker

Theology and Westworld, edited by Juli Gittinger and Shayna Sheinfeld

Theology and Prince, edited by Jonathan H. Harwell and Rev. Katrina E. Jenkins

Theology and the Marvel Universe, edited by Gregory Stevenson

Theology, Religion, and Dystopia

Edited by

Scott Donahue-Martens
Brandon Simonson

LEXINGTON BOOKS/FORTRESS ACADEMIC
Lanham • Boulder • New York • London

Published by Lexington Books/Fortress Academic
Lexington Books is an imprint of The Rowman & Littlefield Publishing Group, Inc.
4501 Forbes Boulevard, Suite 200, Lanham, Maryland 20706
www.rowman.com

86-90 Paul Street, London EC2A 4NE, United Kingdom

Copyright © 2022 by The Rowman & Littlefield Publishing Group, Inc.

All rights reserved. No part of this book may be reproduced in any form or by any electronic or mechanical means, including information storage and retrieval systems, without written permission from the publisher, except by a reviewer who may quote passages in a review.

British Library Cataloguing in Publication Information Available

Library of Congress Cataloging-in-Publication Data Available

ISBN 978-1-9787-1329-1 (cloth) | ISBN 978-1-9787-1331-4 (pbk)
 | ISBN 978-1-9787-1330-7 (ebook)

Contents

Preface ... vii

Chapter 1: Dystopia as Demythologized Apocalyptic ... 1
Brandon Simonson and Scott Donahue-Martens

Chapter 2: The Dystopic Relations of *Interstellar*: A Response from Christian Ecotheology ... 29
Thomas G. Hermans-Webster

Chapter 3: Color-blind Dystopia: *The Giver*, Theology, Race, and Ricoeur ... 43
Scott Donahue-Martens

Chapter 4: Qu(e)erying Posthuman Theologies in *Ghost in the Shell* ... 61
Amanda L. Pumphrey and Nicholaus B. Pumphrey

Chapter 5: Social Life from Scratch: Morality, Religion, and Society in *The Walking Dead* ... 75
Justin F. Martin

Chapter 6: How NOT to Be a Zombie: *The Walking Dead* and Love for the World ... 89
David Penn

Chapter 7: Dystopia in the Apocalypse: Religion and Community in Asimov's *Foundation* Universe ... 103
Brandon Simonson

Chapter 8: Katniss, Christos: Sacrifice and Salvation in Scripture and Young Adult Dystopian Novels ... 119
Shayna Sheinfeld

Chapter 9: Dystopian Festivals, Utopian Fictions: Sovereignty,
　　Sacrifice, and Sanctity in Biblical Jubilee and *The Purge*　　135
　　C. J. McCrary

Chapter 10: The Ability or Inability to Change by the Presence or
　　Absence of *Deus ex Machina*　　149
　　Beáta Gombkötő

Chapter 11: The Spectacle of Hope beyond Capital's Dehumanizing
　　Violence: Reading George Lucas's Dystopian *THX 1138*　　163
　　John C. McDowell

Epilogue　　181

Index　　189

About the Editors and Contributors　　193

Preface

There are perhaps fewer apt times for a book-length study of the intersections of theology, religion, and dystopia than during a global pandemic. The COVID-19 pandemic in which the world currently finds itself frequently reminds us of science's incredibly constructive power, its destructive capabilities, and its limitations. The COVID-19 era witnessed attempts of overthrowing governments, the continuing rise of economic disparity, global supply shortages, military invasions, increased integration and use of technology, and the persistent rise of misinformation. Human frailty and ingenuity were tested simultaneously through this dystopian crucible that initially distinguished people as either essential or nonessential; freedom to work and, therefore, survive was given to the essential workers while the nonessential workers of the world were furloughed. In addition, some political cycles around the globe have resulted in restricted rights and limited basic freedoms.

Dystopia and dystopian themes have risen in popularity and prevalence in popular culture, especially in the years after Hurricane Katrina made landfall in 2005.[1] Suzanne Johnson noted this fact about Katrina in an article for TOR publishing, calling Katrina a critical moment for American authors. On the increased popularity in dystopian works, Johnson writes:

> It's not too hard to understand. The world has had its share of catastrophic events since August 29, 2005, but the images from Katrina, particularly scenes from the long, agonizing drowning of New Orleans, gave us all our first real look at something we'd only imagined before. We saw an American city reduced to chaos, despair, and death. We saw a failure of government. We saw a gut-checking picture of the underbelly of poverty and racial divides that we as a society are all too eager to sweep under the rug. We saw how very quickly our own society could descend into violence and street justice. We saw an American dystopia. Even for authors who weren't among us living the story, the images were impactful.[2] In the first quarter of the twenty-first century, works of dystopian fiction have been written and reimagined as screenplays for blockbuster films and television series in theaters and online streaming services.

In the wake of difficult and tragic world events, humankind has maintained an interest in dystopia.

In the past decade, readers and viewers have been captivated by Katniss's triumph over the capitol in *The Hunger Games*, June's daring escape from Gilead in the Hulu adaptation of *The Handmaid's Tale*, and Wade's journey to another realm through the immersive technology in *Ready Player One*. Beyond aesthetic enjoyment and escapism, dystopia provides a vivid intersection for theological and religious reflection and constructive work. This volume explores some of these vivid intersections that exist among the academic study of theology, religion, and the dystopia genre in popular culture.

Augustine once said that he understood time as long as no one asked him to explain time, writing: "What is time then? If no one asks me, I know. If I would like to explain it to him who asked, I do not know."[3] We suspect Augustine's experience with defining time might resemble how many people engage dystopia. Most people have an intuitive understanding of dystopia that allows it to be recognized yet escape precise articulation. Dystopia is far easier to name than it is to define, even as it often places uncomfortable realities before its reader or viewer. The adjective "dystopian" is thrown around with relative ease on social media, but this casual use of the adjective only breeds familiarity with a disturbingly hazy concept.

In order to clear the air of this haze, this preface serves to orient the reader to the primary contributions of the included chapters and the overall aim of their initial collection.

OVERVIEW OF THE CHAPTERS

As we planned the shape of this volume, we decided against prescribing a single definition of dystopia or a specific critical method of its engagement to the contributors. Instead, we invited each contributor to write their chapter with some engagement of a critical understanding of dystopia and include its concise definition in their work. While a single prescribed definition might have offered clarity and unity to the volume as a whole, we wanted to offer maximal flexibility to the contributors. Dystopia is not an easy term to define and there are many facets to the generic category that a pithy definition would minimize. Instead of one deductive definition, you will encounter many inductive uses of dystopia in these pages.[4] We wanted the authors to bring their diverse perspectives, situations, and insights to the volume in a way that honored their social locations. We hope that the preface and first chapter provide enough depth and perspective to engage the following chapters.

In keeping with the spirit of the series title—Theology, Religion, and Pop Culture—and following a chapter with a greater overview of dystopia studies, this volume is arranged in two parts: chapters that follow theological approaches to the study of dystopia and chapters that follow approaches to the study of dystopia that are grounded in the academic fields of Biblical and Religious Studies. This structure is not meant to be limiting, and several common themes are present in both parts. Readers are free to experience the chapters and parts of the book in the order they see fit. The chapters could have been arranged in several different permutations, but reading them in the order we suggest does present some continuities.

The first chapter, titled "Dystopia as Demythologized Apocalyptic" and co-written by the editors Brandon Simonson and Scott Donahue-Martens, is not intended to be an exhaustive or comprehensive review of the literature included amongst works of the "dystopia" genre in popular culture, to define dystopia or dystopian themes, or to solve scholarly debates on the academic study of dystopia. Instead, the editors hope to provide readers with a basic understanding of the critical study of dystopia so that readers can engage with dystopia as it is presented in both the following chapters and popular culture generally construed. In other words, this chapter aims to orient the reader to major concepts and concerns in dystopian studies and direct them toward important religious and theological intersections. After exploring ways in which dystopia resists neat distinctions and after offering some constructive understandings of dystopia, the first chapter moves to consider what is distinct about dystopian narrative representation and formation. The chapter proposes that the rise of dystopian narratives in popular culture reflects the increasingly dystopian manners in which people across the world are experiencing reality. This allows the reader to consider how the academic disciplines of theology and religious studies inform or respond to dystopian phenomena. In the end, Donahue-Martens and Simonson make a contribution to dystopia studies by proposing that dystopia might be understood as a type of demythologized apocalyptic.

At the beginning of the first part of the book, both chapters 2 and 3 foreground ways in which dystopia invites readers to consider social relating in the world. The second chapter, titled "The Dystopic Relations of *Interstellar*: A Response from Christian Ecotheology," is by Thomas G. Hermans-Webster and discusses dystopia through the movie *Interstellar*. Hermans-Webster explores intersections between eco-theology and the film in order to reconsider planetary well-being and salvation. He hopes that enough time remains to address anthropogenic climate change before the present eco-dystopia intensifies. With rich theological implications, the chapter underscores the planetary web of interconnectedness within which humankind both exists and cannot escape as a part of the created order. Hermans-Webster challenges

Christians to live into the centrality of the Eucharist by considering the sacraments' *earthly* origins as sustenance on a table. The third chapter, titled "Color-blind Dystopia: *The Giver*, Theology, Race, and Ricoeur," explores Lois Lowry's book *The Giver* and the color-blind approach to race in the racialized United States. In this chapter, Scott Donahue-Martens discusses critical functions of memory and forgetting as they concern false utopic promises that preserve dystopic ideologies and realities. The narrative of Cain and Abel serves as a metaphor for more liberative ways of doing theology in connection with histories of the oppressed. Through the work of Paul Ricoeur and the notion of habitus, Donahue-Martens reveals what is at stake in the United States' national debates over history and color-blindness.

In the fourth chapter, titled "Qu(e)erying Posthuman Theologies in *Ghost in the Shell*," Amanda Pumphrey and Nicholaus Pumphrey conduct an intertextual and theological discussion of *Ghost in the Shell* by qu(e)erying posthuman theologies. The chapter contains an especially rich conversation around what it means to be human through body-less manners in a world of increasing technological integration. The chapter correlates Christian normativity, questions surrounding body-mind dualism, and cybernetics in the cyberpunk subgenre with postmodern, queer, and feminist theories and theologies.

The final two chapters in the first part foreground the popular television series *The Walking Dead*. Each chapter discusses the productive capacity of watching a dystopian zombie show on human development. In chapter 5, titled "Social Life from Scratch: Morality, Religion, and Society in *The Walking Dead*," Justin Martin follows Johannes van der Ven in an interactionist approach to morality. He discusses the complexity of morally laden social interactions and religious beliefs through the concept of dystopia and the character Gabriel. Because Gabriel is a priest, his beliefs and actions are especially conducive to the interactionist approach of the chapter. The dystopian situation presented in *The Walking Dead* is morally rife for considering human character, development, and morality. In chapter 6, titled "How NOT to be a Zombie: *The Walking Dead* and *Love for the World*," David Penn invites us to listen to the eternity ghosts haunting popular culture. He recognizes significant shifts that mean ultimate questions are happening with greater frequency around screens rather than congregational settings. Penn wants to avoid the gradual dystopic creep toward zombification through an embrace of wonder, life, and love.

At the start of the second part of the book, two chapters take up the relationship between dystopia and apocalyptic literature. In chapter 7, titled "Dystopia in the Apocalypse: Religion and Community in Asimov's *Foundation* Universe," Brandon Simonson writes about the role of dystopian themes in ancient and modern apocalyptic texts. Arguing that Isaac Asimov's *Foundation* series is a modern form of apocalyptic literature, Simonson explores dystopian elements as they function to form communal and religious identity after the experience of injustice in the same way that they do in ancient apocalyptic works. In chapter 8, titled "Katniss, Christos: Sacrifice and Salvation in Scripture and Young Adult Dystopian Novels," Shayna Sheinfeld explores the role of self-sacrifice in ancient and modern works that might be considered dystopian in nature. Reading two contemporary young adult dystopian trilogies *The Hunger Games* and *Divergent* alongside two first century CE texts *The Testament of Moses* and *Hebrews*, Sheinfeld argues that willing self-sacrifice serves as a path to individual and communal salvation in both ancient and modern literature.

In chapter 9, titled "Dystopian Festivals, Utopian Fictions: Sovereignty, Sacrifice, and Sanctity in Biblical Jubilee and *The Purge*," C.J. McCrary writes about extravagant festivals in the annual calendar, the dystopian themes within them, and the concept of the sovereign in ancient and modern works. McCrary argues that the sacrificial rites in *The Purge* and the biblical stories of the Jubilee and the Sabbatical speak to the necessity and holiness of the sovereign power. In this way, sacrifice makes sovereign power sacred.

The final two chapters consider fascinating themes of human catharsis in dystopian narratives. In chapter 10, titled "The Ability or Inability to Change by the Presence or Absence of *Deus ex Machina*," Beáta Gombkötő explores how the concept of *Deus ex Machina* operates in dystopian works, especially as its presence or absence might either deliver or prevent catharsis in the human actors of that dystopian work. Gombkötő investigates the presence and absence of *Deus ex Machina* in the novels of Hungarian authors György Dragomán (*The White King*) and János Térey (*The Shortest Ice Age*), bringing a fresh perspective on an otherwise Western iteration of dystopia from behind the Iron Curtain. In chapter 11, titled "The Spectacle of Hope Beyond Capital's Dehumanizing Violence: Reading George Lucas's Dystopian *THX 1138*," John McDowell addresses how Lucas's movie *THX 1138* imagines hope. McDowell argues that the film functions as a critical dystopia when it does not offer a possibility for cathartic resolution.

Individually, the chapters in this volume represent diverse approaches, methodologies, and perspectives on dystopia.[5] As a whole, the volume contributes to discussions in the study of Theology, Religion, and Dystopia more generally construed. We invite the reader to make their own connections between these individual contributions first and review the editors' connections in the Epilogue last.

NOTES

1. According to Google Trends, the search term "dystopian" was at an all-time peak at the start of the pandemic from 24 March to 4 April 2020. The search term "apocalyptic" was also at an all-time peak the week of 22–28 March 2020. "Dystopia," on the other hand, had never been searched more than in the wake of Hurricane Katrina in 2005. Google Trends, accessed 27 May 2022, https://trends.google.com/trends/explore?date=all&q=dystopia,dystopian,apocalyptic.

2. Suzanne Johnson, "Hurricane Katrina: Dystopia, in Real Time," TOR.com, 28 August 2015, https://www.tor.com/2015/08/26/hurricane-katrina-dystopia-in-real-time/.

3. Translation of Augustine's Confessions XI, 14 by the editors from the Latin in Augustine of Hippo, *St. Augustine's Confessions* (London: William Heinemann, 1912), 238.

4. Due to the multiple and varied definitions of the term "dystopia" and its function as a generic category, we the editors of this volume decided early in the process of soliciting contributions that we would ask each contributor to define dystopia in their own words and based on their own academic disciplines. Look to each individual chapter for each individual author's concise definition and understanding of dystopia. We recognize the foundational work of Gregory Claeys in defining the genre throughout history and suggested our contributors review his work as they completed their chapters.

5. Yet most kinds of dystopia outlined in this book are clearly *western* iterations of dystopia. This is more clearly addressed in chapter 1 below, but it is important to acknowledge the relative limitations of a volume of this size and scope.

BIBLIOGRAPHY

Augustine of Hippo. *St. Augustine's Confessions.* London: William Heinemann, 1912.
Google Trends. Accessed 27 May 2022. https://trends.google.com/trends/explore?date=all&q=dystopia,dystopian,apocalyptic.
Johnson, Suzanne. "Hurricane Katrina: Dystopia, in Real Time." TOR.com. 28 August 2015. https://www.tor.com/2015/08/26/hurricane-katrina-dystopia-in-real-time/.

Chapter 1

Dystopia as Demythologized Apocalyptic

Brandon Simonson and Scott Donahue-Martens

Literary works help humanity make sense of experiences. Understanding aspects of the literary genre, and the concepts upon which the genre depends, can deepen the resulting experience of reading and understanding that text. This chapter reads the dystopia genre as a demythologized version of the apocalyptic genre. It mutually relates the ancient apocalyptic genre and modern dystopia genre through Bultmann's existential approach of demythologization. The result is a greater understanding of how the two genres can lead to responsible human action and change in the present for well-being. The chapter begins by describing dystopia, especially by discussing its various roles, functions, and related concepts. It then turns to discuss narrative dystopia in the wake of rising dystopian experiences in the twenty-first century. Then, the chapter discusses Bultmann's concept of demythologization before turning to apocalyptic. The chapter includes references to many dystopian and apocalyptic works but does not focus on any one work in particular.[1]

DYSTOPIA: DEFINITION, ROLE, AND FUNCTION

Even beyond the various uses of dystopias in scholarship and popular culture, scholars do not agree on definitions for utopia and dystopia. The various definitions of the term "dystopia" contain an almost equal number of varying nuances or emphases. Dystopia is "derived from two Greek words, *dus* and *topos*, meaning a diseased, bad, faulty, or unfavorable place."[2] To a large extent, dystopia functions to describe real or imagined places or events which are deemed as bad, negative, or beyond the control of humankind. Generally, "the word 'dystopia' evokes disturbing images."[3] Whether it is "the ancient myths of the Flood," the "Divine wrath . . . of the Apocalypse," or "miles of barbed wire broken by guard towers topped with machine guns and searchlights," Gregory Claeys writes, dystopia frightens people and society with known and unknown destruction, degradation, and degeneration.[4] Despite the lack of a single, scholarly definition of the term, "dystopia" is overwhelmingly associated with negative aspects of reality or the imagination.

Common understandings of dystopia that derive from historical and literary sources are often employed to increase the negative perception of all things labeled "dystopian."[5] Even the mere mention of George Orwell's novel *1984* can intensify a negative perception of an unrelated event if used to describe that event.[6] Though there are ancient examples of dystopian themes, dystopia is largely a modern category. It is anachronistic to argue that ancient humans wrote or imagined dystopia like that characteristic of modernity because the concept of dystopia developed in the nineteenth and twentieth centuries of the common era. Of course, ancient writers engaged in imaginative exercises similar to those characteristic of the modern concept of dystopia; these imaginative exercises are especially apparent in ancient apocalyptic, religious, and philosophical writings. Medieval writers also engaged similar imaginative functions in writings about demons, witchcraft, and the monstrous.[7] But it is not a coincidence that dystopia rose to prominence during the general Western shift to philosophical, theological, and religious rationalism.[8] As philosophers and theologians engaged the breakdown of the three-tiered universe, dystopia became a more natural concept that could be used to imagine, interpret, and understand aspects of reality and experience. Coupled with the rise of totalitarian forms of governance, the breakdown of a unified Western religious system for understanding reality created anxiety about the future and human relating which found expression in dystopian literature.[9] Claeys contends, "most of what we associate with 'dystopia' is thus a modern phenomenon, wedded to secular pessimism."[10] Without trust in a direction of history or an *other*, like a god or a divine entity, popular imagination opened spaces where the future is unknown and anxiety-producing.

There is no collective, objective agreement on what a "bad place" is or would be. One person's utopia might contain elements that are dystopian for another. Even more sinister, perhaps, is the reality that utopia for some typically means a dystopia for others. Those familiar with the NBC television show *The Good Place* will readily recognize this last point about how the same place, *topia*, can simultaneously be u-*topia* for some and dys-*topia* for others. *The Good Place* begins in the Good Place, a post-Christian sitcom version of heaven filled with frozen yogurt, the ability to fly, and idealized suburban houses. The toponym "Good Place" itself is meant to evoke imagery of a paradisal afterlife to reward those who have led an ethical life.[11] The overseer of the Good Place, known as the Architect, is tasked with ensuring the happiness of the residents as they live in the afterlife. As the first season unfolds, however, four characters come to realize that they do not belong in the Good Place as they did not live ethical lives. These four main characters fall prey to a series of bad events and mishaps that are ultimately blamed on these four people, one of whom was a moral philosopher who teaches ethics and morals to the main character. The twist of the season finale reveals that the Good Place was actually the demon's experimental realm, constructed in order to discover new ways to torment people in the afterlife. Thus, the Good Place was *good* for the demons running the neighborhood and *bad* for the four humans caught in the experience. Additionally, *The Good Place* plays with a common dystopian device: dystopia as a failed utopia. While *The Good Place* blurs the lines of the dystopia as failed utopia device for the viewer, many dystopian works are more explicit in showcasing how efforts at creating a better society, or a good place, end up becoming dystopian.

Because dystopia and utopia are relative terms, orienting through utopia and dystopia can be difficult. Claeys uses "a spectrum of anxiety, with relative peace, friendship, and the absence of fear at one end, matched by anxiety, paranoia, and alienation on the other" to understand how the terms relate in particular instances.[12] In many dystopian works, there is a "push and pull between utopian and dystopian perspectives."[13] Dystopia often thrives on the back of failed promises or seemingly beneficial trajectories that become malevolent when given totalizing opportunities. This underscores the necessity to discuss utopia, no place or good place, in order to understand dystopia, bad place.

The definition of the term "utopia" is not as clear as it might seem. While dystopia is quite clearly transliterated from the Greek *dus* (δυς) and *topos* (τοπος), "bad place," utopia is not so easily transliterated. There are two distinct possibilities of this term's Greek components: the Greek *ou* (ου) and *topos* (τοπος), meaning "no place," and the Greek *eu* (ευ) and *topos* (τοπος), meaning "good place."[14] While the first recorded use of the term "utopia" was based on historical meaning and etymology just as it does on the former transliteration of *ou* and *topos*, the definition of a word is also dependent on popular usage. Merriam-Webster establishes its definitions of English words based on contemporary and popular usage.[15] The meaning of the word changes as its usage changes. All recent examples listed by Merriam-Webster establish the use of the English word "utopia" in the camp of the latter transliteration, *eu* and *topos* "good place."[16] Some scholars use the term "utopia" to refer to a "no place" and "eutopia" to refer to a "good place," but the use of the "eutopia" spelling is inconsistent. Utopia and eutopia are functionally similar, both terms expressing a "good place" with a singular qualifier: *good for whom*?

Both utopia and dystopia are connected and frequently juxtaposed as opposites in popular opinion. Yet, as Douwe Fokkema opines, "what one may consider eutopian, the other may call dystopian, and vice versa."[17] In addition, many authors blur distinctions between utopia and dystopia within narratives in ways that resist simple definitions. Some works are clearly dystopian *and* utopian.[18] On the relationship between dystopia and utopia, Claeys proffers "the hypothesis that utopia and dystopia evidently share more in common than is often supposed. Indeed, they might be twins, the progeny of the same parents."[19] Thus, one way of understanding more about dystopia is to put it in direct relation with utopia.

While examples or visions of utopia, like Eden in Genesis or in Plato's *Republic*, exist in ancient literature, Sir Thomas More coined the term in his sixteenth-century book, *Utopia*.[20] More's *Utopia*, following the *ou* and *topos* "no place" transliteration, takes place on a fictional island which separated itself from the mainland.[21] The book presents a safe community without private property, tolerant religious communities, six-hour work days, and stability.[22] Characteristic of Renaissance utopias in general, More's Utopia is a model of the kind of promise a rational reorientation of populations and resources poses to Renaissance communities.[23] In this way, utopias that followed More's *Utopia* recognize the potential in society especially when that society might be rearranged according to rationality typical of Renaissance thought. Yet, lurking behind this utopian stability are dystopian realities. On the maintenance of utopias, Claeys writes, "*Utopia*'s peace and plenitude now seem to rest upon war, empire, and the ruthless suppression of others, or in other words, their dystopia."[24] This underscores the complexity of utopia and dystopia as distinct yet interrelated concepts.

Lyman Sargent offers one taxonomy of terms that can help distinguish utopia and dystopia, as well as additional concepts.[25] We offer these taxonomic definitions not as the final word on the topic but in the hope that they offer baseline vocabulary with which to conceive of the otherwise abstract terms in a clear and concise manner. Sargent writes that these understandings are meant to be "porous" boundaries, not restrictive and rigid understandings.[26] Sargent defines utopia as "a nonexistent society described in considerable detail and normally located in time and space that the author intended a contemporaneous reader to view as considerably better than the society in which that reader lived."[27] The definition for dystopia is almost exactly the same; however, it replaces "better" with "worse."[28] Related terms include: *utopianism*, which is defined as "social dreaming"; *utopian satire*, which is defined as a work providing "a criticism of that contemporary society"; *anti-utopia*, which is defined as a work where the "author intended a contemporaneous reader to view as a criticism of utopianism or of some particular eutopia"; and *critical utopia*, which is defined as a work where the author intends readers to view a society "better than contemporary society but with difficult problems that the described society may or may not be able to solve and which takes a critical view of the utopian genre."[29]

While debated, it is necessary to mention that Sargent and other scholars also use the term "critical dystopia." On one hand, Sargent believes the term might be superfluous as he perceives a critical element in all dystopias.[30] On the other hand, Moylan argues that the term helps distinguish the degree to which dystopian works are "emancipatory, militant, open and 'critical' and those that are compensatory, resigned, and quite 'anti-critical.'"[31] We believe Moylan's statement still holds merit concerning the place of critical dystopia. Nuancing the term "critical," Moylan writes that "recent dystopias are strongly, and more self-reflectively, 'critical' does not suggest the appearance of an entirely new generic form but rather a significant retrieval and refunction of the most progressive possibilities inherent in dystopian narrative. The new texts, therefore, represent a creative move that is both a continuation of the long dystopian tradition and a distinctive new intervention."[32] What seems to be distinct about newer forms in the vein of critical dystopia is the sense of urgency to change before impending disaster. Moylan also argues for the appropriateness of the term "critical dystopia" with regard to the response of readers, writing:

> Critical dystopias give voice and space to such disposed and denied subjects [so that] they go on to explore ways to change the present system so that such culturally and economically marginalized people not only survive but also try to move toward creating a social reality that is shaped by an impulse to human self-determinism and ecological health rather than one constricted by the narrow and destructive logic of a system intent only on enhancing competition in order to gain more profit for a select few.[33]

The popularity of dystopian themes and references in popular culture gave rise to the function of critical dystopia in lifting the voices of the marginalized in society.[34]

Dystopia cannot be reduced to a genre or subgenre like young adult literature, science fiction, or myth. Yet, dystopia can traverse typical classification of generic categories. There are works of science fiction that are dystopian just as there are works of dystopian children's literature. Dystopia is capable of synthesizing and integrating features of various genres in novel manners that are revelatory. This makes dystopia an especially malleable device or narrative approach. It is also clear that narratives which are not fully dystopias or utopias can contain dystopian or utopian elements. Claeys identifies three "forms" of dystopia as "the political dystopia; the environmental dystopia; and finally, the technological dystopia, where science and technology ultimately threaten to dominate or destroy humanity."[35] Of course, these three forms often interrelate and many dystopian works include elements from each; however, many dystopian works contain a central focus on one of the three. That is, the main thrust is about how humanity relates socially, whether concerning governance, nature, or technology. These three forms have endured in dystopian literature and are attested in the precursors to dystopia.

Part of the difficulty of developing a comprehensive objective definition of dystopia is that dystopia is subjective. The word dystopia likely conjures different images for different groups of people. Some might picture a horde of undead running towards them in the midst of a postapocalyptic landscape, while others picture natural disasters with such raw power that cities are wiped from the face of the Earth. Culture also plays a major role in understanding, defining, and creating dystopian works. Different cultures and societies around the globe have produced various forms of utopian and dystopian works.[36] Democracy tends to view collectivism with dystopian skepticism while more collective forms of government tend to view the radical individualism that can stem from democracy as dystopian.[37] This not only underscores the subjective quality of understanding and defining concrete examples of dystopia, but it also points to ways in which historical conditions impact dystopia. Both utopian and dystopian works speak from historical moments to historical contexts, even as many of these works have endured beyond their original context.

While the dystopian literature of the past has not predicted the future with perfect precision and accuracy, there is a sense that specific themes and trajectories are coming to fruition before our eyes. Technology and the virtual world increasingly dominate the landscape and consume resources and time as evidenced by the rise of social media, advances in artificial intelligence, augmented and virtual reality devices, and the surge of cryptocurrency untethered to governmental and economic regulations. Melting polar ice caps and increasingly destructive weather events show that the scars of modernity's consumption are not without consequences. Political instability and inabilities to communicate across differences fray the edges of our social fabric charting an unnavigable course.

Douwe Fokkema argues that times of crisis in various historical and cultural settings gave rise to utopian projects.[38] Dystopian writing flourished in abundance amid the rise of a totalitarianism that frequently made utopian promises. It was this historical reality that leads Fokkema to write, "Eutopian narratives propose nearly always an attractive abstraction, are set in faraway times or places, and exist only in the imagination. Dystopian writing, however, is usually inspired by a dreadful sociopolitical reality; in fact, its antiutopian bias is often directed against a half-way materialized, perverted eutopia."[39] As previously stated, what one person considers utopian may be dystopian for others and one person's utopia may depend on a dystopian situation for others. Modern readers look back on Thomas More's classic *Utopia* and rightfully question the inclusion of slavery in society, which illustrates how historical conditions impact an understanding of what is properly utopian and dystopian. In other words, understanding dystopia is not merely an objective interpretive exercise. There is a sense in which history, context, and situation contribute to understanding and experiencing dystopia in ways which resist universalizing definitions. Nonetheless, general characteristics and broad definitions that function descriptively rather than prescriptively can also help the reader identify dystopia.

On the inspiration behind dystopian themes, Tom Moylan argues that "dystopian narrative is largely the product of the terrors of the twentieth century. A hundred years of exploitation, presession, state violence, war, genocide, disease, famine, ecocide, depression, debt, and the steady depletion of humanity through the buying and selling of everyday life provided more than enough fertile ground."[40] Perhaps, then, the rise of dystopia is reflective of the refusal of the wounds of modernity to stay quiet. In this way, dystopia functions as a witness to unspeakable horrors which dominant ideologies would rather forget. When history refused to tell the truth about the horrors of modernity, perhaps, dystopian literature took up the task of remembering on behalf of the dead and oppressed.[41] This form of witnessing, following Ricoeur, might see the horrors of the past continue to haunt society through the liminal space of dystopian literature. To a certain extent, locating a rise in dystopian literature with the terrors of the twentieth century is a helpful step in the delineation of a concise understanding of the role and function of dystopia in popular culture.

DYSTOPIAN NARRATIVE

"Telling stories is as basic to human beings as eating."[42] Richard Kearney's use of metaphor is apt because just as food provides nutrition for our physical bodies, stories shape individual, communal, and social identities. Stories also help reveal the invisible bonds of society that are frequently taken for granted. It is partly through creating and sharing stories that people "become full agents of our history."[43] That is because, as Aristotle argues, stories provide a framework for plotting human action in representative and imitative manners.[44] Stories, and the narrative frame they rely upon, perform a core organizational and revelatory function for individuals, groups, and societies. Stories help humanity make sense of experiences, situations, and our place in the world. This critical function of stories pushes us to consider stories as more than an escape from reality. Stories perform a core representative function that allows for disclosure. Kearney believes that "every life is in search of a narrative. We all seek, willy-nilly, to introduce some kind of concord into the everyday discord and dispersal we find about us."[45] Given the rising political, ecological, and technological concerns about life and the world which produced discordance, the rise in the popularity of dystopian works may not be so surprising. In other words, the present global situation is fertile ground for dystopia.

While works of critical dystopia attempt to elicit some change in the reader or viewer, often to dissuade those in the actual world or a particular society from following a path to a dystopian society, change itself is paradigmatic of dystopia. One of the foremost functions of dystopian media is to render political, social, and technological changes visible and understandable. On the one hand, dystopia can utilize the fear of change and the fear of the unknown for nonproductive ends. On the other hand, dystopia can serve as a warning against uncritical acceptance of certain political, social, or technological changes. Oftentimes, this means that viewers must parse the deeper meaning of dystopias produced for popular culture that retain high levels of entertainment.

The present global situation is fertile ground for dystopia because we live in a world that is rapidly changing and the pace of change has intensified. Technology and globalization have created a human situation that is ripe for dystopia and that often grapples with previous understandings of experience and reality in light of change. For example, a central question of *Ready Player Two* revolves around whether a human soul can live in a virtual reality after the body dies.[46] While the metaphysics of such pondering is largely absent, the novel can invite readers to consider what it means to be human in the virtual age. Does the conception of a soul or consciousness fit considering current technological developments? At what point does technology start consuming life instead of enhancing it?

The Amazon Prime Video series *Upload* (2020) also grapples with these questions through a capitalist lens. In the series, humankind has the decision to "upload" their consciousness to a virtual afterlife, but must make that decision prior to their own death. The series opens with a protagonist surviving a car crash, as he and his significant other make the decision to upload his consciousness before his death. The protagonist finds a luxurious afterlife in a community known as "Lakeview." It falls upon the living to afford this afterlife, however, as each consciousness is only allotted a certain amount of bandwidth based on their families' ability to pay. By the end of the first season, the main protagonist is placed in a simple dormitory on a limited bandwidth that, once expired for the month, renders the individual consciousness suspended in place until that bandwidth is restored.[47]

Dystopian popular culture invites readers to consider these questions as they grapple with change and development. Perhaps one of the most explicit and popular dystopian works that asks these questions is *The Matrix* series. *The Matrix* is more than the run-of-the-mill dystopian work focusing on the fear of technology. It consistently asks the viewer to consider questions of epistemology. How do we know what we know? What are the paradigms upon which knowledge and perception are built? While sense perception is utterly critical to human experience and meaning, it is limited in its capacity to fully describe reality. And yet, humanity has no alternative through which to interpret reality except through sense and interpretation.[48] Productive dystopia takes place at the intersections of a hermeneutics of texts and situations.

Octavia Butler's 1993 dystopian novel *Parable of the Sower* illustrates the centrality of change in dystopia. The novel begins in California in the year 2024. The United States has devolved from greed and ecological degradation. The dystopian world is unstable and unsafe. Addiction, theft, and murder are almost universal. Amid these situational and contextual changes, Bulter weaves in theological changes throughout the novel. The main character, Lauren, "discovers" Earthseed, a new religious philosophy with Christian and Eastern influences.[49] Because Lauren is the daughter of a Baptist minister, she often reflects on traditional Christian theology through a Baptist lens. She finds the traditional theology, and approach to theology, inadequate to adapt to her dystopian context. Therefore, Lauren reimagines God directly in correlation with her experiences of the world. Change is central to Earthseed and change is central to her reimagining of God. Each chapter begins with an excerpt from the religious text Lauren is writing. The text is called "Earthseed: The Books of the Living" and is reminiscent of process theology's understanding of a God who changes in relationship and connection to humanity and Creation. A brief poetic prelude at the start of the first chapter reads:

> All that you touch
> You Change.
> All that you Change
> Changes you.
> The only lasting truth
> Is Change.
> God
> Is Change.[50]

Butler imagines a dystopian world rife with change. Amid the horrors and brutality of droughts, fires, earthquakes, cannibalism, murder, and general distrust, Butler reimagines God as change. The traditional version of God as immutable is unwound by Butler when she writes "We shape God" in the Earthseed excerpt from chapter 3.[51] Change, process, relationality, and adaptation are all central to Earthseed. In this way, the dystopian landscape challenges some traditional forms of theology and invites the reader to engage in theological thinking through a robust dialogue with the present context.

Octavia Butler engages dystopia and theology in a constructive manner. While we are not making a claim about her theological methodology, we do believe it bears similarities to David Tracy's mutual critical correlation approach to theology. Tracy writes, "The history of theology is the history of the ever-shifting relationship between the reality of God and that divine reality as experienced and understood from within a *logos*, i.e., a particular horizon of intelligibility. The theologian is one who attempts the nearly impossible task of correlating *theos* and *logos*."[52] For Tracy, *logos* here refers to the contemporary situation or period which, when correlated in a mutually critical manner with an understanding of God, *theos* becomes theology. Tracy understands that in "modern theology, the *logos* of modern intelligibility was the dominant partner in the correlation."[53] As a theologian, Tracy wants to be sure that theology is not dominated by philosophy or other disciplines even as he recognizes that theology must be in conversation with the world and other disciplines. For Tracy, theology is not done in a vacuum or apart from context and situation. Theology must be open to change based on present human experiences of God and reality. Thus, correlative theology is one especially conducive theological methodology to use when engaging dystopia. Dystopia can be "a particular horizon of intelligibility" for theology to engage God, Creation, and humanity in the present.

We hypothesize that the rise of dystopian works might correlate with the rise of experiences of reality being dystopian. In other words, as people continue to experience life and reality in increasingly dystopian manners, popular culture responds by producing dystopian works. People gravitate toward dystopian works looking for the concordance that narrative typically produces in a dystopian fashion. This function, following Aristotle, is akin to a "creative redescription of the world such that hidden patterns and hitherto unexplored meaning can unfold."[54] Put more directly in terms of the reader or viewer, narratives "offer us a newly imagined way of being in the world."[55] The prominence of dystopia in popular culture reflects a desire for people to navigate the complex contexts and situations involved with twenty-first-century living. The loss of a consensus on which metanarrative is "true" in postmodernity increasingly atomizes in people and places an existential burden of responsibility on the individual. There are benefits to this situation and the burden of responsibility; however, it can be overwhelming. It also raises the question, what type of concordance, if any, does dystopia afford and is it different from genres like comedy, tragedy, and myth? This question is complicated by the subject nature of dystopia.

Dystopia bears similarities with works of tragedy and satire. Frequently, dystopian works portray a tragic protagonist amid dire circumstances. Gottlieb writes, "Yet the tragic elements of the protagonist's fate notwithstanding, the overall strategies of the dystopian novel are those of political satire. The writer offers militant criticism of specific aberrations in our own, present social-political system by pointing out their potentially monstrous consequences in the future."[56] Part of the disclosive productive power of dystopia is the way it draws readers into a narrative world which contains subtle, and not so subtle, critiques of ideologies, governments, societies, or trajectories of society in the actual world. By asking the reader to suspend some aspects of belief for the sake of narrative fiction, readers interact with uncomfortable realities which, when done well, bear significance to the real world.[57] Moylan adds that dystopia's "very textual machinery invites the creation of alternative worlds in which the historical spacetime of the author can be re-presented in a way that foregrounds the articulation of its economic, political, and cultural dimensions."[58] Think of the way William Golding's *Lord of the Flies* describes what could happen if a number of children were isolated on an island and forced to survive on their own.[59] The fear, panic, and factionalism are easily accepted by the reader as a reasonable course of action for children. However, as the reader engages more deeply with the text, they can come to see correlations with the Cold War and nuclear situation. What first appeared to be immature responses of children can be disclosive of global policy. In this way, the alternative world of the narrative is disclosive of the author's, and possibly the reader's, context.

These connections do not have to be exact in order for the viewer or reader to understand their intention. Firemen do not literally need to turn into book burners for us to literarily see the dystopian implications of the portrayal of state-sponsored book banning in *Fahrenheit 451*.[60] Yet, the literary depiction informs our experiences of book censorship. In this way, Moylan reminds us, "Dystopia's foremost truth lies in its ability to reflect upon the causes of social and ecological evil as systemic."[61] By reflecting on the causes of social and ecological evils as systemic, dystopia renders others invisible or obfuscated forces and actions visible. In other words, dystopian works help us understand reality as partly formed by forces and systems in ways that would be inaccessible to human understanding otherwise. Claeys speaks to this point: "Dystopia thus describes negative pasts and places we reject as deeply inhuman and oppressive, and projects negative futures we do not want but may get anyway. In do doing it raises perennial problems of human identity. Shall we be monsters, humans, or machines? Shall we be enslaved or free?"[62] The hope, if there is any, of dystopia is that it can be avoided. Dystopia reveals that the way we live in the present is connected to the past and has implications for the future that impact the well-being of the whole planet. The danger of dystopia is catharsis without change.

Catharsis without change is a warning against the popular consumption of dystopia which renders visible trajectories that reveal human civilization is on destructive paths. Global warming and other anthropogenic changes have altered the sustainability of the planet in substantive manners. Dystopia can reveal the need to change but it must not lead to paralysis if it is going to perform its critical function. The critical function of dystopia is not a guarantee; thus, a theological or religious hope of dystopia is that it leads to responsible human engagement with the world and with each other. In the end, Claeys reminds us that "the task of literary dystopia, then, is to warn us against and educate us about real-life dystopias. It need not furnish a happy ending to do so: pessimism has its place. But it may envision rational and collective solutions where irrationality and panic loom."[63] Dystopia has arisen for such a time as this and hopefully, it can help realize a more just and equitable world.

DEMYTHOLOGIZED APOCALYPTIC

An important element in the mentality of some writers of early Jewish apocalyptic literature is in the resolution at the end of the tale: an injustice of cosmic proportions has taken place, and through the historical apocalypse or otherworldly journey we will find that justice, whether in this world or the next. A key distinction between ancient apocalyptic literature and modern dystopian literature is the presence or absence of that the justice, redemption, or salvation one might expect at the end of a tale of suffering. With an established definition of dystopia and its function in narrative, we would like to suggest that modern works of dystopia can be understood as a demythologized form of apocalyptic literature. In most forms of apocalyptic literature, a divine being or presence in one way or another impacted the resolution of the injustice, bringing about the justice for which those in the narrative yearned; in most forms of dystopian literature the divine being or presence is either absent or fails to act in the world.

In *Dystopian Fiction East and West: A Universe of Terror and Trial*, Erika Gottlieb asserts, "Dystopian fiction is a post-Christian genre."[64] She goes on to say that "if the central drama of the age of faith was the conflict between salvation and damnation by deity, in our secular modern age this drama has been transposed to a conflict between humanity's salvation or damnation by society in the historical arena."[65] She argues that the concept of salvation correlates with a just society and a good government whereas damnation is associated with an unjust society typically under authoritarian rule.[66] Her understanding of post-Christian does not mean that dystopia is without

Christian, religious, or theological concepts and themes. In fact, she is clear that dystopia is largely influenced by conceptions of heaven as a good place and hell as a bad place.[67] There is a sense in which dystopia is heavily influenced by religious and theological themes, motivations, and systems; yet dystopian works typically emphasize human causality, responsibility, and interconnectedness instead of focusing on divine or supernatural forces. In that way, postmodern dystopia might correspond more closely with nontheistic worldviews, religions, faiths, or traditions than theistic ones; however, the dystopian concept and dystopian works can relate to theistic theology and religions. One approach to correlating dystopia with religion and theology is to understand dystopia as a form of demythologized apocalyptic.

Rudolf Bultmann is perhaps most well-known for developing the concept of demythologization. Bultmann recognized that ancient texts, including the Christian and Jewish scriptures, were written with an ancient worldview and prescientific understanding prevalent at that time. These texts present a world and an interpretation of the world rooted in its historical context. In hermeneutical terms, the preunderstandings from worldviews and conceptions of the cosmos impact how both ancient and modern people interpret events and write about them. If a person believes that a deity controls the weather, as opposed to weather resulting from natural forces, they might be prone to interpret changes in the weather as significant reflections of their relationship with the deity. For Bultmann, "mythical thinking is the opposite of scientific thinking. It refers certain phenomena and events to supernatural, 'divine' powers, whether these are thought of dynamistically or animistically or are represented as personal spirits or gods."[68] This type of thinking views world events as directly impacted by outside forces, often thought of in terms of gods, deities, or higher powers not bound by human limitation.

Mythical thinking, the notion that outside powers directly cause, change, and impact nature and events, was common in the ancient world. In fact, the involvement of deities, and the interpretation of involvement through natural means was a core part of ancient science.[69] This understanding of science is not congruent with modern and postmodern paradigms; however, it shaped reality and how it was experienced in the ancient world. Writing about modern thinking, Bultmann said, "scientific thinking, by contrast, is performed in the 'work thinking' that also reckons with a closed continuum of cause and effect."[70] Modern scientific thinking views the world as a closed system of natural cause and effect. No otherworldly powers or agents of higher power shape world events or the weather. It is important to note that Bultmann does argue that all traditions, ancient and modern, "are relative and that any world picture worked out either yesterday, today, or tomorrow can never be definitive."[71] In this way, Bultmann recognizes the limitations of all paradigms, not just ancient understandings. While many scholars focus on the ways in which demythologization functions to remove mythical elements from premodern texts, Bultmann cautions against totalizing objective views of science in the modern world too. He is especially wary of the inadequacy of modern scientific language to speak objectively about transcendence. Thus, modern scientific worldviews and precritical scientific worldviews are *both* limited paradigms which, nonetheless, can existentially disclose aspects of reality and transcendence.[72]

Myth, according to Bultmann, "objectifies the transcendent into the immanent."[73] It is necessary to speak about transcendence. However, such a move is always limited because anything transcendent, especially something conceived of like the god of sacred texts, cannot be reduced to immanent concepts and causality. This presents two major problems for Bultmann. How do we talk immanently about transcendence and how do we engage ancient texts written in a worldview that is no longer assumed? A basic example of this second problem is the three-tiered universe. In this worldview, the three tiers are heaven above, earth, and Hades or hell beneath. With very rare exceptions, the three-tiered order is no longer taken literally in the modern world, but it still holds great metaphorical and imaginative sway over people. Thus, the three-tiered system is existentially important even if it is no longer taken for literal fact. This move, something being existentially significant while not being literally valid, is crucial to demythologization.

In sometimes problematic language, Bultmann viewed demythologization as a way of bringing out the existential reference of texts and stories by displacing the cultural confines in the sense of texts and stories. In hermeneutics, this is sometimes referred to as removing the cultural husk to get to the existential kernel. Bultmann writes, "Demythologizing seeks to bring out the real intention of myth, namely, its intention to talk about human existence as grounded in and limited by a transcendent, unworldly power, which is not visible to objectifying thinking."[74] Demythologizing argues that the mythology imbued within the text needs to be interpreted for modern readers to understand its significance. Not all aspects of the text carry over in the interpretation. Bultmann wants to retain what he sees as a deeper meaning through interpretation, which allows for some carry over despite different methodological approaches to the world. The aim of demythologizing is not to eliminate the mythological saying and elements, it is to interpret them and understand their deeper meaning. For Bultmann, this demythologizing process takes place hermeneutically and existentially: "Positively, demythologizing is existentialist interpretation, in that it seeks to make clear the intention of myth to talk about human existence."[75] It is also the existential approach, which understands ancient myths as speaking to us, that invites interpretation for Bultmann.

Bultmann writes that "demythologizing wants an understanding of scripture that is free of every world picture projected by objectifying thinking, whether it is that of myth of that of science."[76] While we are skeptical that such a positivist and objectivist approach to interpretation and demythologization is possible, we find the overall method interesting in light of the development of the dystopia genre. Gottlieb writes, "While the medieval morality play implies that the fate of the human soul will be decided at the Last Judgment, the modern dystopian narrative puts the protagonist on an ultimate trial where his fate will be decided in confrontation with the Bad Angel in his secular incarnation as the Grand Inquisitor, high priest of the state religion and God-like ruler of totalitarian dictatorship."[77] In many ways, dystopia is a form of demythologized apocalyptic. Demythologization reveals that, existentially speaking, apocalyptic texts and dystopian texts bear great similarities. In fact, we argue that the modern scientific worldview exemplified through the dystopia genre functions as a demythologized version of a mythological apocalyptic. "This scandal lies in the fact that God's word calls us out of all our anxiety as well as all our self-contrived security to God, and thereby to our own authentic existence, to freedom from the world that we take possession of by the objectifying thinking of science in such a way that we thereby give it power over us."[78] Because dystopian anxiety underscores human responsibility and causality, it can fall victim to the objectifying tendencies of modernity. Authentic existence does not come purely from mythology or science, apocalyptic or dystopia, but in relating to transcendence and immanence. Part of what dystopia can do is inspire human responsibility and agency for the well-being of Creation. Even when dystopian works do not explicitly engage the divine, or another religious system, they can still be existentially revelatory.

Like dystopia, the generic category "apocalyptic" is a modern invention. In 1832, Gottfried Lücke used the term *Apokalyptik* in reference to the Book of Revelation.[79] Since that time, distinctions between the terms apocalyptic, apocalypse, and apocalypticism have been further delineated.[80] The English term apocalypse itself comes from the Greek *apokalupto* (ἀποκαλύπτω), meaning "to reveal" or "to disclose."[81] As a literary genre, apocalyptic was defined toward the end of the twentieth century. The classic definition of the apocalyptic genre in Biblical Studies can be traced to the work of the Society of Biblical Literature Genres Project as it was reported in the journal Semeia. An "apocalypse" is defined as "a genre of revelatory literature with a narrative framework, in which a revelation is mediated by an otherworldly being to a human recipient, disclosing a transcendent reality which is both temporal, insofar as it envisages eschatological salvation, and spatial insofar as it involves another supernatural world."[82] Apocalyptic as a generic category can therefore define several ancient Jewish and Christian texts in the Hebrew

Bible, New Testament, and extrabiblical material that share many of the same generic features.

John Collins argues that the literary function of all apocalypses is to address an underlying problem in society.[83] For many apocalyptic texts, that problem deals with a community's inability to reconcile their present circumstances with their overall conception of divine justice in their world. In the ancient Near East, justice was often defined as a return to equilibrium.[84] If a person was wronged, that wrong would be righted in an equivalent way. This is also known as *lex talionis*, a legal principle that states the punishment should resemble the offense in kind and severity. The classic phrase "an eye for an eye" might be better interpreted as a call to make the compensation equal the severity of the crime rather than an imperative to blind or otherwise wound the offender. The Hebrew Bible nuances this conception of justice by prescribing justice for specific circumstances.

Therefore, apocalyptic texts answer the question: what happens when justice is not served? In the books of the Maccabees, a protoapocalyptic work, a final judgment and resurrection is promised to all those who do not receive justice in the real world and during their lifetimes. Set in the Hellenistic period, 2 Maccabees begins by relaying the stories of despair and struggle under the reign of Antiochus IV Epiphanes, ultimately leading to the eventual Maccabean revolt and the historical origins of the festival of Hanukkah. In 2 Maccabees 6 the temple in Jerusalem is used for sacrifices to both the god of Israel and the Greek gods, an abhorrence to contemporaneous ritual purity laws regulating temple practice. In this process, Eleazar the scribe is killed after refusing to eat pork. The concept of theodicy, or divine justice, appears most prominently in 2 Maccabees 7, where a mother watches as each of her seven sons are tortured and killed when they, like Eleazar, refuse to violate early Jewish dietary laws. At the death of one of her sons, the steadfast mother proclaims, "Therefore the Creator of the world, who shaped the beginning of humankind and devised the origin of all things, will in his mercy give life and breath back to you again, since you now forget yourselves for the sake of his laws" (2 Maccabees 7:23, NRSV). This promise of justice at an end of time, here juxtaposed with the image of the god of Israel as the creator of the universe, is prototypical of apocalyptic texts. Despite the immense amount of suffering endured by the protagonists of this narrative, there is hope in the promise of justice at the time when the judgment will take place.

A defining generic feature of nearly every example of early Jewish apocalyptic literature is judgment, which often takes the form of a punishment meted out upon those deserving of said punishment. Collins shares what is common amongst all apocalyptic texts:

Dystopia as Demythologized Apocalyptic   17

the world is mysterious and revelation must be transmitted from a supernatural source, through the mediation of angels; there is a hidden world of angels and demons that is directly relevant to human destiny; and this destiny is finally determined by a definitive eschatological judgment. In short, human life is bounded in the present by a supernatural world of angels and demons and in the future by the inevitability of a final judgment.[85]

In all apocalyptic texts, life is governed by beings and events in the supernatural world and a final judgment happens in one or more of three distinct ways: judgment that leads to the destruction of the wicked, judgment that leads to the destruction of the world, and judgement that leads to the destruction of otherworldly beings.

The book of 1 Enoch 1–36, an example of an apocalyptic otherworldly journey dated to the 3rd century BCE, is a deuterocanonical text that originally appeared in Aramaic, but is most extant in a version written in the Ethiopic language of Ge'ez.[86] Chapters 1–36 is also known as the Book of the Watchers. The Watchers are better known as the angels who fathered the "sons of the gods" (*bene elohim*, בני אלהים) with human women in Genesis 6:1–4.[87] At the beginning the book, Enoch is selected as a righteous man who would receive visions about the final judgment as they were interpreted by the angels. In chapters 6–11, it is revealed to Enoch that all of the vices and evils of the world were brought about as these Watchers disseminated secret knowledge to humankind. These corruptions led to humankind's victimization. Enoch is then chosen to be a prophet of justice (chapters 12–16) and is subsequently led on a journey exploring where the righteous will be rewarded and the wicked will be punished. The secret knowledge relayed to Enoch by the divine is meant as a critique of the vices currently present in the world and a preview of the final judgment of the wicked, the world, and otherworldly beings.

The book of 4 Ezra, an example of an historical apocalypse from the end of the first century CE, is primarily concerned with the Roman destruction of the temple in Jerusalem.[88] The book contains seven visions that were presented to Ezra the scribe as he lived in Babylon. Like most other historical apocalypses, the narratives are often set in the past in order to speak about the present. Ezra speaks about theodicy and the lack of divine justice in the world that people of ancient Israel inhabit. Ezra laments:

> For when I came here I saw ungodly deeds without number, and my soul has seen many sinners during these thirty years. And my heart failed me, because I have seen how you endure those who sin, and have spared those who act wickedly, and have destroyed your people, and protected your enemies, and have not shown to anyone how your way may be comprehended. Are the deeds of Babylon better than those of Zion? Or has another nation known you besides

Israel? Or what tribes have so believed the covenants as these tribes of Jacob? Yet their reward has not appeared and their labor has borne no fruit. For I have traveled widely among the nations and have seen that they abound in wealth, though they are unmindful of your commandments. Now therefore weigh in a balance our iniquities and those of the inhabitants of the world; and it will be found which way the turn of the scale will incline. When have the inhabitants of the earth not sinned in your sight? Or what nation has kept your commandments so well? You may indeed find individuals who have kept your commandments, but nations you will not find. (2 Esdras 3:29–36, NRSV)

In this part of the narrative, Ezra is living in a dystopian world. While not always acting according to the laws dictated to them in their scriptures, the people in Ezra's community in exile are indeed still the chosen people of their god. Ezra wonders why they must live in misery while others who are not the chosen people and also disobey these same laws are given a pass. After Ezra makes the above lament, the angel Uriel responds to him. At this point, the dystopian text becomes an apocalyptic text as Uriel eventually reveals how resolution in the form of a final judgement will come about.

Dystopian literature lacks this final judgment. Problems that would have been solved either in this world or in the next world in apocalyptic literature instead remain unsolved in dystopian literature. Humankind is forced to deal with suffering and difficult situations without divine intercession or outside help in dystopian literature. Characters in dystopian literature come to terms with suffering whereas characters in apocalyptic literature hold out hope for justice that will come. This lack of final judgment is precisely related to the lack of a divine intercession in dystopian literature. When the divine intercession is removed from apocalyptic, so is the judgment and resolution that might occur within the narrative. What remains are either the evils of the world (e.g., as they appeared in 1 Enoch 1–36) or the persecution of the protagonists (e.g., as it appeared in 4 Ezra).

As the onus for improvement within the narrative itself seemingly shifts from the divine in apocalyptic literature to the human in dystopian literature, we still find one key similarity between the genres. Apart from narratives of misery and suffering, dystopian literature shares something very important with apocalyptic literature: the imperative to change is simultaneously placed upon the *reader* of the literature. In an apocalyptic narrative, secret knowledge permeates from the divine realm into the human realm by divine intercession, but the reader is one with the most to gain from that interaction. Secret knowledge is presented from the divine representative to the human representative, but it also passes to the human readers of the apocalyptic narrative itself. In dystopian literature, that secret knowledge is not passed from divine to human realms, but instead is present in the dystopian narrative itself as an example of what kind of sufferings and miseries are possible. The suffering and miseries in some dystopian literature might bear resemblance to lived realities in the real world, but in others they could be exaggerated or extended on a much grander scale. In both of these instances, they provide the imperative for the reader: there is no justice in this possible way of life, and it is up to the reader to implement appropriate change.

In this way dystopia might be best understood as a sort of demythologized apocalyptic. Where the divine entity or representative intercedes on behalf of the protagonists in order to bring about divine justice and provide an example for a reader in apocalyptic literature, the removal of that divine intercessor and absence of appropriate justice providing the reader an example of such lack of justice in dystopian literature might also preserve the same kind of function. Both apocalyptic literature and dystopian literature aim to inspire the reader to make changes in their own lives in order to achieve a certain end, yet the means by which they reach this point vary.

In *The Lord of the Flies*, a group of school children is stuck alone on an island. They come to be afraid of something they refer to as the beast. Fear of the beast dominates their existence on the island and continually leads to more violent ways of relating with each other. Throughout the story, the children debate the existence of the beast; however, even those who deny the beast, existentially fear its power and experience the impact of the beast regardless of its metaphysical existence. In a profound realization, one character says,

> "Life," said Piggy expansively, "is scientific, that's what it is. . . . I know there isn't no beast—not with claws an all that, I mean—but I know there isn't no fear either."
> Piggy paused.
> "Unless—"
> Ralph moved restlessly.
> "Unless what?"
> "Unless we get frightened of people."[89]

The scientific approach to life leads Piggy to conclude that the existence of a beast is impossible, yet he realized that fear of other people is itself a beast. This conclusion is correct. For there is no beast on the island with the children except the beast they created and enacted by hunting and hurting each other. Science shows there is no apocalyptic beast and yet, dystopia thrives existentially just as it would under an apocalyptic beast. Toward the end of the book, Simon has an imagined encounter with the Lord of the Flies, which is a dead pig's head. The Lord of the Flies says, "'Fancy thinking the Beast was something you could hunt and kill!' said the head. For a moment or two the forest and all the other dimly appreciated places echoed with the parody of laughter.

'You knew, didn't you? I'm part of you?'"[90] Simon learned that the terror and horror of the island were of the children's making. The one responsible for death, despair, and destruction was not a mythical beast but the children. The significance of this correlates with geopolitics in the real world but also serves as an example of demythologization. The beast, the Lord of the Flies is not real but really impacts reality. The Lord of the Flies is so important that the book is titled after it. In *Dictionary of Deities and Demons in the Bible* under the entry *Baal Zebub*, a Semitic god who came to be associated with the Christian devil Beelzebub, is the title "Lord of the Flies."[91] The Lord of the Flies is not metaphysically real in Golding's dystopia but existentially it is just as powerful as an opposing supernatural force in apocalyptic literature. To us, this suggests a process akin to existential demythologization in action. The beast of the apocalypse is the dystopian reality created by human hands.

CONCLUSION

Regarding their existential impact, dystopia and apocalyptic function similarly such that demythologization helps connect the ancient and modern genres. Both wrestle with difficult, overwhelming, and possibly traumatic realities that often appear out of human control. While the apocalyptic genre frequently emphasized otherworldly agents of power, dystopia underscores how systems function in similar confining manners. Predatory capitalism is not a willful agent like an ancient demonic force; however, it existentially oppresses as a system of domination. Humans frequently appear powerless before totalizing forces, whether supernatural or natural in their respective genres, and struggle to respond meaningfully. In a certain sense, both genres are widened through demythologization by allowing existential purposes to surface. What does responsible human action do in the face of insurmountable oppression, destruction, or lack of purpose when all seems lost?

Both ancient writers and modern writers were concerned with justice, well-being, and societal ordering such that they turned to apocalyptic and dystopia, respectively, for expression and understanding. The literary genres become ways of expressing worldviews and seek to address "why" questions that pervade the human experience. Like all literary genres and concepts, understanding their forms and rules should impact how we interpret and engage the texts and concepts. The form is essential to the meaning that results from the intersection of writer, written work, and reader. With greater attention to the form of apocalyptic and dystopia, modern readers can claim the critical function of *both* apocalyptic and dystopia. With Bultmann, we find demythologization helpful because it seeks to relate the ancient and modern existentially in ways that avoid totalizing objectivity or subjective fantasy. In fact, it might just be the intersection between the faith of the past in some transcendent aspect of reality or understanding of humanity that correlates with the modern focus on immanent causality that allows for a healthy mixture of science and the humanities, faith and reason, and responsibility and action in the face of dystopia.

NOTES

1. Though this chapter functions as a stand-alone essay on the generic categories of dystopia and apocalyptic, it is the hope of the authors that this chapter might help prepare the reader to encounter the rest of the chapters in this volume.

2. Gregory Claeys, *Dystopia: A Natural History* (Oxford: Oxford University Press, 2017), 4.

3. Claeys, *Dystopia: A Natural History*, 3.

4. Claeys, *Dystopia: A Natural History*, 3.

5. Claeys, *Dystopia: A Natural History*, 7.

6. One of the most famous uses of dystopian imagery in the history of marketing is Apple Computer's introduction of the Macintosh in 1984, metaphorically using dystopian imagery to describe the current state of the personal computer marketplace. Directed by Ridley Scott, the commercial displayed stereotypical dystopian images of uniformed people sitting attentively and paying attention to big brother manifest on a projector screen. As she is chased by the authorities, a heroine emerges in full color, tossing a hammer into screen and shattering the representation of big brother. Captions appears on the screen: "On January 24th, Apple Computer will introduce Macintosh. And you'll see why 1984 won't be like '1984.'" *Apple Mac: 1984*, directed by Ridley Scott, https://www.imdb.com/title/tt4227346/.

7. See the relevant discussion in Claeys, *Dystopia: A Natural History*, 80–109.

8. See chapter 2, titled "Monstrosity and the Origin of Dystopian Space," in Claeys, *Dystopia: A Natural History*, 58–109.

9. Claeys, *Dystopia: A Natural History*, 113–120.

10. Claeys, *Dystopia: A Natural History*, 4.

11. Upon entry into the afterlife in the first episode of the show, the character Eleanor gesticulates upward and downward asking where she ended up. She is met with the response: "Well, it's not the heaven or hell idea that you were raised on. But generally speaking, in the afterlife, there's a Good Place and there's a Bad Place. You're in the Good Place." *The Good Place*, season 1, episode 1, "Everything is Fine," directed by Drew Goddard, written by Michael Schur, aired September 19, 2016, https://www.netflix.com/watch/80191852, 02:39–03:00.

12. Claeys, *Dystopia: A Natural History*, 8

13. Erika Gottlieb, *Dystopian Fiction East and West: A Universe of Terror and Trial* (Montreal: McGill-Queen's Press, 2001), 8.

14. For ευ, see Henry George Liddell and Robert Scott, *A Greek-English Lexicon* (Oxford: Oxford University Press, 1996), 704; for ου, see Liddell and Scott,

A Greek-English Lexicon, 1266–67; and for τοπος, see Liddell and Scott, *A Greek-English Lexicon*, 1806.

15. For insight into the lexicographic process, cf. Kory Stamper, *Word By Word: The Secret Life of Dictionaries* (New York: Pantheon, 2017).

16. Merriam-Webster, "Utopia," accessed May 29, 2022, https://www.merriam-webster.com/dictionary/utopia.

17. Douwe Fokkema, *Perfect Worlds: Utopian Fiction in China and the West* (Amsterdam: Amsterdam University Press, 2011), 21.

18. Tom Moylan, *Scraps of the Untainted Sky: Science Fiction, Utopia, Dystopia* (New York: Routledge, 2018), 188.

19. Claeys, *Dystopia: A Natural History*, 7.

20. Thomas More, *Utopia*, trans. Clarence H. Miller (New Haven, CT: Yale University Press, 2001). Cf. chapter 30, titled "Brave New Worlds: Utopias and Dystopias," in John Sutherland, *A Little History of Literature* (New Haven, CT: Yale University Press, 2013), 195–96.

21. More's "utopia" is a deliberate play on the possible transliterations *outopos* and *eutopos* and could be interpreted as effectively one and the same in his work.

22. More, *Utopia*.

23. Cf. Antonis Balasopoulos, "Celestial Cities and Rationalist Utopias," in *The Cambridge Companion to the City in Literature*, ed. Kevin R. McNamara (Cambridge: Cambridge University Press, 2014), 25–29.

24. Claeys, *Dystopia: A Natural History*, 6.

25. Lyman Sargent, "The Three Faces of Utopianism Revisited," *Utopia Studies* 5, no. 1 (1994): 1–37.

26. Sargent, "The Three Faces of Utopianism Revisited," 12.

27. For a brief but helpful taxonomy of these terms, see Sargent, "The Three Faces of Utopianism Revisited," 9–12. An alternative continuum that could be helpful is found in Moylan, *Scraps of the Untainted Sky*, 195.

28. Sargent, "The Three Faces of Utopianism Revisited," 9.

29. Sargent, "The Three Faces of Utopianism Revisited," 9.

30. Sargent, "The Three Faces of Utopianism Revisited," 9.

31. Moylan, *Scraps of the Untainted Sky*, 188.

32. Moylan, *Scraps of the Untainted Sky*, 188.

33. Moylan, *Scraps of the Untainted Sky*, 189

34. In part, it is this very transversive nature of dystopia that served as impetus behind our interest in compiling this volume. As mentioned in the preface to this volume, the dystopia genre gained popularity at two crucial points in the last twenty years: when hurricane Katrina made landfall in August 2005 and the start of the COVID-19 pandemic in 2020. Cf. Google Trends, accessed 27 May 2022, https://trends.google.com/trends/explore?date=all&q=dystopia,dystopian,apocalyptic.

35. Claeys, *Dystopia: A Natural History*, 5.

36. A comprehensive analysis of ways in which different cultures understand utopia and dystopia is beyond the scope of this introduction. Readers interested in an example of a text that compares Western and Chinese understandings of utopia and dystopia should see: Fokkema, *Perfect Worlds*. One difference that the author notes

is relative to time. Many Western examples of utopia envision it in the future, Eden and other founding myths being exceptions; many Chinese utopian works, on the other hand, position the utopic society in the past. Fokkema, *Perfect Worlds*, 16–26.

37. Gottlieb, *Dystopian Fiction East and West*, 6–7.
38. Fokkema, *Perfect Worlds*, 15–18.
39. Fokkema, *Perfect Worlds*, 20.
40. Moylan, *Scraps of the Untainted Sky*, xi.
41. Ricoeur argues that memory can serve critical functions on behalf of the dead for the sake of justice. Paul Ricoeur, *Memory, History, and Forgetting*, trans. Kathleen Blamey and David Pellauer (Chicago: University of Chicago Press, 2004), 86–89.
42. Richard Kearney, *On Stories* (New York: Routledge, 2002), 3.
43. Kearney, *On Stories*, 3.
44. Kearney, *On Stories*, 3.
45. Kearney, *On Stories*, 4.
46. Ernest Cline, *Ready Player Two* (New York: Ballantine Books, 2020).
47. *Upload*, season 1, episode 10, "Freeyond," directed by Daina Reid, written by Greg Daniels, aired on May 1, 2020, on Amazon Prime Video, https://www.amazon.com/Upload-Official-Trailer/dp/B08BYYSF6M/.
48. This is the intersection of hermeneutics and phenomenology that Richard Kearny writes about in the introduction to *Carnal Hermeneutics*. Readers interested in exploring this line of thinking more thoroughly should read Richard Kearney, "The Wager of Carnal Hermeneutics," *Carnal Hermeneutics*, ed. Richard Kearney and Brian Treanor (New York: Fordham University Press, 2015), 14–16.
49. Lauren prefers the description "discover" to "invent" when other characters ask her about the origins of Earthseed. See her conversation with Bankole for one example of this. Octavia Butler, *Parable of the Sower* (New York: Grand Central Publishing, 2019), 261.
50. Butler, *Parable of the Sower*, 3.
51. Butler, *Parable of the Sower*, 17.
52. David Tracy, *On Naming the Present: Reflections on God, Hermeneutics, and Church* (Maryknoll, NY: Orbis Books, 1994), 36.
53. Tracy, *On Naming the Present*, 37.
54. Kearney, *On Stories*, 5
55. Kearney, *On Stories*, 5.
56. Gottlieb, *Dystopian Fiction East and West*, 13.
57. For hermeneutical support of this position of a narrative, see Paul Ricoeur's *Interpretation Theory: Discourse and the Surplus of Meaning* (Fort Worth, TX: Texas Christian University Press, 1976), especially his understanding of the dialectic of sense and reference.
58. Moylan, *Scraps of the Untainted Sky*, xii.
59. William Golding, *Lord of the Flies* (New York: Penguin Books, 2006).
60. Sutherland, *A Little History of Literature*, 199–200.
61. Moylan, *Scraps of the Untainted Sky*, xii.
62. Claeys, *Dystopia: A Natural History*, 498.
63. Claeys, *Dystopia: A Natural History*, 501.

64. Gottlieb, *Dystopian Fiction East and West*, 3.
65. Gottlieb, *Dystopian Fiction East and West*, 3.
66. Gottlieb, *Dystopian Fiction East and West*, 41–45.
67. Gottlieb, *Dystopian Fiction East and West*, 3.
68. Rudolf Bultmann, *New Testament and Mythology: And other Basic Writings*, ed. and trans. Schubert M. Ogden (Philadelphia: Fortress Press, 1984), 95.
69. In order to ferret out divine will, ancient kings and leaders would employ an educated class of professional interpreters known as "diviners." These diviners were experts in the contemporaneous science known as "extispicy," a process or reading animal entrails in order to learn about the divine will regarding the outcome of events in the real world. For a general and accessible overview, see Ivan Starr, "Omens in the Ancient Near East," in *The Anchor Bible Dictionary*, ed. David Noel Freedman (New Haven, CT: Yale University Press, 1992), 5:15–17.
70. Bultmann, *New Testament and Mythology*, 96.
71. Bultmann, *New Testament and Mythology*, 97.
72. In the words of Mac from the series *It's Always Sunny in Philadelphia*, "Science is a LIAR sometimes." Mac continues, "Mr. Reynolds, these were all the smartest scientists on the planet. Only problem is, they kept being wrong. Sometimes." *It's Always Sunny in Philadelphia*, season 8, episode 10, "Reynolds vs. Reynolds: The Cereal Defense," directed by Richie Keen, written by Rob McElhenney, Glenn Howerton, and Charlie Day, aired December 20, 2012, on FX, Hulu, https://www.hulu.com/watch/f0643cf6-e4dc-4f0b-ac57-2d5beb111e24.
73. Bultmann, *New Testament and Mythology*, 99.
74. We would like to point out that demythologizing has been used harmfully in supersessionist interpretations by Christians. We are not endorsing this use of demythologizing nor do we use it in a way that presumes the cultural and technological superiority of the modern world vis-à-vis the ancient world or one tradition over another. Bultmann, *New Testament and Mythology*, 99.
75. Bultmann, *New Testament and Mythology*, 99.
76. Bultmann, *New Testament and Mythology*, 102.
77. Gottlieb, *Dystopian Fiction East and West*, 4.
78. Bultmann, *New Testament and Mythology*, 102.
79. Friedrich Lücke, *Versuch einer vollständigen Einleitung in die Offenbarung Johannis und in die gesammte apokalyptische Litteratur,* Litteratur, Commentar über die Schriften des Evangelisten Johannes, v. 4/1 (Bonn: Eduard Weber, 1832).
80. For a concise overview of the term "apocalyptic," see: John J. Collins, "What Is Apocalyptic Literature?" in *The Oxford Handbook of Apocalyptic Literature*, ed. John J. Collins (Oxford: Oxford University Press, 2014), 1–16.
81. Liddell and Scott, *A Greek-English Lexicon,* 201.
82. John J. Collins, ed., *Apocalypse: The Morphology of a Genre*, Semeia 14 (Missoula, MT: Scholars Press, 1979).
83. Collins, *Apocalyptic Imagination*, 51.
84. For a general overview of law in the ancient Near East, Hebrew Bible, and correcting economic wrongs (typified by the *mišārum* edict), see Douglas Knight,

Law, Power, and Justice in Ancient Israel, Library of Ancient Israel (Louisville, KY: Westminster John Knox, 2011), 217–22.

85. Collins, *Apocalyptic Imagination*, 9.

86. The Ethiopic version of the Book of Enoch is canonical to the both Christian and Jewish traditions emerging out of Ethiopia. Cf. George W.E. Nickelsburg and James C. VanderKam, *1 Enoch: The Hermeneia Translation*, Hermeneia (Minneapolis, MN: Fortress Press, 2012); and Collins, *Apocalyptic Imagination*, 61–75.

87. Following the popular culture theme of this volume, one might note that this section of the Book of Enoch is most similar to a work of fan fiction. During its time and in the following centuries, this form of interpreting books of the biblical canon was quite common.

88. 4 Ezra occupies the deuterocanonical book of 2 Esdras 3–14, which is persevered in the Apocrypha.

89. Golding, *Lord of the Flies*, 84.

90. Golding, *Lord of the Flies*, 143.

91. Wolfgang Herrman, "Baal Zebub," in *Dictionary of Deities and Demons in the Bible*, ed. Karel van der Toorn, Bob Becking, and Pieter W. van der Horst (Grand Rapids, MI: Eerdmans, 1999), 154.

BIBLIOGRAPHY

Apple Mac: 1984, directed by Ridley Scott, https://www.imdb.com/title/tt4227346/.

Balasopoulos, Antonis. "Celestial Cities and Rationalist Utopias." In *The Cambridge Companion to the City in Literature*, edited by Kevin R. McNamara, 17–30. Cambridge: Cambridge University Press, 2014.

Bultmann, Rudolf. *New Testament and Mythology: And other Basic Writings*. Selected, edited, and translated by Schubert M. Ogden. Philadelphia: Fortress Press, 1984.

Butler, Octavia. *Parable of the Sower*. New York: Grand Central Publishing, 2019.

Claeys, Gregory. *Dystopia: A Natural History*. Oxford: Oxford University Press, 2017.

Cline, Ernest. *Ready Player Two*. New York: Ballantine Books, 2020.

Collins, John J. *The Apocalyptic Imagination: An Introduction to Jewish Apocalyptic Literature*. Third Edition. Grand Rapids, MI: Eerdmans, 2016.

———. "What Is Apocalyptic Literature?" In *The Oxford Handbook of Apocalyptic Literature*, edited by John J. Collins, 1–16. Oxford: Oxford University Press, 2014.

Collins, John J., ed. *Apocalypse: The Morphology of a Genre*. Semeia 14. Missoula, MT: Scholars Press, 1979.

Fokkema, Douwe. *Perfect Worlds: Utopian Fiction in China and the West*. Amsterdam: Amsterdam University Press, 2011.

Golding, William. *Lord of the Flies*. New York: Penguin Books, 2006.

Good Place, The. Season 1, episode 1, "Everything is Fine." Directed by Drew Goddard. Written by Michael Schur. Aired September 19, 2016. https://www.netflix.com/watch/80191852.

Google Trends. Accessed May 27, 2022. https://trends.google.com/trends/explore?date=all&q=dystopia,dystopian,apocalyptic.
Gottlieb, Erika. *Dystopian Fiction East and West: A Universe of Terror and Trial.* Montreal: McGill-Queen's Press, 2001.
Herrman, Wolfgang. "Baal Zebub." In *Dictionary of Deities and Demons in the Bible*, edited by Karel van der Toorn, Bob Becking, and Pieter W. van der Horst, 154–56. Grand Rapids, MI: Eerdmans, 1999.
It's Always Sunny in Philadelphia. Season 8, episode 10. "Reynolds vs. Reynolds: The Cereal Defense." Directed by Richie Keen. Written by Rob McElhenney, Glenn Howerton, and Charlie Day. Aired December 20, 2012, on FX. Hulu, https://www.hulu.com/watch/f0643cf6-e4dc-4f0b-ac57-2d5beb111e24
Kearney, Richard. *On Stories.* New York: Routledge, 2002.
———. "The Wager of Carnal Hermeneutics." In *Carnal Hermeneutics*, edited by Richard Kearney and Brian Treanor, 15–56. New York: Fordham University Press, 2015.
Knight, Douglas. *Law, Power, and Justice in Ancient Israel.* Library of Ancient Israel. Louisville, KY: Westminster John Knox, 2011.
Liddell, Henry George, and Robert Scott. *A Greek-English Lexicon.* Oxford: Oxford University Press, 1996.
Lücke, Friedrich. *Versuch einer vollständigen Einleitung in die Offenbarung Johannis und in die gesammte apokalyptische Litteratur.* Litteratur, Commentar über die Schriften des Evangelisten Johannes, v. 4/1. Bonn: Eduard Weber, 1832.
Merriam-Webster. "Utopia." Accessed May 29, 2022. https://www.merriam-webster.com/dictionary/utopia.
More, Thomas. *Utopia.* Translated by Clarence H. Miller. New Haven, CT: Yale University Press, 2001.
Moylan, Tom. *Scraps of the Untainted Sky: Science Fiction, Utopia, Dystopia.* New York: Routledge, 2018.
Nickelsburg, George W.E., and James C. VanderKam. *1 Enoch: The Hermeneia Translation.* Hermeneia. Minneapolis, MN: Fortress Press, 2012.
Ricoeur, Paul. *Interpretation Theory: Discourse and the Surplus of Meaning.* Fort Worth, TX: Texas Christian University Press, 1976.
———. *Memory, History, Forgetting.* Translated by Kathleen Blamey and David Pellauer. Chicago: University of Chicago Press, 2004.
Sargent, Lyman. "The Three Faces of Utopianism Revisited." *Utopia Studies* 5, no. 1 (1994): 1–37.
Stamper, Kory. *Word By Word: The Secret Life of Dictionaries.* New York: Pantheon, 2017.
Starr, Ivan. "Omens in the Ancient Near East." In *The Anchor Bible Dictionary*, ed. David Noel Freedman, 5:15–17. New Haven, CT: Yale University Press, 1992.
Sutherland, John. *A Little History of Literature.* New Haven, CT: Yale University Press, 2013.
Tracy, David. *On Naming the Present: Reflections on God, Hermeneutics, and Church.* Maryknoll, NY: Orbis Books, 1994.

Upload. Season 1, episode 10. "Freeyond." Directed by Daina Reid. Written by Greg Daniels. Aired on May 1, 2020, on Amazon Prime Video. https://www.amazon.com/Upload-Official-Trailer/dp/B08BYYSF6M/.

Chapter 2

The Dystopic Relations of *Interstellar*

A Response from Christian Ecotheology

Thomas G. Hermans-Webster

Though many of the questions and ideas for this chapter are long in the making, an eerie sense of timing has gathered around my writing. It is July, 2021. On the radio today, there were stories of food and water shortages, crop failures, drought and record heat, preparations for and damages from a young-but-active season of wildfires in North America, dramatic shifts in the amount of energy our planet radiates back out into space, and recent flooding in New York and New England that was caused by the remnants of a tropical storm that hit Cedar Key, Florida, only a few days and a thousand miles earlier. These are only some of the many headlines of the climate crisis that faces Earth, our common home. And, while countless human people and our other-than-human relatives are suffering amid these dynamic conditions, there are billionaires locked in a race to see who can reach space first, fly the highest, and establish operational space tourism companies.

Christopher Nolan's 2014 film *Interstellar* is a visually stunning work of science fiction that captured my imagination the first time I saw it on the big screen, reigniting a wondrous longing toward the stars. Yet after today's radio stories and so many other recent ones like them, the film doesn't inspire me to interstellar travel. It doesn't even inspire me to pursue a ticket for whichever space tourism company is able to get its ship safely into and back from space. Instead, I am struck by the dystopic sense of it all. Anthropogenic climate change has turned Earth into a bad place, and I doubt that colonizing another planet will truly save humanity. Yet humanity and our other-than-human relatives can be saved, and the ecocatastrophic dystopia of *Interstellar* presents

Christian theology with the opportunity to articulate and cultivate salvation in terms of ecological well-being here and now.

In this chapter, I argue that *Interstellar* is a dystopian film that proposes answers to questions of ultimate concern in the dynamic and tumultuous conditions of anthropogenic climate change on our planet. I argue that the film's dystopic setting serves an apocalyptic purpose with theological implications. *Interstellar* uses widespread ecological catastrophe to reveal how human communities might suffer following the collapse of modern societies and wrestles with how human interrelatedness is an inescapable reality that can influence the world for ill or for good. Furthermore, these revelations challenge the viewer to consider the ecocatastrophe at hand in the twenty-first century with the question: "How adequate is the film's message of salvation in the face of current struggles for life and ecological well-being?" Finally, I respond to this question and the film's proposals for human flourishing from the perspective of a Christian ecological theology. Because apocalyptic stories are not statements of deterministic doom upon future events, my proposal is offered in the hope that the dystopic setting of *Interstellar* can be avoided. There are other options before us than the film presents, but we must act for justice, and we must act now.

DYSTOPIA IN *INTERSTELLAR*

Earth has become a dystopia, a bad place. Though the year is not precisely known, *Interstellar* opens sometime in the middle of the twenty-first century.[1] A decade has passed since major events brought down national military command centers. Remnants of extensive militarization in the late twentieth and early twenty-first centuries, like drone aircraft and guard robots, have been either abandoned or repurposed for civilian needs. These same events, the viewer is led to believe, have contributed to dramatic crashes in human population and societal infrastructure, jeopardizing planetary food systems. This is an ecocatastrophic dystopia.[2]

The main character of the film, Cooper (who goes by "Coop" for much of the film), is a former engineer and pilot. Now, he, like almost all his neighbors, is a corn farmer.[3] Cooper was widowed after his wife died from a cyst in her brain that could have been detected by MRI machines prior to the catastrophe. Cooper has two children, Tom and Murphy (who goes by "Murph"), and they live with Cooper's father-in-law, Donald, in their farmhouse. The children attend their local school and work around the farm where needed. In an early scene, Cooper attends a parent-teacher conference at the school to learn about the results of Tom's recent test scores and discuss Murph's disruptive behavior in class. This meeting weaves the dystopic threads of blighted crops, dust storms, population decline, and wayward military machinery together for the first time and sets a dystopic tone for the film.

ECOLOGICAL ANXIETY AND SOCIETAL NEED

Tom's test scores are good and show a high aptitude for farming, but "Tom's score simply isn't high enough" to be accepted into the university given how few students are annually accepted and how few resources are provided for their education.[4] The news angers Coop. How could one test foreclose the possibility of further education for his son? How could this one test effectively measure the child's future and how he can help meet society's needs? "Right now," the principal says, "we don't need more engineers. We didn't run out of television screens and planes. We ran out of food. The world needs farmers. Good farmers, like you. And Tom."[5] "Uneducated farmers," Coop retorts.[6]

This conflict of visions begins to reveal underlying anxieties about both the fragility of human life and the purpose of human living that have persisted through traumatic events within Coop's generation. These anxieties locate *Interstellar* within the broad dystopia genre. More specifically, the dystopic approach of *Interstellar* taps into ecological anxieties that Brian Stableford argues have "played a central role in futuristic fiction" in the latter third of the twentieth century and on into the twenty-first century.[7] Director Christopher Nolan heightens the film's ecological anxieties by including interview footage from Ken Burns's 2012 documentary miniseries *The Dust Bowl* at various points in both the exposition and conclusion of the film. By including the ecocatastrophic experiences of the Dust Bowl in the film, Nolan captivatingly blurs the lines between fictional storytelling and actual events in *Interstellar*. What has happened before may be happening again and with more devastation, he seems to suggest.

With this decision, Nolan brings ecocatastrophic dystopia together with science fiction in *Interstellar*. He incorporates the experiences of people who lived through the calamitous droughts and dust storms that ravaged prairie lands across the United States and Canada in the 1930s as if they are speaking about the present realities of Coop's world. In so doing, Nolan is able "to reflect or express our hopes and fears about the future, and more specifically to link those hopes and fears to science and technology."[8] Whether in plumes of smoke from burning okra fields or the candor of the principal's criticism of engineering, *Interstellar* makes a possible future, one full of pervasive ecological anxieties about our current planetary climate crisis, a stark reality.

MACHINE ANXIETY AND ECOCATASTROPHE

As the parent-teacher conference continues, the focus turns to Murph. Her teacher, Miss Hanley, expresses concern for Murph and hands Coop a book that Murph brought to class. It's an old textbook of his, and Miss Hanley has opened it to the section on NASA's Apollo missions and the lunar landings. "She always loved the pictures," Coop says with a smile.[9] Miss Hanley responds without reciprocating Coop's pleasure at seeing his old textbook. "It's an old federal textbook. We've replaced them with the corrected versions," she states.[10] These new books argue that the Apollo missions were faked, "a brilliant piece of propaganda," an effective ploy by the United States government because "the Soviets bankrupted themselves pouring resources into rockets and other useless machines," Miss Hanley responds.[11] In this exchange, Nolan echoes dystopic concerns about regimes that work to control and revise history and introduces another familiar dystopic theme into the film: anxiety toward mechanization.

In dystopic literature, as Gregory Claeys chronicles, anxiety toward mechanization has taken many forms. Claeys argues that "The Threat of the Machine" rose as a prominent theme during the industrializations of Britain and the United States and especially in response to World War I.[12] "Possessing the technological edge was essential to building the world's largest empire. But always there was ambiguity," Claeys writes.[13] The machine was useful for a human society as long as it wasn't capable of disrupting the society's mythic journey of progress towards eutopia—a good place. Referencing the automatic machine gun, Claeys argues that the machine "was a source of boastfulness *so long as it was deployed in imperial slaughter*."[14] When this ignorant positivity towards the machine was transgressed, when the machine was used against the society's so-called progress, "doubt, suspicion, skepticism, anomie, and anxiety stepped into the place of the vacuous optimism of the technophiles."[15] Miss Hanley's remarks about the "useless machines" that became capital drains on the Soviet Union reflect a particular kind of skepticism and anxiety towards mechanization that is important for understanding how *Interstellar* conceives of the struggle for human life and ecological well-being on Earth.

Human design, use of, and overreliance upon machines carries with it the distinct possibilities of intensifying ecocatastrophe in *Interstellar*; intensifying both the catastrophic events in the film's world and reiterating the dystopic theme that runs through the film's story. Exemplifying what Fitting calls the second contribution of science fiction to utopian literature, Miss Hanley and the principal each recognize "the role of technology as a tool for social transformation" without admitting positive or progressive outcomes as the necessary results of technological impacts.[16] They represent similar interpretations of the human problem: *whatever societal and ecological catastrophes happened were and are the results of human failures to relate well to the planet as the source of food.*

Their wariness towards "useless machines" signals a profoundly pragmatic anthropocentrism that undergirds their stances towards the mechanical and frames their solution to the struggle for human life and well-being. Does the machine assist in the rebuilding of human society by promoting food security? If so, then it should be understood and used. If not, then humanity can do without it. Using some machines can correct problems that emerged when using other machines, but this is a vicious cycle that never rules out the possibility that future ecological disasters may occur through human use of machines to relate to the planet. Humanity has both influenced and been influenced by machines to such an extent in the film that Miss Hanley and the principal take for granted that salvation from the human problem can only happen through one particular ethical framework: "We're a caretaker generation, Coop. And things are getting better," the principal puts it.[17] This is the film's earliest option for salvation from suffering in an ecocatastrophe.

DIRT, STARS, AND SALVATION

The principal explicitly calls their collective identity "a caretaker generation,"[18] and Miss Hanley tells Coop that, "if we don't want a repeat of the excess and waste of the twentieth century, then we need to teach our kids about this planet not tales of leaving it."[19] To be caretakers of the planet in *Interstellar*, however, is presented less like some recent interpretations of the "dominion language" in Genesis 1:26–28 and more like a hesitancy to venture—conceptually and physically—too far away from the dirt under one's feet.[20] Unlike other examples of the threat of the machine, Miss Hanley's skepticism and anxiety towards machines is shaped by this hesitancy to move too far away from corn cultivation. Her anxiety presents as a reaction to the traumatic experiences that happened as the result of "excess and waste."[21] Reliable food security assures human salvation, and all human and other-than-human systems and structures should be directed toward this goal. This first option for salvation in the midst of the struggle for life and ecological well-being is not adequate for Cooper, however.

Later that day, he expresses his frustration to Donald, and the second soteriological option in *Interstellar* emerges. "It's like we've forgotten who we are . . . explorers, pioneers, not caretakers . . . We used to look up in the sky and wonder at our place in the stars . . . now we just look down and worry about our place in the dirt."[22] Framed as an antagonism between "the stars" and "the dirt" that drives human responses to planetary food shortages, drastic climate change, loss of biodiversity, and catastrophic population collapse, *Interstellar* proposes two competing options for well-being in response to ecocatastrophic dystopia: escape to another planet or ignorantly struggle within this one, hoping that fortunes may turn. As the film progresses, the former becomes the only viable option.

Following Coop's meeting with Miss Hanley and the school principal, he and Murph find themselves on an adventure, tracking down geographic coordinates that they have mysteriously received through dust encoded in binary. The coordinates lead them to the secret headquarters of NASA, where they learn just how dire the planetary situation truly is. NASA is, seemingly, researching how to save the world because the only food that humans are still able to grow is corn. Blight killed wheat seven years earlier, is killing okra at the beginning of this growing season, and is predicted to become an existential threat to the global corn crop within seven years before threatening atmospheric oxygen levels themselves. "The last to starve will be the first to suffocate," Professor John Brand, a physicist at NASA and Coop's former mentor, tells him.[23]

This brief encounter with Professor Brand gives the viewer significant insight into the extent of the devastation that has occurred in the ecocatastrophe that frames *Interstellar*. Agriculture has become corn-growing, for maize is now the only crop that survives. The modern, colonial pattern of monoculture plantation has reached its idealized vision, and this is not good news. Loss of biodiversity across the planet means that humans are one of only a few species that are referenced in the film at all, and the human diversity in the film also reflects modern, colonial desires for white, heteronormative supremacy. Set within the context of monocultured disaster, Coop's longing for the stars ought to be witnessed as a potent, even if uncritical, advance of the settler-colonizing patterns that have inflicted ecological devastation on the whole planet, including on his and his neighbors' farms. The option for well-being by escaping the planet to settle on a new one cannot be separated from the histories of settler-colonization that turned Earth into a dystopia.

Yet, Professor Brand introduces and recruits Cooper to a crew of astronauts who have been assembled to pursue the salvation of humanity through just such an escape. "Plan A," as it's called, seeks to locate, settle, and colonize an inhabitable planet beyond our solar system. Should this work, NASA will be prepared to evacuate humanity to the newfound planet, leaving behind Earth and its increasing hostility toward human life. If Plan A won't work, then "Plan B" will travel with the crew. This plan calls for the laboratory incubation of fertilized embryos to begin to grow a new human community on the suitable planet. These are the live options for salvation as Professor Brand and NASA understands the situation, and they are pursued through the film's interstellar journey. By the end of the film, Murph has led the NASA mission that has saved the human species. They now live in a space station that orbits Saturn, near the opening of a wormhole to another galaxy. Coop has journeyed through that wormhole to locate Professor Brand's daughter, Dr. Amelia Brand, one of the astronauts in his crew, on a habitable planet as she begins the settler-colonial project anew.

ECOLOGICAL WELLBEING IN DYSTOPIA

Interstellar engages themes that are familiar to Christian theologies, including questions of ecological well-being and reflection on human experiences of our own finitude, contingency, and relatedness. In this sense, *Interstellar* is also firmly dystopic rather than anti-utopic, for it critiques contemporary society in such ways that imply the need for change before catastrophe of some kind befalls our world.[24] I have said above that the film's dystopia is also apocalyptic in the most fundamental way: the dystopic circumstances reveal ways that humans relate to one another and to our other-than-human relatives in our planetary moment. Some have used the term *Capitalocene* to critique how the interlocking oppressions of this period depend on the transnational movement of capitalist economic resources to support the extraction and exploitation of "natural resources." The dystopic circumstances of *Interstellar*, however, illustrate relational complexities that require a more comprehensive analysis of interconnectedness and oppression than the *Capitalocene* offers. Proposed by Anna Tsing and others, *Plantationocene* is a term that provides this needed thoroughness, naming how transnational accumulation and movement of financial resources further depends upon coercively alienating creatures from their biodiverse home ecosystems for the benefit of a limited number of human people.[25]

Our current ecological crises are replete with relationships that are dis-eased under the oppressive weight of Plantationocene activities that follow the extractive pattern of commodification and alienation of biotic and abiotic communities alike. Furthermore, the dystopic setting of *Interstellar* reveals possibilities for the struggle for liberation in response to these multifarious cruelties even after unspeakable loss and devastation. In the language of Christian theology, it could be said that *Interstellar* proposes an understanding of both sin and salvation in an ecocatastrophic dystopia.

The great focus of the film is on the human species' journey into salvation. From what, however, is humanity to be saved? One interpretation of the epic interstellar mission might propose that the human race is to be saved from Earth itself, from Nature, from the radical contingencies and finitudes that have been exacerbated by ecocatastrophe. While on the mission, Dr. Amelia

Brand responds that such an interpretation is woefully incorrect. Nature can be "formidable, frightening, but not evil," for humanity is who has introduced evil into the equation of life.[26] Evil is what humanity has taken with us on our journeys around the world. With Dr. Brand's brief insight, *Interstellar* proposes that space exploration for the salvation of the human race is to save humanity from ourselves. This notion of sin stands in contrast to the first theory of salvation—caretaking hesitancy that focuses on the dirt—and to an annihilationist interpretation of the second theory of salvation—we humans are victims who leave Earth behind because Earth will destroy itself.

Dr. Brand's notion of sin and evil is, however, inadequate in two ways. First, she fails to articulate an accurate history of which humans and human societies have furthered evil through ecological catastrophe. Tsing frames this inadequacy well, writing, "'Man' does not mean humans, but a particular kind of being invented by Enlightenment thought and brought into operation by modernization and state regulation" and commodification and genocide of humans who were not quite white, Christian, and "Man" enough.[27] Second, Dr. Brand never explains how the very humans who are violently estranged from their relatives on their home planet will not reinscribe the same necrotic violence in their new settlements. Through Dr. Brand's description of evil and the mission's settler-colonizing goals, *Interstellar* fails to offer an adequate message of salvation in the face of current oppressions of life and ecological well-being on Earth. The film's vision, while foregrounding a collectivist effort to save the species, depends upon the very modern exceptionalism and colonialism that wreaked havoc upon the well-being of the planet in the first place.

For both Plan A and Plan B, salvation depends on patterning the human person as excepted out of the cosmic web of relations, licensed to then "'take out' whatever impedes [the] ascent" towards the other world where we can start afresh.[28] *Anthropic exceptionalism*, as Catherine Keller phrases it, operates as the "normative separation of the human from the nonhuman, from the animal, from 'nature.'"[29] The separation of the human out from our other-than-human relatives throughout the cosmos is itself sinful. In *Interstellar*, this exceptionalism is most evident in the theme that particular human individuals can be the exceptions to the fray of nature both as nature's masters and as idols for other humans who are still caught in nature's struggles.[30] Yet, when confronted with anthropogenic ecocatastrophe, salvation-through-abandonment fails to save anyone. Instead, it perpetuates the insidious lie that humanity and nature happen apart from one another, that we are not all connected within an emerging cosmos.

Along with many Christian ecological theologians, I am convinced that ecological well-being will only come when we abandon this dangerous exceptionalism. I echo Norman Pittenger. He wrote that to prioritize selfish exceptionalism "is to blaspheme: it is to deny in practice that the love of God is indeed reflected in and part of the reality of love of the neighbor."[31] The ecologic of salvation in the Christian sense recognizes that, from the dirt under our feet to the stars of the farthest galaxy, we are all related to one another and are all influential in each other's lives. This includes God. The Christian message of love, then, is misunderstood whenever it is relegated to a sentimental sweetness. Christian ecotheology asserts that love-in-action reconciles each of us with one another, other-than-human creatures, and God through Christ's incarnation, life, death, and resurrection. Love is the creative and restorative justice that is necessary for promoting the healing of the dis-eased relationships that pervade our world. The possible ecocatastrophe that occupies *Interstellar* should be particularly concerning for Christians because a meal is a centering experience of Christian reconciliation and love: the Eucharist, Holy Communion, or Last Supper. *Interstellar* warns that the Plantationocene's continued reliance upon and expansion of industrial transnational agriculture will not bear sustainable, just, or healthy fruit.[32]

The Eucharist teaches Christians that meals are more than biological acts of calorie acquisition. Meals reveal and enact how communities value and prioritize the relationships that constitute them in the world. As more extreme climatic events occur and threaten food supplies across the planet, meals that intensify the experiences of God's priorities for love and justice will be gifts of salvation through ecological well-being in love and for the life of the world. Such meals will happen when people, especially those of us who eat in what has been called the Western Diet, become better relatives to the people who are intimately involved in food production and to the plants, animals, and fungi whom we eat. This planet is our common home, and we can become good relatives in love that overcomes suffering. Our salvation need not come as we flee to a space station.

CONCLUSION

Interstellar inspires a different adventure than one of interstellar colonization. Responding to ecocatastrophic dystopia, Christian ecological theology challenges each of us to recognize that human integration within the interconnected cosmos means that ecological well-being can only happen through our reconciled participation in the restoration of the world. Salvation will not happen by abandoning suffering but through participative healing, through attending to the wounded of the world in confession, repentance, reparation, and transformed living. Rather than dreams of conquest or settler-colonial fantasies of "A New World," wondering with Coop about our place in the stars will inspire dynamic, responsive, and participative acts that reveal God's love for life of the world and attune each of us to the health and well-being of the dirt from whom our food grows. This is a different adventure, yet it overflows with zest and peace, beauty and truth, love and creativity that weave us into abundant life.

NOTES

1. Regarding the chronological setting of the film, I assume that Donald, the grandfather, was born sometime between 1993 and 2004. This would mean that he was between seven and eighteen years old when the human population on Earth crossed over into seven billion people. Early in the film, he says, "When I was a kid, it felt like they made something new every day. Some gadget or idea. Like every day was Christmas. But six billion people, just try to imagine that. And every last one of them trying to have it all." Assuming a generation gap of twenty-five to thirty years, then Donald would be between sixty-five and seventy-five years old with grandchildren aged fifteen and ten years old, respectively. If Donald was born in 1993 and is seventy-five—the oldest possible age I can figure in this scenario—at the beginning of the film, then the film opens in 2068 at the latest. *Interstellar*, directed by Christopher Nolan, (Paramount Pictures and Warner Brothers, 2014), featuring Matthew McConaughey, Anne Hathaway, Jessica Chastain, and Michael Caine, DVD (Warner Home Video, 2015), 0:16:15; United Nations, Department of Economic and Social Affairs, Population Division (2019), "World Population Prospects 2019," accessed July 1, 2021, https://population.un.org/wpp/DataQuery/.

2. I understand *Interstellar* to fit within Stableford's description of ecocatastrophic dystopia because the film lacks "the slightest vestige of trust in the possibility that the exercise of moral restraint might slow the catastrophe down, let alone prevent it proceeding to its climax." Yet, the good place—eu/topia—is still possible according to *Interstellar*. The possibility of eutopia is what makes the film a dys-topia rather than an anti-utopia, a genre that, according to Fitting, critiques the very notion that there is a good (or even better) place for which to hope, imagine, and work. As Stableford notes with other ecocatastrophic dystopias in the early twenty-first century, the eutopia in *Interstellar*, however, is "necessarily postponed until the aftermath of an environmental collapse." I add that it is also postponed until the colonizing humans centered in the film can construct their haven away from the collapse. Brian Stableford, "Ecology and Dystopia," in *The Cambridge Companion to Utopian Literature*, ed. Gregory Claeys (Cambridge: Cambridge University Press, 2010), 278–79; Peter Fitting, "Utopia, Dystopia, and Science Fiction," in Claeys, *The Cambridge Companion to Utopian Literature*, 141.

3. Cooper's neighbor, Nelson, decided to grow okra instead of corn for the season, but he ends up setting the crop aflame to combat blight. "They're saying it's the last harvest for okra. Ever." Donald remarks. "He should have planted corn like the rest of us," Cooper responds. *Interstellar*, 0:04:48–55.

4. *Interstellar*, 0:10:30–0:10:48.

5. *Interstellar*, 0:11:10–0:11:21.
6. *Interstellar*, 0:11:21.
7. Stableford, "Ecology and Dystopia," 273.
8. Fitting, "Utopia, Dystopia, and Science Fiction," 138.
9. *Interstellar*, 0:11:50.
10. *Interstellar*, 0:11:51.
11. *Interstellar*, 0:11:51–0:12:15.
12. Gregory Claeys, *Dystopia: A Natural History* (Oxford: Oxford University Press, 2017), 313.
13. Claeys, *Dystopia*, 314.
14. Claeys, *Dystopia*, 314. Emphasis mine.
15. Claeys, *Dystopia*, 314.
16. Fitting, "Utopia, Dystopia, and Science Fiction," 139.
17. *Interstellar*, 0:11:25.
18. *Interstellar*, 0:11:26.
19. *Interstellar*, 0:12:20.
20. Countless biblical scholars and ecological theologians have highlighted the Genesis 1:26–28 pericope as they have wrestled with Hebrew and Christian relationships to the other-than-human world. Alternatives to what Phyllis Trible has called "The Dilemma of Dominion" have proposed words like "stewardship" and "caretakers" to characterize God's desire for the human's relationship to our common world. There is not space in this chapter to adjudicate those discussions. I only want to note the shared language between the film and these more recent biblical interpretations. Phyllis Trible, "Ecology and the Bible: The Dilemma of Dominion," *Canon & Culture* 6, no. 2 (2012): 5–19.
21. *Interstellar*, 0:12:20.
22. *Interstellar*, 0:15:50–0:16:00.
23. *Interstellar*, 0:29:30.
24. Fitting writes of the difference that "the anti-utopia is, on the other hand, explicitly or implicitly a defense of the status quo" because it is a critique of the very idea of imagining a better world. Fitting, "Utopia, Dystopia, and Science Fiction," 141.
25. Building on Noboru Ishikawa's work regarding cycles of capital in human societies as they relate to cycles of nitrogen and other materials in transnational corporate agriculture plantations, Donna Haraway discusses different names than the Anthropocene that might further thicken an ecotheological account of and responsibility to histories of commodification in racial capitalism: the Capitalocene and the Plantationocene. Citing Andreas Malm's origination of the term in 2014, Haraway describes the Capitalocene as capable of insisting upon a longer, more complex, and contextually situated analysis of the epoch or transition event in which we find ourselves than can the Anthropocene—especially given the latter's ambiguity regarding the generalization of actions to the whole species. Anna Tsing adds that the Capitalocene provides a critical analysis of how capital moves through and across societies to influence ecologies even at tremendous distances away from the site of the capital or the capitalist. This alienating movement is at the heart of the term I use in this chapter: the Plantationocene. Tsing rightly notes that, "we need to understand the dynamics

through which plants and animals are abstracted in order to become resources that can be used for investment. Plantations and feedlots are places where this happens." The Plantationocene is a useful frame for this chapter's analysis of human interconnectedness with our planetary relatives because it recognizes the toll of commodification upon human, other-than-human, and divine lives as we become with one another, through the meeting of basic bodily and societal needs through food. Furthermore, because it can account for both contextuality and complexity in these relationships, the Plantationocene can also be understood as an apocalyptic event that can be ended through the struggle for liberation. Learning from Theodore Walker, Jr., I argue that the Plantationocene's greatest usefulness, then, is its ability to adequately analyze the multitude of imbricating oppressions that characterize modernity—"the increasing commodification of the world, starting with the emergence of transatlantic slavery in the fifteenth century" chief among them—so that they can be overcome through the struggle for liberation. Donna Haraway, Noboru Ishikawa, and Anna L. Tsing, "Anthropologists are Talking—About the Anthropocene," *Ethnos* 81, no. 3 (2016): 555–57; Theodore Walker, Jr., *Mothership Connections: A Black Atlantic Synthesis of Neoclassical Metaphysics and Black Theology* (Albany, NY: State University of New York Press, 2004), 15.

26. *Interstellar*, 0:52:00.
27. Tsing, "Anthropologists are Talking—About the Anthropocene," 541.
28. Catherine Keller, *Political Theology of the Earth: Our Planetary Emergency and the Struggle for a New Public* (New York: Columbia University Press, 2018), 48.
29. Keller, *Political Theology of the Earth*, 48.
30. "This crew represents the best of humanity," Dr. Amelia Brand says to Coop, singling out the leader of the previous mission, Dr. Mann, as an exemplar of the species. *Interstellar*, 52:17.
31. Norman Pittenger, *Catholic Faith in a Process Perspective* (Maryknoll, NY: Orbis Books, 1981), 112.
32. Nor, apparently, will it bear grapes, and that could be a problem for a meal of bread and wine.

BIBLIOGRAPHY

Claeys, Gregory. *Dystopia: A Natural History*. Oxford: Oxford University Press, 2017.
Claeys, Gregory, ed. *The Cambridge Companion to Utopian Literature*. Cambridge: Cambridge University Press, 2010.
Fitting, Peter. "Utopia, Dystopia and Science Fiction." In Claeys, *The Cambridge Companion to Utopian Literature*, 135–53.
Haraway, Donna, Noboru Ishikawa, and Anna L. Tsing. "Anthropologists are Talking—About the Anthropocene." *Ethnos* 81, no. 3 (2016): 535–64.
Interstellar. Directed by Christopher Nolan. Paramount Pictures and Warner Brothers, 2014. DVD. Warner Home Video, 2015.
Keller, Catherine. *Political Theology of the Earth: Our Planetary Emergency and the Struggle for a New Public*. New York: Columbia University Press, 2018.

Pittenger, Norman. *Catholic Faith in a Process Perspective*. Maryknoll, NY: Orbis Books, 1981.

Stableford, Brian. "Ecology and Dystopia." In Claeys, *The Cambridge Companion to Utopian Literature*, 259–81.

Trible, Phyllis. "Ecology and the Bible: The Dilemma of Dominion." *Canon & Culture* 6, no. 2 (2012): 5–19.

United Nations, Department of Economic and Social Affairs, Population Division (2019). "World Population Prospects 2019." Accessed July 1, 2021. https://population.un.org/wpp/DataQuery/.

Walker, Theodore Jr. *Mothership Connections: A Black Atlantic Synthesis of Neoclassical Metaphysics and Black Theology*. Albany, NY: State University of New York Press, 2004.

Chapter 3

Color-blind Dystopia
The Giver, *Theology, Race, and Ricoeur*

Scott Donahue-Martens

The Giver is an award-winning children's book that imagines a carefully designed society gone awry. The book addresses coming of age, euthanasia, memory, conformity, and utopia. Like many dystopian works, it blurs the lines between utopia and dystopia by requiring the reader to determine whether narrative elements are utopic or dystopic. The reader's perspectives and positions impact the process of making sense of these elements. Both the process of making sense and the narrative elements evolve in a correlative manner through the reading of the novel. What first appears as a well-structured and ideal society turns out to be a place of restricting utilitarianism. The society maintains conformity to its ideals due to an intentional move to "Sameness" where significant elements of difference were altered.[1] Sameness was created through a deliberate process of forgetting that took place in the community's past. Careful control over memory and history led to a habitus of Sameness that refused to engage meaningfully with meaningful matters of differences. The attempt to achieve utopia through an intentional forgetting of the past turned into dystopic uniformity. Parallels between Sameness and forgetting exist in the color-blind approach to race in North America. Like Sameness in *The Giver*, the promised utopia of the color-blind approach to racial inequality is actually dystopic in the ways it fails to account for racialization and racial equity. Lois Lowry's, *The Giver*, reveals that memory can serve critical and constructive functions to imagine a more equitable world, which also serves as a theological imperative stemming from the gospel to actualize racial equity.

There are numerous significant topics to explore in *The Giver*, but the focus of this chapter is on forgetting and memory regarding race and racism.

The community in *The Giver* is postracial because of genetic altering, literal color-blindness, and forgetting. These three factors coalesce to form a habitus of Sameness because elements of alterity were selectively purged. Habitus is a concept I draw from Pierre Bourdieu as a way of exploring the embodied impact of hermeneutical schematization on individual and community systems. Habitus is a "system of durable, transposable dispositions, structured structures predisposed to function as structuring structures."[2] Habitus is a largely invisible paradigm that shapes individual and communal identity. It exerts itself by forming the "schemes of perception, thought and action" of individuals and communities in ways that seek to "guarantee the 'correctness' of practices and their constancy over time."[3] Thus, habitus is a formative shaper of human perception, thought, and action. Like a watershed fed by diverse collections of water, habitus allows for degrees of freedom and unique expressions but attempts to direct the flow of perception, thoughts, and actions toward a collective constant. Once formed, habitus reinforces itself through established norms. It can also be thought of as an embodied hermeneutical lens which is largely unconscious and formed in direct connection with social situations.

In many ways, habitus is an enactment of history through social living in the present; however, *The Giver* raises interesting questions about the relationship between a falsified history or past on present being. *The Giver* offers a glimpse into a narrative reality where past racialized trauma is misremembered to form a particular mode of being in the present, which impacts the way habitus is "a present past that tends to perpetuate itself into the future."[4] In other words, one way of achieving changed action and perception of the present is to manipulate the past. The manipulation of the past allows for the formation of a habitus which preserves the desired ideologies.[5] Once formed, the habitus enacts itself socially and regulates itself through community life, but *The Giver* underscores the danger of a false habitus which presents itself as utopic but is actually dystopic. While such a modification of social being is clearly dystopian in the way that identity is manipulated, the racialized forgetting and minimization of difference in *The Giver* has direct parallels with the present-day North American color-blind approach to race and racism. The drive to Sameness and intentional manipulation of the past to shape the present may be better obfuscated by present-day America for portions of the American public, but it desperately attempts to shape the habitus of American life in similar ways to the habitus produced in *The Giver*. *The Giver* and Sameness reveal part of what is at stake over current book banning, debates surrounding Critical Race Theory (CRT), and revisionist history.

In *The Giver*, only the main character and one other person are aware of the concept of color and remember a time "when flesh was many different colors."[6] The interplay between racial Sameness and forgetting has correlations with the work of race theorist Eduardo Bonilla-Silva. Bonilla-Silva argues that the dominant racial ideology in the United States is color-blind racism. Much like the drive to Sameness in *The Giver*, color-blind ideologies minimize race by claiming not to see race or by claiming to be race-neutral.[7] Color-blind ideologies deny the ongoing significance of race and racism in the United States. Color-blind racism thrives by its invisibility and its assurance that covert racialized structures will replace overt actors in the new racialized system. In addition to minimizing race in the present, color-blind ideologies stem from a frame that argues "the past is the past" in order to deny the ongoing prevalence of racism and to support a false claim of a utopic, postracial society in the United States.[8] Denying the significance of the past on the present is an attempt of communal forgetting akin to the collective forgetting in *The Giver*. What Lowry imagines in a fictive world without remembered history and race parallels Bonilla-Silva's understanding of the dominant racial ideology of color-blind racism in the actual world. At stake in both worlds are identity, well-being, truth, and difference.

In order to address present racial inequality, histories of oppression cannot be forgotten, and resistance must be remembered; remembering can lead to liberation in the present. The hope of liberation discloses critical constructive functions of memory. Liberating efforts struggle against elements of the dominant ideologies of color-blind racism. The church must take a role in rejecting white-washed versions of history, including ones that minimize the harms of colonial Christianity. In order to discern and proclaim the Gospel, the church must support the oppressed in dismantling ideologies of modern oppression which persist. *The Giver* offers critical insights and constructive paths toward dismantling racialized minimization. Minimization is a frame of the dominant color-blind ideology which denies the prevalence and salience of race in the present.[9] I previously argued that minimization can be understood in hermeneutical terms. "The hermeneutic of minimization has become a closed loop that justifies and reinforces itself by latching onto non-racial factors. It presumes that situation X cannot be about race; therefore, it explains situation X in non-racial terms."[10] Minimization is especially problematic because of its general ethnocentric orientation, and it is not confined to hermeneutics alone. Minimization is a core part of a habitus of whiteness which is bodily enacted every day. Minimization tends to flatten difference by appealing to assumed universal commonalities, which makes it difficult to identify and subvert. *The Giver* offers insight into a society which minimized difference to such extremes that it was socially engineered out of existence. Carter Hansen writes, "Lowry's world is an engineered Utopia gone wrong due to its extinction of aesthetics and personal choice, and through her protagonist's alienation from his society and resistance to it, the novel offers hope for a better future."[11] For the present world, hope for a better future comes through truthful remembering of the oppressed and for the oppressed. This remembering can lead to dismantling harmful ideologies in the present with deep roots in the past. The Gospel calls the church to participate in this truthful remembering and dismantling for the sake of liberation.

THE GIVER

The Giver begins with the preteen main character, Jonas, and his family discussing their feelings as they are required to do every evening. Jonas searches for the right language to describe his experience of waiting to be assigned his job at the upcoming "Ceremony of the Twelve." The reader quickly learns that Jonas lives in a well-regulated and mostly self-contained community. Rules govern almost every aspect of life, and everyone is constantly watched. Infractions of rules are accompanied by reminders over a speaker system that community members are forbidden from turning off. Children and adults are acutely aware that their lives are always watched and that they are expected to conform to the rules which govern the community. Yet, this way of life appears normal to Jonas and everyone in the community. Their habitus has been formed to accept this way of living and being as normal. For the most part, there is no awareness that anything is missing or that an alternative way of living would be desirable.

Even the population of the community is "perfectly" regulated so that everyone has food and shelter. Controlled birth rates and euthanasia ensure that the right number of people live in the community at any given time. Citizens are regularly euthanized for a variety of reasons, like rule breaking, after a period of retirement, if requested, or if born as the smaller twin. Children are not raised by their biological parents, nor do they have awareness of being in relationship with their assigned parents as a bonded family.[12] They are given to couples whose job is to help them be productive citizens. Thus, the family unit primarily serves civil functions. It is presumed that parents do not have romantic feelings for each other or emotional bonds with the children assigned to them. In addition to other methods of population control, people are regulated by medication that suppresses emotions and desires. This impacts the everyday lives of people, especially how they relate to each other. Many readers might wonder what the point of such existence is as Lowry challenges the reader to consider the costs of utopia.

In addition to biological control and influence, a committee makes the most significant choices in the lives of citizens and orders the community. This underscores that free will, agency, and autonomy are major themes of the book. This committee, as well as the rules, maintain order. The regulation of order is a source of comfort to the citizen. Throughout the book, people refer to the constancy of the rules and community in positive manners. While the committee has some power to make new rules, Lowry does not give the reader much insight into how existing rules were put into place. Largely, the committee seems to be responsible for maintaining a well-structured society. There is nearly complete trust between the citizens of the community and the regulations. This trust is revealed when Jonas contemplates whether he would fit into the community as he matured. Jonas thinks to himself, "How could someone not fit in? The community was so meticulously ordered, the choices so carefully made."[13] Even with the most significant choices of his life being made for him, Jonas clearly likes being a part of his community. As the plot develops, freedom to choose and choice itself become increasingly complicated. Eventually, Jonas learns to differentiate himself from the community, which results in a breakdown of the communal structured habitus in Jonas' life.

As with many dystopian novels, the relationship between the individual and community is central in *The Giver*. Unlike other dystopian works, the affiliation is largely marked by symbiosis. Citizens have their basic needs met and accept the life provided to them. The ruling committee does not benefit from their power or explicitly abuse their power. The committee makes decisions in a way that largely preserves the established order, which underscores that the society functioned well for a long time by many metrics. This is different from dystopian works which emphasize the political ramifications of totalitarianism and abuses of power. Lowry largely invites the reader to consider the social implications of dystopia in a seemingly benign situation where power is not politically misused but socially creates an unvaried existence through the elimination of difference.

One way of creating and regulating order was by eliminating differences that were viewed as causing conflict. Lowry underscores the social implications of this in a scene where the reader learns it was considered rude to draw attention to differences or seek attention for being different.[14] The rejection of difference extended to many areas beyond the social realm, including terraforming and climate control. Many of the reasons for rejecting difference have utilitarian purpose; for instance, crop production necessitated weather control.[15] While seemingly benign, these contribute to a habitus of Sameness and conformity where difference is exchanged for stability. A more extreme version of this trade is the mandatory feeling-suppressing pills which prevent attachment and other potential causes of conflict stemming from choice and difference. Citizens are required to take these pills at the onset of puberty and throughout the rest of their lives. Despite the pressure to ignore what differences existed in the community, Jonas was acutely aware of difference because of his eyes. From birth, Jonas' eyes set him apart because, with few exceptions, almost everyone in the community has the same eyes. This difference is why Jonas was chosen by the committee for a special job within the community.

At the "Ceremony of Twelve," each twelve-year-old is assigned their future career. Jonas was given the job "Receiver of Memory." Jonas learns that the Receiver advises the committee and is exempt from some of the rules which govern the society. There is only one Receiver at a time and only people with eyes like Jonas can be the Receiver. The Receiver lives differently from the community because the Receiver has something the community lacks, memory and open access to books. As previously noted, in order to overcome difference, the community underwent processes of change, including communal forgetting. A core part of avoiding conflict and difference stemmed from intentionally forgetting the past. Community members did not know about the past and were locked into the present which avoided polarization. Each person had memories of their individual life, but the community lacked a real sense of the past or present. Famine, wars, geography, and history were all selectively and intentionally forgotten by everyone except the Receiver of Memory. The Receiver of Memory was tasked with holding the collective memories of the past on behalf of the community. The Receiver bore the pains of the past so that the community could live without pain in the present. Because there can only be one Receiver at a time, when Jonas was assigned the role, the previous Receiver named himself "The Giver."[16] When his role was explained to him by the Giver, Jonas responded, "I thought there was only us. I thought there was only now."[17] Jonas learned of the past and remembered events forgotten by the community through the Giver.

As the novel unfolds, the Giver and Jonas eventually have a different relationship than is possible for anyone else; one by one, the Giver transfers the community's past memories to Jonas. At first, the Giver only transmits happy memories like sledding, snow, and Christmas. As time moves on, Jonas must receive painful memories like sunburn, war, and famine. These memories are excruciating because the process of transmission is not passive. The Giver explains that he can re-experience memories from the past, including memories that go back much farther than his life, and that by passing memories to Jonas, Jonas experiences them vicariously. Jonas feels the memories as if they were happening, which reveals the cost of remembering painful events. The community is unwilling to pay the cost of remembering, even as they benefited from the memories because of the role of Receiver. The Giver and Jonas enjoy a special relationship that would not be possible apart from the memories they share. It is through memories that they know of love and family.[18] Their relational interdependence stems from their capacity to remember beyond their biological lives. Because they hold memories of the past, they relate to each other differently in the present.

When recounting the history of their community, the Giver refers to the founding event as moving to "Sameness."[19] He acknowledged that the move to Sameness came with significant losses, but also resulted in significant control that served utilitarian purposes. The move to Sameness extended even to seeing color, which no one but Jonas and the Giver can do. The community intentionally chose to be without certain aspects of life to meet their basic needs and for order. Through memories, Jonas felt true emotions for the first time and started to see the limitations of rejecting difference. Jonas evaluates the costs of "utopia," especially concerning choice and decision-making capacity. From a developmental perspective, this coincides with Jonas' coming of age, which also involves increased decision-making. In the story, Jonas has the capacity to see beyond, which means that he can catch glimpses of color; however, it is through memory that this capacity solidifies. In their article, Han and Lee assert that Jonas' unfolding capacity to see color enhances his capacity to engage in meaningful meaning-making.[20] Jonas comes to understand something like "selfhood" by engaging memory and color which allow for greater depths of recognition than Sameness allows.[21] The "color blind" that Han and Lee write about is literal color-blindness; however, there are thematic similarities with racial-blind ideologies. These thematic similarities are also potentially relevant in the world of the reader. It is significant that racial and literal color-blindness are both linked with memory and forgetting.

Lowry engages serious themes through her adolescent character, which connects the critical function of dystopia with adolescent readers entering similar life stages as Jonas. Jonas notes how Sameness removed significant aspects of life. In a profound exchange, the Giver and Jonas discuss how freedom and choice can lead to people making wrong choices. The early assumption was that wrong choices would lead to an unsafe community.[22] As Jonas receives more memories, however, he comes to realize that memory and meaning are intimately connected. Memories provide a sense of purpose and meaning to life.[23] When critiquing the structure of the community, the Giver indicates that "without memories it's all meaningless."[24] Remembering can be a core process of being. While remembering and especially freedom of choice involve risk, they are enriching components of being. Jonas concludes that people should be free to make wrong choices rather than have their choices made for them and be regulated by strict control.

The Giver and Jonas devise a plan for releasing the memories back into the community. They hoped that knowledge of the past would allow for a more meaningful being in the present. Jonas and the Giver felt that the pain and burden of memories were worth paying to abolish Sameness. This underscores that the cost of truthful grappling with the past is worth paying; rather than, taking the color-blind shortcut of forgetting. The plan required Jonas to leave the community. Jonas hoped that the community would be a place where memories, color, love, and family were once again present. Jonas and the Giver determine that Sameness was not a price that people should be willing to pay for a regulated and controlled life. While Sameness brought about a sense of collectivism, it also depended on atomized individualism as social connections between people were utilitarian. Jonas and the Giver saw that life has a quality of depth that refused to be systematized uniformly. This means that freedom of choice should be an element of meaningful and complex being. Their plans were disrupted and Jonas took great risks when he was forced to improvise. Jonas makes significant personal sacrifices as he attempts to bring about the desired change of returning memory to the community. The ending of the book is ambiguous, and until the publications of sequels, readers were left wondering what happens to Jonas.

MEMORY AND COLOR-BLIND IDEOLOGIES

Dystopia can be a revelatory genre or tool for considering life in the real world. While there are a variety of uses of dystopia, "Dystopia's foremost truth lies in its ability to reflect upon the causes of social and ecological evil as systemic."[25] What I find so promising about *The Giver* and racialization is the way it reveals that the color-blind habitus cannot bring about racial equity through forgetting. Dystopian literature allows the reader to imagine an alternative world or horizon that often represents core elements of the reader's world. Often, the truth revealing function of dystopian literature shows readers structural elements of the real world that negatively impact populations. *The Giver* reveals the danger of selective forgetting for the sake of a supposed collective good. *The Giver* also challenges white-washed narratives which deny difference and refuse to engage honestly with the past. Both forgetting and minimizing difference are core elements of color-blind ideologies. *The Giver* underscores how a habitus, like a habitus of whiteness or color-blindness, can appear true and good but actually depend on misremembering the past and result in further inequalities.

Race theorist Bonilla-Silva argues the present racial structure in the United States is marked by color-blind ideologies which attempt to avoid accounting for the significance of race on modern living. Color-blind ideologies reinforce dominant ideologies of whiteness by affording material and immaterial benefits to some while enforcing detriments upon others. By attempting to ignore race, Bonilla-Silva argues that the dominant group can receive benefits from racist structures and ideologies while viewing themselves as not racist. Hence, he refers to the present situation as "racism without racist" in order to explore how color-blind racism allows racial inequality to persist in the United States.[26] Color-blind structures and ideologies present a narrative about the past and present where race no longer matters. It purports to be progressive or racially neutral, often proof-texting figures like Martin Luther King Jr., for support and depending on a hermeneutic that constantly minimizes race.[27]

One element from Bonilla-Silva's extensive argument is especially revelatory for consideration of the present topic. Bonilla-Silva recounts how color-blind racism relies on "fable like" storylines which are taken as "factual" by the dominant ideology.[28] These storylines are crucial to the collective influence and permeation of color-blind ideologies because they offer avenues for non-racial interpretations that are treated as true, even if they are not. One of these storylines is "the past is the past" which attempts to deny the ongoing significance of past oppression on people and structures in the present.[29] This storyline is used in response to counternarratives that attempt to account for the significance of past racial oppression on the present. In other words, when nonwhite people point out how the system of slavery and economic order continues to benefit some, they are often told that their analysis is flawed on individual and historical levels. The storyline argues that the past is no longer relevant and that things are better today than they ever have been. The storyline attempts to erase race by refusing to see its significance on modern life. The storyline is an intentional attempt at forgetting the past by failing to account for the past's impact on the present. By attempting to cut past racialization, the present habitus of whiteness disconnects itself from the past. In doing so, even when done with good intentions, it embodies a harmful and false habitus. Lowry's *The Giver* offers a window into a world where history and memory are also forsaken for the sake of dominating Sameness, including racial Sameness. Rather than remember the pains of the past, they are forgotten for the sake of anesthetization in the present. Both *The Giver* and Bonilla-Silva offer insight into modes of intentional forgetting of the past that serve dominating ideologies of Sameness in the present.

In *The Giver*, genetic altering and forgetting removed the concept of race from the community in the book, similar to how color-blind ideologies attempt to remove it from society in the real world. As a concept, race did not fit into the ideology of Sameness, so it was dismissed as a divisive difference. While not to be equated with race, Jonas only learns about biological differences in skin color through memories. When reflecting on the color of people's skin, the Giver said, "There was a time, actually—you'll see this in memories later—when flesh was many different colors. That was before we went to Sameness. Today flesh is all the same."[30] Ethnic and racial diversity is absent from the community that values conformity, uniformity, and Sameness. Color-blind ideologies attempt to negotiate matters of difference by denying difference or denying the significance of difference. This functions much like Sameness. Susan Lea sees "*The Giver* as an investigation of universal fears of the unknown and of difference, and its implications for our historical and current notions of race, colorblindness, and social injustice."[31] She notes how the dominant culture of whiteness in the actual world is afforded the privilege of forgetting past atrocities and labeling race-conscious perspectives as being divisive. Selective memory and control of the present narrative afford whiteness a powerful dominant position.[32] Lea argues, "There is an eerie consistency between Jonas' community and the colorblind stance in its inability to appropriately assimilate difference."[33] She continues, "The colorblind perspective seeks to ignore race and ignore difference so that they become invisible to achieve an illusory state of equality. Such an orientation implies that any difference is a cause of discomfort and therefore, must be ignored, denied, or eradicated."[34] Color-blind ideologies claim to be race-neutral or even progressive by promoting egalitarian values in theory. In actuality though, Bonilla-Silva argues that they allow dominant structures to maintain systems of oppression against nonwhite people. The community and Sameness can be seen as a metaphor of whiteness which exerts itself as a minimizing hermeneutic denying the existence and prevalence of race. In both cases, difference is a threat to a dominant order.[35] *The Giver* exposes the false storyline of a postracial society's color-blindness on two major levels: it warns against the danger of color-blind Sameness and asserts the significant role of the past on the present.

HISTORY AND REMEMBERING

Modernity and the Enlightenment brought about so-called advances for the largely white West on the backs of nonwhite people. In many ways, Christianity received benefits by attaching itself to the "progress" of modernity in exchange for participating in the systematic killing and enslavement of people to bring about a new socio-economic order. Once established, this new socio-economic order became largely self-sustaining and nearly unassailable.[36] Modernity promised utopia but actualized dystopia. Nevertheless, modernity's utopian lies persist in ideologies, structures, and as a habitus of whiteness. Similar to how Jonas was stuck in the present and had no choice in the move to Sameness, present-day dominant structures persist by largely remaining invisible in their influence. This could only happen through the intentional forgetting of racist and oppressive origins or periods of history. *The Giver* cautions against such forgetting. Carter Hansen writes, "*The Giver* warns against the dangers of cultural amnesia by depicting the suppression of historical memory as a tool of static totalitarian control."[37] As a theologian, my interests in this are not only historical and social, but they are also theological. From a theological perspective, the "gospel" of white American exceptionalism is imbued with cultural amnesia and suppresses historical memory to maintain modes of domination in the present. This false gospel attaches itself to capitalism and democracy in manners that are theologically incongruent with Christianity. This dangerous "gospel" has done irreparable harm to the world and must be forsaken. For memory to serve critical and constructive theological functions in the present, honest engagement with the past is necessary.

I believe elements from the Cain and Abel narrative from Genesis can be understood as a metaphor of colonial modernity and forgetfulness in the age of postmodernity. The narrative especially indicts versions of American Christianity which wed American exceptionalism with divine providence. Genesis four tells the story of two brothers, Cain and Abel. Each of the brothers gave an offering to God from their labors but God looked upon Abel and his offering with favor. This angered Cain to the point that he murdered his brother. When confronted by God concerning the whereabouts of Abel, Cain responded, "Am I my brother's keeper?" (Gen. 4:9b). Cain not only committed an atrocity against his brother, he hid behind clever rhetoric to escape its implications. At that moment, Cain's assertion could only be maintained through willful ignorance, which often leads to willful forgetting.[38] Certainly, Cain knew where Abel's murdered body was, but he refused to answer honestly. Versions of history told by victors often resemble the willful ignorance and willful forgetting of Cain. By nature of being alive, Cain is the one who gets to respond to God. In other words, Cain gets to tell the story of what happened, even if his telling of the story avoids narrating the actual events. This correlates to versions of history told through triumphal whiteness that reinforces whiteness. The abuses and harms of the past are intentionally forgotten or glossed over, even while historical whiteness demands the celebration of perpetrators.

History is not only told from the perspectives of the victors; it contributes to the cementation of colonizing ideologies. Liberation theologian Gustavo Gutierrez writes, "Human history has been written by a white hand, a male hand from the dominating social class. The perspective of the defeated in history is different."[39] Remembering the perspective of the defeated is necessary to deconstruct ideologies of domination. The work of remembering and deconstructing is obfuscated by the intentional forgetting and misremembering of whiteness. Whiteness has a stake in telling its version of history to maintain the present structures of domination. Gutierrez continues, "Attempts have been made to wipe from their minds the memory of their struggles. This is to deprive them of a source of energy, of an historical will to rebellion."[40] Gutierrez underscores that the version of history narrated by whiteness supports past and present ideologies of domination partially by misremembering and forgetting. Much like Cain who avoids honestly recounting the past, history told from whiteness is perspectival and limited. It serves not to recount events honestly and objectively but to uphold systems of oppression. In many ways, it is also a form of mis-remembering for the sake of the ideology of whiteness.

In recent years, postcolonial theology, liberation theology, CRT, and other disciplines have offered counternarratives to these dominant ideologies and structures. These counternarratives attempt to deconstruct false and harmful ideologies while holding the dominant structures accountable to past and present harms. Central to this work is truthful remembering of the past for the sake of liberation in the present.[41] These efforts are largely met with resistance from those with economic control and social power. Dominant ideologies and structures resist truthful, liberating counternarration. Current iterations of dominant ideologies resisting truthful engagement with the past are exampled by efforts at banning CRT at the state and federal levels, the accusation that counternarratives are just reflective of cancel culture, and that faithful remembering is rewriting history. These efforts to control the narrative about race by the dominant structures are an example of intentional forgetting of the past for the sake of continued domination in the present. This forgetting attempts to foster a utopia of whiteness; however, the color-blind utopia of whiteness is actually a death-dealing dystopia. In the Genesis narrative of Cain and Abel, God was not fooled by Cain's response. "And the Lord said, 'What have you done? Listen; your brother's blood is crying out to me from the ground!'" (Gen. 4:10, NRSV). God knew of the murder of Abel because the ground cried out to God. The ground crying out serves as a countermemory and counternarration to the version of events proffered by Cain. The ground cries out to God and God remembers. The past is not merely the past. The blood crying out from the ground must haunt the habitus of whiteness in order to dismantle its domination.

The Giver reveals that memories of the past are a core part of understanding the present. Without some connection to memory, being in the present is substantively altered. While this is true on the individual level, it is also significant from a collective standpoint. From a narrative standpoint, Jonas' capacity to interact with the world is enhanced when he received new memories. This led to Jonas actively questioning the foundations of the community differently from the Giver because of his desire to relate meaningfully with people. In other words, memory is not a panacea to Sameness in and of itself. It is because Jonas *chooses* to be formed and informed by memories that he can imagine a better world than the "utopia" offered to him. Thus, memory serves a critical and constructive function. Jonas can critique the current structures he is a part of and imaginatively works to construct a world where different outcomes were possible. Jonas receives from memory the capacity to critically engage with the present because memory offers him perspective.

Jonas chooses to embrace painful perspectives rather than anesthetized versions controlled by his society. The memories enabled him to imagine a world with different possibilities. This world rejected Sameness in favor of free will and choice. This constructive imagining only occurred through faithful remembering of the past. Just as the dominant structure of Sameness denied free will to people in Jonas' community, agency and autonomy are limited by color-blind structures and ideologies.

RECKONING WITH RICOEUR: MEMORY AND JUSTICE

The church in the United States has a responsibility to remember past traumas, including the traumas it actively or passively caused. Addressing present racial inequalities and structures of oppression require hearing the voices of the marginalized in the past and present. The way forward is not to do away with difference because difference has been racialized and abused in the past. In fact, the ongoing minimization of racialized difference without material change contributes to a racist structure. While history has often been the domain of the oppressor, lived memory can be a place of resistance for the oppressed. Paul Ricoeur argues that every telling of history or recounting of memory is a selective process.[42] History is not a pure objective copy of the past. The selective process stems from the perspectives and social locations of the narrator; thus, it is likely to support the ideologies of the speaker. For some white people, selectively narrating and remembering the past, especially when done in minimizing and color-blind manners, amounts "to selective ignorance."[43] Selective ignorance can be intentional and willful; yet it appears innocent or omissive. It thrives on intentionally misremembering and misunderstanding to preserve the dominant ideology. Ricoeur refers to this as "strategic" and I think it helps illustrate Bonilla-Silva's argument that the present color-blind ideology is a racist system which no longer requires militant overt racists. The habitus of whiteness no longer requires as much overt racism but still provides a racialized schema for moving through life. The way the past shapes the present, and especially how the past is narrated and remembered, is illustrated by national debates over confederate monuments and school curriculum.

The glorification of the founding of the United States as an "exceptional" and "Christian nation" glosses over and justifies the violence against people indigenous to America and people from Africa. While nations tend to glorify their founding narratives by glossing over acts of violence and oppression, American Christianity's embrace of the founding "Christian" nation is theologically problematic. Ricoeur says that founding narratives often legitimize violent acts and even celebrated them to legitimate present systems and power structures.[44] They are a means of reinforcing a national habitus. "What we celebrate under the heading of founding events are, essentially, violent acts legitimated after the fact by a precarious state of rights . . . The same events are thus found to signify glory for some, humiliation for others."[45] By embracing an ethnocentric minimizing hermeneutic, white American Christianity proclaimed itself God's elected chosen people and interpreted world events through this lens in manners which benefits white Americans. The dual collective forgetting of past harms and glorification of the founding events constitute an "abuse of memory."[46] The founding history of the United States has attached itself to a false and racist gospel of American exceptionalism, which persists through storylines that attempt to deny the ongoing significance of race. Much like the stories of conquest in the Bible, white Anglo-Saxons interpreted history in a way that justified killing and enslaving other people.[47] This past continues to live through dominating structures and ideologies, despite the claims of color-blind ideologies. Therefore, American Christianity needs to reconsider how it engages its past in order to seek racial justice in the present.

While there is no purely objective form of remembering the past, Ricoeur challenges us to remember in ways that honor the dead and the victims of history. Justice for *the other* is the priority of memory. "The duty of memory is the duty to do justice, through memories, to an other than the self."[48] Thus, where the church has misremembered its complicity in racism, intentionally and unintentionally, it has denied justice. It has obfuscated the blood of Abel crying out to God. In the aftermath of the Genesis account of Cain and Abel, God places a mark on Cain which prevents people from killing him (4:15). Throughout history, there have been numerous speculations about the mark, some of which claim it was black skin. In these interpretations, black skin is typically understood as a curse from God, which some white interpreters used to justify American slavery.[49] Color-blind minimization downplays the tragic history of white supremacy and American Christianity. It tells a story about the present and past which glosses over injustices. Reckoning with this heritage requires reworking theological priorities and norms, in addition to developing racial consciousness. Ignoring the racialized system through color-blind minimization does not lead to racial equity and justice. When writing about responding with justice to the past, Ricoeur writes, "the moral priority belongs to victims."[50] This means, for many white people, moving forward requires a posture of listening and learning. While Ricoeur understands this responsibility with regard to human responsibility, I claim it is central to the Gospel. Christians are responsible to the past, present, and future by virtue of participation in the Divine economy. The Gospel calls us to love God and neighbor which shifts the responsibility from civic to theological. The color-blind ideology is a form of forgetting that many white people are comfortable with because it preserves a system which benefits them; however, color-blindness is antithetical to the Gospel given the present situation of whiteness. The color-blind ideology promises utopia for some, while preserving dystopia for others. However, Ricoeur and the Gospel are clear that responsibility is to others.

CONCLUSION

Just as characters in dystopian works come to recognize their perceived "good" situation as actually "bad," readers can undergo a similar process when interacting with dystopian works.[51] *The Giver* draws us into a bad place in a manner that can lead to a better place in the actual world if readers embrace the critical and constructive tasks of memory. Part of what *The Giver* reveals is the intimate connections between memory, the past, and the present. The work maintains that memories, even painful and overwhelming ones, cannot merely be forgotten. The "gospel" of white American exceptionalism and the myths of color-blind ideologies must be critically rejected and replaced. Remembering does not have to be merely a cognitive event or lifting forgotten details of history; it is a challenge to structures of domination in the present which thrive on misremembering and color-blind ideologies. Neither the efforts of forgetting the traumas of the past in the actual world nor a color-blind approach to race leads to justice and equality for victims of racial oppression. Just as the ground cried out to God with Abel's blood, it cries out today against dominating whiteness. The path to a more equitable society lies not in forgetting the past but in remembering for the sake of liberation in the present. God is not color-blind and God is listening.

NOTES

1. Lois Lowry, *The Giver* (New York: Dell Laurel-Leaf, 1993), 94.
2. Pierre Bourdieu, *The Logic of Practice*, trans. Richard Nice (Stanford, CA: Stanford University Press, 1992), 55–65.
3. Bourdieu, *The Logic of Practice*, 54.
4. Bourdieu, *The Logic of Practice*, 54.
5. Paul Ricoeur writes about how memory and the past can be manipulated through narrative to achieve ill ends. Paul Ricoeur, *Memory, History, Forgetting*, trans. Kathleen Blamey and David Pellauer (Chicago: University of Chicago Press, 2006), 448.
6. Lowry, *The Giver*, 94.

7. Eduardo Bonilla-Silva, *Racism without Racists: Color-Blind Racism and the Persistence of Racial Inequality in America,* 5th ed. (Lanham, MD: Rowman & Littlefield, 2017), xiii-xv, 1–4.

8. Bonilla-Silva, *Racism without Racists*, 97–100.

9. Bonilla-Silva, *Racism without Racists*, 70.

10. Scott Donahue-Martens, "Beneath the Veneer: Critical Race Theory's Challenge to White Color-Blind Preaching," *Wesleyan Theological Journal* 55, no. 2 (Fall 2020): 29.

11. Carter F. Hanson, "The Utopian Function of Memory in Lois Lowry's The Giver," *Extrapolation* 50, no. 1 (2009): 45–60, 45.

12. Lowry's latest book in the quartet, *Son*, develops family relationships further than *The Giver* and other books in the series; although, family life and relationships are themes present in all four works. The main focus of *Son* is a mother's desire to be in a real family relationship with her son.

13. Lowry, *The Giver*, 48.

14. Lowry, *The Giver*, 38.

15. Lowry, *The Giver*, 83.

16. Lowry, *The Giver*, 87.

17. Lowry, *The Giver*, 78.

18. Lowry, *The Giver*, 125, 135.

19. Lowry, *The Giver*, 94.

20. Kyoung-Min Han and Yonghwa Lee, "Philosophical and Ethical Significance of Color in Lois Lowry's *The Giver*," *The Lion and the Unicorn* 42, no. 3 (2018): 351.

21. Han and Lee, "Philosophical and Ethical Significance of Color in Lois Lowry's *The Giver*," 351.

22. Lowry, *The Giver*, 98–99.

23. Lowry, *The Giver*, 105.

24. Lowry, *The Giver*, 105.

25. Tom Moylan, *Scraps of the Untainted Sky: Science Fiction, Utopia, Dystopia* (Boulder, CO: Westview, 2000), xii.

26. Bonilla-Silva, *Racism without Racists*, xiii-xv, 1–4.

27. Donahue-Martens, "Beneath the Veneer," 31.

28. Bonilla-Silva, *Racism without Racists*, 97.

29. Bonilla-Silva, *Racism without Racists*, 99.

30. Lowry, *The Giver*, 94.

31. Susan Lea, "Seeing Beyond Sameness: Using The Giver to Challenge Colorblind Ideology," *Children's Literature in Education* 37, no. 1 (March 2006): 52.

32. Lea, "Seeing Beyond Sameness," 59.

33. Lea, "Seeing Beyond Sameness," 60.

34. Lea, "Seeing Beyond Sameness," 60.

35. Donahue-Martens, "Beneath the Veneer," 28–32.

36. Catherine Keller, Michael Nausner, and Mayra Rivera, eds., *Postcolonial Theologies: Divinity and Empire* (St. Louis, MO: Chalice Press, 2004), 5–12.

37. Hanson, "The Utopian Function of Memory in Lois Lowry's The Giver," 45–46.

38. Ricoeur, *Memory, History, Forgetting*, 448.

39. Gustavo Gutierrez, "Where Hunger Is, God is Not," *Witness* 69 (April 1976): 6.
40. Gutierrez, "Where Hunger Is, God is Not," 6.
41. Richard Delgado, and Jean Stefancic, *Critical Race Theory: An Introduction*, 3rd ed. (New York: New York University Press, 2017), 49–52.
42. Ricoeur, *Memory, History, Forgetting*, 448.
43. Ricoeur, *Memory, History, Forgetting*, 447.
44. Ricoeur, *Memory, History, Forgetting*, 82–83.
45. Ricoeur, *Memory, History, Forgetting*, 82.
46. Ricoeur, *Memory, History, Forgetting*, 86.
47. Kelly Brown Douglas, *Stand your Ground: Black Bodies and the Justice of God* (Maryknoll, NY: Orbis Books, 2015), 97–107.
48. Ricoeur, *Memory, History, Forgetting*, 89.
49. Nyasha Junior takes a different racialized understanding of the mark of Cain by exploring ways in which black interpreters consider the mark white skin. In both interpretations, the mark is racialized. The article does engage ways in which the mark was used to justify the enslavement of black bodies. Nyasha Junior, "The Mark of Cain and White Violence," *Journal of Biblical Literature* 139, no. 4 (2020): 661–66.
50. Ricoeur, *Memory, History, Forgetting*, 89.
51. Moylan, *Scraps of the Untainted Sky*, xiii.

BIBLIOGRAPHY

Bonilla-Silva, Eduardo. *Racism without Racists: Color-Blind Racism and the Persistence of Racial Inequality in America*, 5th ed. Lanham, MD: Rowman & Littlefield, 2017.

Bourdieu, Pierre. *The Logic of Practice*. Translated by Richard Nice. Stanford, CA: Stanford University Press, 1992.

Brown Douglas, Kelly. *Stand your Ground: Black Bodies and the Justice of God*. Maryknoll, NY: Orbis Books, 2015.

Delgado, Richard, and Jean Stefancic. *Critical Race Theory: An Introduction*, 3rd ed. New York: New York University Press, 2017.

Donahue-Martens, Scott. "Beneath the Veneer: Critical Race Theory's Challenge to White Color-Blind Preaching." *Wesleyan Theological Journal* 55, no. 2 (Fall 2020): 26–38.

Gutierrez, Gustavo. "Where Hunger Is, God is Not." *Witness* 69 (April 1976): 4–7.

Han, Kyoung-Min, and Yonghwa Lee. "Philosophical and Ethical Significance of Color in Lois Lowry's *The Giver*." *The Lion and the Unicorn* 42, no. 3 (2018): 338–58.

Hanson, Carter F. "The Utopian Function of Memory in Lois Lowry's *The Giver*." *Extrapolation* 50, no. 1 (2009): 45–60.

Junior, Nyasha. "The Mark of Cain and White Violence." *Journal of Biblical Literature* 139, no. 4 (2020): 661–73.

Keller, Catherine, Michael Nausner, and Mayra Rivera, eds. *Postcolonial Theologies: Divinity and Empire*. St Louis, MO: Chalice Press, 2004.

Lea, Susan. "Seeing Beyond Sameness: Using *The Giver* to Challenge Colorblind Ideology." *Children's Literature in Education* 37, no. 1 (March 2006): 51–67.

Lowry, Lois. *The Giver*. New York: Dell Laurel-Leaf, 1993.

Moylan, Tom. *Scraps of the Untainted Sky: Science Fiction, Utopia, Dystopia*. Boulder, CO: Westview, 2000.

Ricoeur, Paul. *Memory, History, Forgetting*. Translated by Kathleen Blamey and David Pellauer. Chicago: University of Chicago Press, 2006.

Chapter 4

Qu(e)erying Posthuman Theologies in *Ghost in the Shell*

Amanda L. Pumphrey and Nicholaus B. Pumphrey

CYBORGS AMONG US

One of the most influential anime, Masamune Shirow's *Ghost in the Shell (GITS)*, envisions a postnuclear, cyberpunk world where humans have cybernetic enhancements. The series was first created as a manga in 1989, followed by several films, television series, and video games, spanning from 1995 to the present. *Ghost in the Shell* explores what it means to be human in a posthuman context and engages multifaceted questions of identity including techno-theological embodiment within complex elements of AI, cyborgs, robots, and humans.[1] The main protagonist, Major Motoko Kusanagi, or the Major, is completely cybernetic. Without a physical body, Major Kusanagi's mere existence challenges traditional understandings of mind-body dualism and what it means to be less human and more machine.

The entire series highlights a government agency, Public Security Section 9, which prevents cybercrime and terrorism. The *Stand Alone Complex (SAC)* investigates cyberbrain hacking. Section 9 is primarily staffed with cybernetic enhanced individuals, mostly men who are ex-military. The agency is headed by Daisuke Aramaki and the team led by Major Kusanagi, featuring a cast of supporting characters including the former ranger, Batou, and former detective, Togusa. *GITS*'s concepts of cyberpunk dystopia, cybernetic brains, and posthumanism were extremely influential if not the main inspiration for American blockbuster sci-fi films of the late 1990s and early 2000s like *The Matrix* trilogy and *Avatar*.[2]

As a multimedium series developed over several decades, *Ghost in the Shell* itself is an intertextual cyborg consisting of philosophical, ethical, theological, postmodern, and posthuman components that are not easily separated out by readers and contain complex signifiers discovered based on the readers' contexts. In Japanese manga or American comic books, there is a continuity of characters and ideas that are built by multiple authors and artists who completely alter the text through their own intertextual makeup, regardless of the presumed linear tradition of continuity. Readers often allow one text to supersede the continuity of others, typically ignoring the minor discrepancies that simultaneously co-exist and co-mingle. Cultural memory impacts and shifts (meta)narratives and how readers create their own continuity regardless of what is categorized as the main narrative or the original creators' intention.

Although first published as a manga by Shirow, the films *Ghost in the Shell* and *Ghost in the Shell 2: Innocence* by Mamaru Oshii attracted wider attention to the series. These earlier works spawned the television series *SAC* by Kenji Kamiyama and *Arise* by Tow Ubukata. The title originates from the works of Gilbert Ryle, who coined the phrase "ghost in the machine," and Arthur Koestler who wrote a philosophical treatise on the concept.[3] Oshii's work is influenced by Donna Haraway's "Cyborg Manifesto," in which she uses the notion of cyborg as an act of reclamation.[4] All installments of *GITS* simultaneously allow for multiple readings of liberation, restrictions, or both of the cyborg's agency and gender.[5]

Ghost in the Shell presents a future without physical bodies. From a theological analysis, this presentation disrupts preconceived constructions of the soul in connection to embodiment. Cybernetic enhancements blur "boundaries between mind and machine, body and machine" and "provide new ground upon which to argue that gender and its representations are technological productions."[6] Therefore, in this chapter, we explore the implications of a bodiless or "body-less" theology which challenges notions of a fixed identity and deconstructs the limits of the body as a physical site of theo-politicization and forced constructs. We develop a framework of "body-less" theology by qu(e)erying *Ghost in the Shell*'s posthumanism utilizing the lenses of scholars of postmodern, queer, and feminist theories and theologies.[7] Focusing upon key thematic elements within the entire series, we weave together a discussion based on our cybernetic readings of these texts.

THEOLOGY AND DYSTOPIA IN *GHOST IN THE SHELL*

The devastating context of global war, nuclear fallout, and pandemic situates *GITS* in a postapocalyptic, dystopian genre. Etymologically, dystopia derives from the Greek words *dys* and *topos* literally meaning to be out of place or located within a bad place. In terms of genre, dystopian literature traditionally parrels a troubled dystopian context with an idealized utopian society, and similarly to the subgenre of cyberpunk, the dystopian setting functions to reveal that the futuristic utopia is unattainable. As a literary device, dystopia often blends the dualistic nature of societies, combining the damning realities, to show that perfection is built on the subjugation and exploitation of beings through horrifyingly extreme systems of dominance, power, and control. Science fiction and dystopia often reflect current social realities while focusing upon technological futurity and advancements to emphasize the destructive nature of contemporary capitalist society.[8] *GITS* is also set within the cyberpunk subgenre popularized by William Gibson's *Neuromancer* and *Sprawl* trilogy which was influenced by Philip K. Dick, especially the novel *Do Androids Dream of Electric Sheep?*, later adapted to film as *Blade Runner*. Japanese creators further developed the genre through their lived reality of a postnuclear dystopia.[9] Therefore, cyberpunk functions to unmask the ugly dystopian aspects of a seemingly progressive utopian future.

Ghost in the Shell questions if a cybernetic, inorganic-bodied being has a soul. The characters constantly existentially reflect throughout the series: Do I have a ghost? Is my body only a tool for myself and the government/capitalism? Can my ghost perpetually live on the net? What truly separates robot, AI, cyborg, and human, especially with cybernetic enhancements? Existing within a transitional, liminal space, the posthuman/postbody world of *GITS* positions all bodies in multiconversations with one another. As gender and theology are "technologies placed on the body," *GITS* portrays how gender is read, performed, and (re)produced when bodies are cybernetic with "permanently partial identities"[10] which are "always becoming."[11] Interestingly enough, the term *dystopia* also functions in a medical context to refer to the malposition of organs.[12] Therefore, if we read this definition of dystopia along with *GITS*, we can develop a richer understanding of how dystopia relates to bodies. Here, we draw upon the co-mingling of understandings of dystopia in its multiple uses in order to analyze and problematize the common temporal and permanent notions of bodies, minds, and ghosts.

A ghost is not a metaphysical concept of soul; instead, it is the scientific concept of the soul, or the "spectral machine."[13] The ghost is a scientific data-system, capable of being mapped or hacked, making up the individuality of a being. In *Arise*, Batou states, "Ghosts are the most fundamentally independent things in this world. Even if someone takes control of another person's ghost, at its core it is still stand alone."[14] The ghost is what gives individuality to all beings. In the original film from 1995, Kusanagi states, "My thoughts and memories are unique only to me. And I carry a sense of my own destiny. Each of those things are just a small part of it. I collect information to use in my own way. All of that blends to create a mixture that forms me and gives rise to my consciousness. I feel confined. Only free to expand myself within boundaries."[15] While this is complicated throughout the series, "all things in nature have 'ghosts,'" including robots, AI, and other nonorganic beings.[16] There is no universal definition of a ghost throughout the series, and Shirow acknowledges ghosts are too complex to be categorized within the simple dualistic framework of ghost/body.[17]

(UN)READING MIND-BODY DUALISM: "GHOST" AND "SHELL"

Cartesian mind-body dualism is the assumption of a binary, polar-opposite framework in which the mind and the body exist in separate, fixed categories. Using proto-cyborg imagery, Descartes established the complete separation of the mind and the "mechanical" body, readily garnishing criticism because both voluntary and involuntary actions involve the brain as an organ, thus a part of the body.[18] Gender and queer theorist Jack Halberstam asserts that cyborg media immediately engages the mind-body debate which is linked to constructions of class and gender as social privilege is "dependent upon stable categories of gender" as well as other binaries.[19] Kwasu Tembo claims the "heterotopic space" of science fiction allows for conflicting narratives and multiple truths that dismantle the absolutist, dualism of modern thought.[20] *Ghost in the Shell* and the existence of the Major challenge the rigid binaries of Cartesian dualism and breakdown theological dichotomies, especially regarding gender and bodies.

Descartes presupposed the existence of a Christian soul based on Paul and Neoplatonism, influencing his idea that the mind equates the soul. Criticizing this theological framework, Ryle's and Koestler's understandings are rooted in biological determinism, functionalism, and behaviorism. Ryle notes the "absurdity" of the "dogma of the Ghost in the Machine" is that a human mind is part of the body and cannot be fully separated.[21] Postmodernists like Haraway and sci-fi writers such as Shirow and Oshii strategically blend a variety of theologies and religious concepts found in pagan, Shinto, Buddhist, and Christian frameworks with posthumanism in order to construct a dystopian analysis that disrupts solely Christian-based dualisms.

Haraway argues that humans have evolved beyond simple organic beings and that machines are "haunted" with a ghost.[22] *Ghost in the Shell* complicates the notion of a soul through a myriad of questions without providing direct answers to who acquires a ghost and how. The suggestion in *SAC* is that organic material is necessary. One cannot have humanity, exemplified by a ghost, without at one time being organic or having the presence of organic matter. The Major, Batou, and Togusa all have ghosts because they are human regardless of their level of cyberization: Togusa is fully human, Batou is partly cybernetic, and Kusanagi is fully cybernetic with a cyberbrain. However, the organic necessity is complicated when individuality is linked to ghost creation in the inorganic.

The tachikomas are the AI "think-tanks" of *SAC* who never had an organic body; yet, they achieve a ghost, either through contact with organic oil or through individual memory storage. Signs of tachikomas developing ghosts happen when they begin to exhibit emotion, mourn the loss of friends, express individuality, and even sacrifice themselves, defying all presuppositions. However, *Stand Alone Complex 2* (*SAC2*) portrays ghosts as more related to individuality. Due to cyberbrains, most humans are driven toward collectivity. AI are void of an individual self and the tachikomas sync with each other at night to keep a collective mind. During *SAC2*, attempts to harness individuality are linked to terrorist groups and depicted negatively. This specific series constantly reinforces, especially through AI and Major Kusanagi's characters, that individuality signifies the presence of a ghost, but seeking that specified individuality is almost "sinful." The tachikomas never had an organic body, and while god/creator is too complex a concept, they still discuss the presence of an afterlife on the net.

The AI antagonist from the first animated film, the Puppet Master, also has the presence of a ghost; although, they were never truly an organic being from originating in/on the internet. Unlike the tachikomas, who are allowed to see their own mechanical body avatars in the net after obtaining a ghost, the Puppet Master cannot conceive of themselves as having any bodily form.[23] The Puppet Master only takes corporeal form after being trapped and gains a ghost through individuality. Therefore, ghost is not synonymous with soul or mind, shell does not equate body, and the nonhuman/posthuman can obtain a ghost. The multilateral structures of ghost/mind/body(less) inherently disrupt the binary, especially that of a Christian soul, and becomes further complicated when the body is cybernetic, robotic, inorganic, or only existing online in cyberspace.

READING POSTHUMAN THEOLOGIES IN *GHOST IN THE SHELL*

The concept of the cyborg/posthuman challenges traditional aspects of Christian theology, especially Christianity's fundamental problems with the body.[24] The mind/soul is trapped in an imperfect "shell" that can corrupt or become corrupt, jeopardizing the quality of the soul. Cyberization offers the ability to gain the perfect body or rid oneself of the negative influence on the soul. Rooted in Greco-Roman constructions of gendered bodies, Christian theology has devalued bodies that are assigned as female or considered as feminine.[25] Facets of Christianity have rendered women as unable to achieve liberation or adequately lead others to salvation. In short, Christianity both historically and contemporarily has major theological problems with the body, especially relating to gender, sexuality, and spiritual (un)cleanliness precisely through embodiment. These theological constructions that moralize specific bodies over others are further problematized by the existence of the cyborg.

When analyzing gender and posthuman theologies, the "domains of gendering practices [are] contingent upon shape, color, function and sociolinguistic convention."[26] Gender is not biological, often bodiless,[27] and a culturally created "technology" that is placed upon bodies.[28] Major Kusanagi, the epitome of cyborg, exists in a liminal space which strategically confuses both the reader and the characters within the texts. It is within the locus of liminality that she questions her own identity and be-ing.[29] With characters existing from "fully" human to "completely" cybernetic, *GITS* forces a posthumanist discussion based on the cybernetic bodiless, or body-less, human; and gender directly intersects with this body-less range.

Togusa is attached to his humanity and masculinity through his family and children, and he is ridiculed for it. Batou, as partially cybernetic, clings to what he views as human. His gender identity and gender performance are hypermasculine.[30] Appearing strikingly cyborg with cybernetic eyes, Batou fixates on masculine-human performance through weightlifting or wearing "human" clothes. As a complete cyborg and liminal being, the Major is scrutinized by her Section 9 team who do not understand her masculine gender expression. Referring to Kusanagi as "the Gorilla Woman," "Queen Kong," or "macho," the members of Section 9 do not understand her gender performativity and attempt to quantify and categorize it.

In Japanese and English, Kusanagi uses masculine speech, while the non-human beings like the tachikomas and other robots use feminine speech patterns.[31] Batou presses the Major for not switching to a "male" body and the entire team jokes about Kusanagi's love life because she frequently switches partners who are portrayed as women and men. Tembo reads the series as having a "double-bind," where a genderless body is possible yet there are patriarchal projections "onto the space of an idealized female body."[32] The cyborg has the capability to exist beyond society's cisheteronormative restrictions but cannot fully escape a false binary reduction. Kusanagi can be read as liberated from dualist limitations; although, her male colleagues do not read her this way. *GITS* exemplifies the posthuman/postmodern notion of gender as situated between the fixed universalism of modernism while acknowledging the ever-present liminality.

Along with critiques of monogamous parallel partnerships, another thematic element which theologizes and genders the cyborg is the way in which bodily nudity is constructed and categorized in another false binary. Either a naked body is sexualized and shamed, or a nude body is childlike and innocent. Haraway proclaims a cyborg was not born in "the Garden" which is significant to the second film's title, *Innocence*. While many sources and cyborg films focus primarily on the female cyborg as Eve, Haraway's reluctance to link cyborgs to Eden is a result of the dualisms and gender binary interpreted in Genesis 2–3.[33] However, these are very particular Christian readings of Eden that have long been disputed by feminist and queer Christian theologians as well as Jewish sources.[34] Eden does not have to be read as binary.

First, Kusanagi has no creator and except for Kuze in *SAC2*, the Major has no binary opposite.[35] Commentary on the series attempts to draw parallels among the characters: Togusa and Kusanagi, Batou and Kusanagi, or the Puppet Master and Kusanagi; however, the fact that Kusanagi must be partnered with an opposite or parallel character suggests these dualistic readings are forced. There is no Adam and Eve in *GITS* and there is no "Fall." Authors take the Eden narrative and recreate it with the creator/Adam/masculine figure and their perfect partner/Eve/feminine figure, such as the premise of *Tomorrow's Eve, Ex Machina*, and *Weird Science*. As Halberstam asserts, the cyborg is a new myth "of multiple genders, of variegated desires" that is a "post-Christian" myth.[36] Those strict dualistic character categorizations and creation narratives that reinforce a gender binary simply do not exist in *GITS*. The Major lacks a singular creator and a singular partner to adhere to and her nakedness is not inherently shameful or innocent, although it could potentially be read as simultaneously both.

There are problems regarding voyeurism, the male gaze, and the hypersexualization of Kusanagi's nudity as depicted throughout the series; however, the nakedness of the Major reveals her un-humanity. Kusanagi is not aware of her body because technically she is body-less. She feels no shame of her nudity because she has no knowledge of why she should. In *SAC*, the Major wears thong bodysuits and skin-revealing clothing in contrast to Togusa and Aramaki's business suits and Batou's bomber jacket. In the series, she only wears full-coverage clothing when she wears her military uniform. An iconic portion of the film is the optic camouflage that many characters use. The characters wear it as hooded jackets, but Kusanagi's optic camouflage is a form-fitted, nude bodysuit creating the allusion/illusion that she is naked. While nakedness in Eden is linked to childlike innocence, Haraway rejects this concept, and the Major is not characterized as such. However, the opening scene in the first film depicts her body being reborn paralleling her portrayal as a doll-like child in the movie's final scene, yet Kusanagi is not a child. Therefore, it is significant that she quotes 1 Corinthians 13:11 stating to "put away childish things." The Major's ghost is not a child either, and the creators strategically utilize the signifiers of gender performativity, innocence, and nakedness in contention with one another.

CONCLUSION: BODY-LESS THEOLOGY? OR WE ARE NOT ALL CYBORGS

From Pope John Paul II's *Theology of the Body* (1979–1984) to the Council on Biblical Manhood and Womanhood's *Danvers Statement* (1987) and follow-up *Nashville Statement* (2017), Christianity continues to fight to control theologies of bodies. The body is a site of theo-politicization. While we can attempt to intellectualize "body-less" and posthuman theologies in *Ghost in the Shell*, we cannot escape the context in which these categories and theories are developed. Therefore, there is no dystopia—or utopia—in which these epistemologies and theologies are not co-existing and co-mingling which intertextually influence our understandings of be-ing. The assumed "goal" of separating the mind from the body attempting to neutralize it, rendering one postgender, postracial, posthuman, etc. can never fully occur as we are bound to the body as a socio-cultural, religiously constructed site of contestation. As Halberstam and Livingston state, the posthuman body does not "represent an evolution or devolution of the human [body]. Rather it participates in redistributions of difference and identity."[37] The separation of gender, sexuality, and race among other intrinsic identity factors from the (sub)consciousness or soul cannot be the ultimate goal if we read Major Kusanagi as a strategically queer, femme, Japanese person.[38]

Regardless of her own self-understanding and self-identity, the Major is still read and consumed by both the dystopian society in which she exists and by the readers. There are multiple projections upon her "ghost" and her "shell" as readers interpret Kusanagi's be-ing precisely through her feminized physical form, her masculinized speech, actions, and gender performance, and her fluid (bi)sexuality as her partners are depicted as male and female. If we are to promote this discussion it must be said that a "body-less" theology should never erase the body but problematize the ways in which the dominant cultural discourse constructs and politicizes the body. In this regard, it is more appropriate to read *GITS* through the lens of a "body-and" theology that recognizes the significance of both the corporeal experience as well as the (sub)conscious aspects of be-ing.

Major Kusanagi challenges us to reconceptualize our own presuppositions of the construction of bodies and souls as fixed, independent factions.

As the late queer, feminist theologian, Marcella Althaus-Reid suggests, we must interrogate and deconstruct what normative theology has positioned as "decent" and in turn, reconstruct a theology that is "indecent."[39] The process of qu(e)erying posthuman theologies in *GITS* is an attempt to disrupt binaries, including our own inquiry of a body-less theology. Regarding the posthuman/ cyborg, Claudia Springer states, "The cyborg appears to rest on a dichotomy between mind and body, but it actually supersedes the dichotomy and makes it anachronistic in a new vision of fusion and symbiosis with electronic technology."[40] However, it is necessary to continue to move beyond Haraway's notion that "we are all cyborgs" so as to not erase embodied experiences of oppression and ignore structural and individual levels of power and privilege.[41] Although, the prospect of multiple categories of intrinsic be-ing is promising. Major Kusanagi signifies the presence of existing both corporally and temporally within an infinite potential of fluidity beyond the dichotomies of mind/body, male/female, human/cyborg, gay/straight, and organic/ inorganic. Despite the context of a dystopian, cyberpunk world, *Ghost in the Shell* and the Major present to the reader glimmers of multispecies queer, trans-futurities; ones in which the struggle for bodily autonomy and liberation is ongoing, yet to be fully realized materially but potentially achievable beyond our current imaginations and ghosts.[42]

NOTES

1. The 2017 American live-action film's attempt to depict a postracial future was poorly developed and heavily criticized. The ability to switch bodies allows change in appearance; although, the casting of a white actor, Scarlett Johannsen, in a Japanese heroic role was problematic to say the least. There was only one Japanese actor cast in a major role, "Beat" Takeshi Kitano who plays Daisuke Aramaki. The movie was released shortly before the U.S. saw an alarming increase in anti-Asian racism and hate crimes. It is critical to note that the first animated film from 1995 opens with the line: "society has not yet been too computerized to erase nations and races." *Ghost in the Shell*, directed by Mamoru Oshii (Los Angeles: Manga Entertainment, 2002), DVD, and *Ghost in the Shell*, directed by Rupert Sanders (Glendale: Dreamworks, 2017), Blu-ray.

2. Steve Rose, "Hollywood is haunted by Ghost in the Shell," *The Guardian*, Guardian News & Media Limited, October 19, 2009, https://www.theguardian.com/ film/2009/oct/19/hollywood-ghost-in-the-shell.

3. Shirow references Koestler's holons, something that is simultaneously part of a system but whole by itself. Masamune Shirow, *The Ghost in the Shell 1* (New York: Kondasha Comics, 2009), 267. Koestler believed that the human mind often used illusions of dualisms to understand; however, those dualisms were not necessarily true. Arthur Koestler, *Ghost in the Machine* (New York: Random House, 1982).

4. The dialogue of *Ghost in the Shell 2: Innocence* is primarily quotes from philosophers, authors, and scientists such as Dawkins, Villers, Gogol, and Asimov. Oshii even names a scientist Haraway, and the title is a reference to "Cyborg Manifesto." *Ghost in the Shell 2: Innocence*, directed by Mamoru Oshii (Glendale, CA: Dreamworks Video, 2004), DVD. Donna Haraway, "A Cyborg Manifesto: Science, Technology, and Socialist-Feminism in the Late Twentieth Century," in *The Transgender Studies Reader*, ed. Susan Stryker and Stephen Whittle (New York: Taylor & Francis, 2006), 103–18.

5. Carl Silvio, "Refiguring the Radical Cyborg in Mamoru Oshii's 'Ghost in the Shell,'" *Science Fiction Studies* 26, no. 1 (1999): 54–72. Silvio provides two different readings. Using Haraway, the initial reading is of the "radical cyborg" that offers liberation from boundaries of gender. Silvio's second reading purposely contradicts the first to show how the cyborg can be read through exploitation and objectification, which reaffirms gender norms. As evident in our methodology, our readings of *GITS* result from our respective canons of influence that can also be contradictory.

6. Jack Halberstam, "Automating Gender: Postmodern Feminism in the Age of The Intelligent Machine," *Feminist Studies* 17, no. 3 (2007): 439–40.

7. Our understanding and method of queering/questioning is based upon the work of Cheri DiNovo in *Qu(e)erying Evangelicalism: Growing a Community from the Outside In* (Cleveland, OH: The Pilgrim Press, 2005), 25. As well as Robert E. Goss' notion of queer as a verb meaning to disrupt, challenge, spoil, and interfere with normative ideologies and theologies in *Queering Christ: Beyond Jesus Acted Up* (Eugene, OR: Resource Publications, 2002), xiv.

8. Jean Baudrillard, "Simulacra and Science Fiction," trans. Arthur B. Evans, *Science Fiction Studies* 18, no. 3 (1991): 309–13; Stephanie Peebles Tavera, "Utopia, Inc.: A Manifesto for the Cyborg Corporation," *Science Fiction Studies* 44, no. 1 (2017): 21–42; Istvan Csicsery-Ronay, Jr., "The SF of Theory: Baudrillard and Haraway," *Science Fiction Studies* 18, no. 3 (1991): 387–404; and Sharalyn Orbaugh, "Sex and the Single Cyborg: Japanese Popular Culture Experiments in Subjectivity," *Science Fiction Studies* 29, no. 3 (2002): 436–52.

9. Susan Napier, *Anime: from Akira to Princess Mononoke* (New York: Palgrave, 2001).

10. Haraway, "Cyborg," 107.

11. Halberstam, "Automating Gender," 451.

12. *The Encyclopedia of Cosmetic and Plastic Surgery*, Second Edition, s.v. "dystopia."

13. Gilbert Ryle, *The Concept of Mind* (London: Routledge, 2009), 9.

14. *Ghost in the Shell: Arise*, episode 4, "Ghost Stands Alone," directed by Susumo Kudo, written by Tow Ubukata, aired September 6, 2014 (Japan), https://www.funimation.com/en/shows/ghost-in-the-shell-arise/border-4-ghost-stands-alone/.

15. Here, the Major's quote is from the 1995 film. See *Ghost in the Shell*, directed by Mamoru Oshii (Los Angeles: Manga Entertainment, 2002), DVD.

16. Shirow, *The Ghost in the Shell 1*, 33.

17. Shirow explains that the ghost is similar to Shinto concepts of the "*Ikumsubi* or conscious self, the *Tarumusubi* or unconscious self, and the *Tamazumemusubi* or

the self that transcends self." *The Ghost in the Shell 1*, 267. As a result, the mind and ghost are separated in a multilayer structure, which the tachikomas in *SAC2* reaffirm.

18. Rene Descartes, *Meditations on First Philosophy* (South Bend, IN: Informations Inc., 2000).

19. Halberstam, "Automating Gender," 439.

20. Tembo, "Death, Innocence, and the Cyborg," 108.

21. Ryle, *The Concept of Mind*, 11.

22. Haraway, "Cyborg Manifesto," 106.

23. Lyotard explains the body-less mind by calling the body the "hardware of the complex technical device that is human thought." The article is based on the idea that a solar disaster would eventually destroy the bodies, and like Descartes, he believes the mind is too complex to be on the same level as the body. Jean-François Lyotard, "Can Thought Go on Without a Body?" trans. Bruce Boone and Lee Hildreth, *Discourse* 11, no. 1 (1988–1989): 78.

24. Francesco Paolo Adorno, "Against posthuman ideology: Aesthetics and the finitude of the individual," *RES: Anthropology and Aesthetics* 57/58 (2010): 344–54.

25. For further discussion, see Caroline Vander Stichele and Todd Penner, *Contextualizing Gender in Early Christian Discourse: Thinking Beyond Thecla* (London: T & T Clark, 2009) and Peter Brown, *The Body and Society: Men, Women, and Sexual Renunciation in Early Christianity* (New York: Columbia University Press, 1988).

26. Robertson elaborates that gender is placed on the mechanical beings as a result of the creators; however, returning to Haraway's logic, the cyborg has no genesis and no one to "originate" gender. Cyborgs can be read with gender, but their gender identities or performances of gender do not come from a creator source. Jennifer Robertson, "Gendering Humanoid Robots: Robo-Sexism in Japan," *Body & Society* 16, no. 2 (2010): 2. The notion that cyborgs lack a creator and therefore an origin for gender that cannot be linearly traced fits well with Judith Butler's discussion on gender performativity as a reproduction for which there is no origin. See Judith Butler, *Gender Trouble: Feminism and the Subversion of Identity* (New York: Routledge, 1990).

27. Allison describes that her students struggle with associating cyborgs with gender because of cyborgs not having a "real" body. Anne Allison, "Cyborg Violence: Bursting Borders and Bodies with Queer Machines," *Cultural Anthropology* 16, no. 2 (2001): 250.

28. Halberstam, "Automating Gender," 443.

29. Willow Maclay, "Mannequins: On the Power of the Original 'Ghost in the Shell,'" *Roger Ebert*, April 7, 2017, https://www.rogerebert.com/features/mannequins-on-the-power-of-the-original-ghost-in-the-shell.

30. Note that gender identity and gender expression are distinctive contributors to one's be-ing that do not have to neatly align with one another. In other words, one's expression of gender or performance of gender does not necessarily equate or directly correlate to one's (a)gender(s), gender identities, and/or assigned sex(es). See Butler's theories of gender performativity in *Gender Trouble*. For a richer discussion that problematizes the normative categories of "sex" and "gender" see the work of Anne Fausto-Sterling in *Sexing the Body: Gender Politics and the Construction of Sexuality*

(New York: Basic Books, 2000) and *Sex / Gender: Biology in a Social World* (New York: Routledge, 2012).

31. Japanese distinguishes speech patterns between *danseigo* and *joseigo*, masculine and feminine or even hard and soft. The Major employs the masculine speech patterns.

32. Tembo, "Death, Innocence, and the Cyborg," 123.

33. Haraway, "Cyborg Manifesto," 104–5.

34. For example, see Phyllis Trible, *Texts of Terror: Literary-Feminist Readings of Biblical Narratives* (Philadelphia, PA: Fortress Press, 1984); Robert E. Goss and Mona West, eds., *Take Back the Word: A Queer Reading of the Bible* (Cleveland, OH: Pilgrim Press, 2000); Deryn Guest, Robert E. Goss, Mona West, and Thomas Bohache, eds., *The Queer Bible Commentary* (London: SCM Press, 2006). Also, note there are many historical and contemporary Jewish interpretations suggesting the human created in Genesis 1 was a singular androgynous being. This is evident in rabbinical Midrash and even in the biblical paintings of Marc Chagall.

35. Like the Major, the Puppet Master also has no creator, and was "spontaneously created from the sea of information" of the net. *Ghost in the Shell* (1995). And as previously stated, the tachikomas cannot fathom the concept of a creator.

36. Halberstam, "Automating Gender," 457.

37. Jack Halberstam and Ira Livingston, "Introduction: Posthuman Bodies," in *Posthuman Bodies*, ed. Jack Halberstam and Ira Livingston (Bloomington, IN: Indiana University Press, 1995), 10.

38. Lyotard, "Can Thought Go On," 85.

39. Marcella Althaus-Reid, *Indecent Theology: Theological Perversions in Sex, Gender, and Politics* (New York: Routledge, 2000).

40. Claudia Springer, *Electronic Eros: Bodies and Desire in the Postindustrial Age* (Austin, TX: University of Texas Press, 1996), 19.

41. Haraway, "Cyborg Manifesto," 116. Note Springer's critique of Haraway's construction of cyborg as universal or representing "all women." Springer includes Haraway's later commentary which takes a more intersectional approach, *Electronic Eros*, 66. For another critique of Haraway regarding cyborgs and race see Malini Johar Schueller, "Analogy and (White) Feminist Theory: Thinking Race and the Color of the Cyborg Body," *Signs* 31, No. 1 (2005): 63–92.

42. Here, we are building upon the notion of queer futurity developed by Muñoz and multispecies futurities articulated by @QueerNature, @Cyberpunkecology, and @QueerQuechua. See José Esteban Muñoz, *Cruising Utopia: The Then and There of Queer Futurity* (New York: NYU Press, 2009) and the work of Pınar Ateş Sinopoulos-Lloyd and So Sinopoulos-Lloyd at https://www.apocalypticecology.com/ and https://www.queernature.org/. Also see, Sophia and Pınar Ateş Sinopoulos-Lloyd, "Animism(s) And Our Need For Beyond-Human Kinship," in *Nature Is A Human Right: Why We're Fighting for Green in a Grey World*, ed. Ellen Miles (London: DK, 2022), 67–68.

BIBLIOGRAPHY

Adorno, Francesco Paolo. "Against posthuman ideology: Aesthetics and the Finitude of the Individual." *RES: Anthropology and Aesthetics* 57/58 (2010): 344–54.

Allison, Anne. "Cyborg Violence: Bursting Borders and Bodies with Queer Machines." *Cultural Anthropology* 16, no. 2 (2001): 237–65.

Althaus-Reid, Marcella. *Indecent Theology: Theological Perversions in Sex, Gender, and Politics*. New York: Routledge, 2000.

Baudrillard, Jean. "Simulacra and Science Fiction." Translated by Arthur B. Evans. *Science Fiction Studies*, 18, no. 3 (Nov. 1991): 309–13.

Brown, Peter. *The Body and Society: Men, Women, and Sexual Renunciation in Early Christianity*. New York: Columbia University Press, 1988.

Butler, Judith. *Gender Trouble: Feminism and the Subversion of Identity*. New York: Routledge, 1990.

Conway, Colleen M. "Eve as Cyborg: The Eden Myth as Blueprint for Artificial Women." *Postscripts* 11, no. 2 (2020): 145–74.

Csicsery-Ronay, Jr., Istvan. "The SF of Theory: Baudrillard and Haraway." *Science Fiction Studies* 18, no. 3 (1991): 387–404.

Descartes, Rene. *Meditations on First Philosophy*. South Bend, IN: Informations Inc., 2000.

DiNovo, Cheri. *Qu(e)erying Evangelicalism: Growing A Community from the Outside In*. Cleveland, OH: The Pilgrim Press, 2005.

Fausto-Sterling, Anne. *Sexing the Body: Gender Politics and the Construction of Sexuality*. New York: Basic Books, 2000.

———. *Sex / Gender: Biology in a Social World*. New York: Routledge, 2012.

Goss, Robert E. *Queering Christ: Beyond Jesus Acted Up*. Eugene, OR: Resource Publications, 2002.

Goss, Robert E. and Mona West, eds. *Take Back the Word: A Queer Reading of the Bible*. Cleveland, OH: The Pilgrim Press, 2000.

Grey World. https://www.queernature.org/.

Guest, Deryn, Robert E. Goss, Mona West, and Thomas Bohache, eds. *The Queer Bible Commentary*. London: SCM Press, 2006.

Halberstam, Jack. "Automating Gender: Postmodern Feminism in the Age of The Intelligent Machine." *Feminist Studies* 17, no. 3 (2007): 439–60.

Halberstam, Jack, and Ira Livingston. "Introduction: Posthuman Bodies." In *Posthuman Bodies*, edited by Jack Halberstam and Ira Livingston, 1–19. Bloomington, IN: Indiana University Press, 1995.

Haraway, Donna. "A Cyborg Manifesto: Science, Technology, and Socialist-Feminism in the Late Twentieth Century." In *The Transgender Studies Reader*, edited by Susan Stryker and Stephen Whittle, 103–18. New York: Taylor & Francis, 2006.

Koestler, Arthur. *Ghost in the Machine*. New York: Random House, 1982.

Lyotard, Jean-François. "Can Thought Go on Without a Body? Translated by Bruce Boone and Lee Hildreth." *Discourse* 11, no. 1 (1988–1989): 74–87.

Maclay, Willow. "Mannequins: On the Power of the Original 'Ghost in the Shell.'" *Roger Ebert*. April 7, 2017. https://www.rogerebert.com/features/mannequins-on-the-power-of-the-original-ghost-in-the-shell.

Muñoz, José Esteban. *Cruising Utopia: The Then and There of Queer Futurity*. New York: NYU Press, 2009.

Napier, Susan. *Anime: from Akira to Princess Mononoke*. New York: Palgrave, 2001.

Orbaugh, Sharalyn. "Sex and the Single Cyborg: Japanese Popular Culture Experiments in Subjectivity." *Science Fiction Studies*, 29, no. 3 (2002): 436–52.

Oshii, Mamoru. *Ghost in the Shell*. 1995; Los Angeles: Manga Entertainment, 2002. DVD.

———. *Ghost in the Shell 2: Innocence*. 2004; Glendale, CA: Dreamworks Video, 2004. DVD.

Robertson, Jennifer. "Gendering Humanoid Robots: Robo-Sexism in Japan." *Body & Society* 16, no. 2 (2010): 1–36.

Rose, Steve. "Hollywood is haunted by Ghost in the Shell." *The Guardian*, Guardian News & Media Limited. October 19, 2009. https://www.theguardian.com/film/2009/oct/19/hollywood-ghost-in-the-shell.

Ryle, Gilbert. *The Concept of Mind*. London: Routledge, 2009.

Sanders, Rupert. *Ghost in the Shell*. Glendale, CA: Dreamworks, 2017. Blu-ray.

Schueller, Malini Johar. "Analogy and (White) Feminist Theory: Thinking Race and the Color of the Cyborg Body." *Signs* 31, no. 1 (2005): 63–92.

Shirow, Masamune. *The Ghost in the Shell 1*. New York: Kondasha Comics, 2009.

Silvio, Carl. "Refiguring the Radical Cyborg in Mamoru Oshii's 'Ghost in the Shell.'" *Science Fiction Studies* 26, no. 1 (1999): 54–72.

Sinopoulos-Lloyd, So. https://www.apocalypticecology.com/.

Sinopoulos-Lloyd, Sophia "So" and Pınar Ateş Sinopoulos-Lloyd. "Animism(s) And Our Need For Beyond-Human Kinship." In *Nature Is a Human Right: Why We're Fighting for Green in a Grey World*, edited by Ellen Miles, 67–68. London: DK, 2022.

Springer, Claudia. *Electronic Eros: Bodies and Desire in the Postindustrial Age*. Austin, TX: University of Texas Press, 1996.

Tavera, Stephanie Peebles. "Utopia, Inc.: A Manifesto for the Cyborg Corporation." *Science Fiction Studies* 44, no. 1 (2017): 21–42.

Tembo, Kwasu D. "Death, Innocence, and the Cyborg: Theorizing the Gynoid Double-Bind in Mamoru Oshii's *Ghost in the Shell II: Innocence.*" *American, British and Canadian Studies* 29 (2017): 103–25.

Trible, Phyllis. *Texts of Terror: Literary-Feminist Readings of Biblical Narratives*. Philadelphia, PA: Fortress Press, 1984.

Ubukata, Tow, writer. *Ghost in the Shell: Arise*. Episode 4, "Ghost Stands Alone." Directed by Susumo Kudo. Aired September 6, 2014 (Japan), https://www.funimation.com/en/shows/ghost-in-the-shell-arise/border-4-ghost-stands-alone/.

Vander Stichele, Caroline, and Todd Penner. *Contextualizing Gender in Early Christian Discourse: Thinking Beyond Thecla*. London: T & T Clark, 2009.

Chapter 5

Social Life from Scratch

Morality, Religion, and Society in The Walking Dead

Justin F. Martin

When the opportunity to reflect on what keeps me glued to *The Walking Dead* (*TWD*) for this volume presented itself, I could not wait to dive in. In line with Social Cognitive Domain Theory (SCDT),[1] I believe we develop moral concepts through interactions with our environments and these environments often include events that vary in moral complexity (e.g., consisting of competing considerations). Two ways we try to make sense of these events, and our place within them, are through weighing different priorities or considerations against one another and judging an act based on our assumptions about the world/reality, others, and so forth. For the purposes of this chapter, it is worth making explicit that religious beliefs are one category of assumptions. I hope to correlate the interactive and dynamic view of moral understanding reflected through the character Gabriel in the *TWD*, and the chapter's focal philosopher and theologian Johannes van der Ven.[2]

OVERVIEW

I aim to advance two interrelated arguments. One is that, as suggested by van der Ven, to be human is to grapple with, reflect on, and interrogate the complexities inherent in many morally laden social interactions. This occurs regardless of the ways these interactions may differ in degree, like how often we may face what we consider to be moral dilemmas. These interactions can also differ in kind, like whether we find ourselves the perpetrator, victim, or observer of a morally relevant act. The second is that dystopian narratives such as *TWD* can serve as useful representations to explore these processes of grappling, reflecting, and interrogating. Dystopia is especially conducive to this exploration because of the way it reimagines relationships between morality, society, and religion. To illustrate the latter, events from the narrative journey of *TWD*'s Father Gabriel Stokes will be discussed through van der Ven's interactionist approach to moral understanding. Morality is defined as largely consisting of three concepts that help govern our interactions with others. The concepts are harm, justice, and rights or liberties. Harm is closely identified with welfare and violence, justice with fairness and equality, and rights or liberties with civil and human domains.[3] Quotes from Gabriel in relation to some of these events will serve as section headings.[4]

"THE WORLD ISN'T BUILT FOR THE WAY WE USED TO BE."

Before discussing van der Ven, some features of dystopian fiction and their relevance to *TWD* should be highlighted.[5] The first is that through opposing the utopian view that humans can construct perfect societies, dystopian fiction generally operates from the assumption that humans are inherently and deeply flawed. These flaws are reflected in societies that are horrifically grim and oppressive, which makes for potentially complex morally laden social interactions. Amid these dark social configurations, however, lies another important feature of dystopian fiction: hope. By prioritizing societal improvement over societal perfection, and human cooperation with the goal of creating a better society over an ideal society, dystopian fiction creates space within the narrative for some characters to hope and strive for moral progress. By exploring human social relations in ways that acknowledge despair-laden realities and hopeful possibilities, dystopian narratives provide meaningful contexts to explore the complexities and nuances of human morality.

TWD television series is based on the comic book created by Kirkman and Moore and tells the story of people trying to survive a zombie apocalypse. Kirkman made it clear that *TWD* is also a story about *us*, about what it means to be human.[6] With this view of the zombie apocalypse serving as the contextual backdrop in mind, I think it is easier to focus less on the zombies as a threat to survival and civil society, and more on how survivors try to get by. The focus on survivors considers the efforts to rebuild some semblance of a civil society.

I believe the events in *TWD* are relevant for thinking about what it means to conceive of social relations, moral understanding, and the relationship between the two, as interactive and dynamic. This is largely because of two types of relationships examined throughout the series. The first deals with the person-environment relationship, or the relationship between the individual and society. This relationship is approached in at least four ways: isolated individuals/families encountering and subsequently joining larger communities, individuals leaving one community and joining another, intact communities relocating and growing into larger communities, and interactions between communities in both cooperative and conflictual ways. The second pertains to the relationship between morality and religion, as implied through some of the recurring themes. Like the relationship between persons and their environments, this relationship can be approached in multiple ways. One is through the theme of killing, where questions and debates about the sanctity of life, of humans and zombies alike, are frequent and robust. Other themes are human and divine retribution, forgiveness, and change. Often, these themes interact as individuals and communities constantly navigate the violent realities of this new world.

These diverse acts (e.g., of retribution and forgiveness) and social configurations (e.g., individuals joining and leaving groups of varying size) highlight both features of dystopian fiction mentioned above. As far as showing humanity's flaws, *TWD* frequently portrays characters treating others inhumanely due to fear, trauma, or adopting a new philosophy on life that devalues others for the sake of survival. In terms of hope, certain consistent themes reverberate amid these inhumane acts, such as the power and promise of nonviolence, or at least not killing, forgiveness, and treating others as means and not simply ends.

These acts and configurations highlight two additional features of dystopian fiction as well. For one, the show's exploration of the relationship between morality and religion generally aligns with dystopian fiction's tendency to include parallels between religious and secular themes and conflicts. Second, the frequent discussions and disagreements about matters pertaining to the sanctity and potential of human life function as a warning of what could happen if grave injustices are not corrected.[7] This interrogation of the value of human life across religious and secular dimensions provide myriad opportunities for viewers to witness characters justify, debate, and alter positions on morally relevant matters, partly as a function of their social interactions with individuals and communities. The potential benefit of observing these interactions becomes clearer with van der Ven's approach to moral understanding which suggests that diverse social interactions are important for understanding what it means to be moral agents attempting to do life with others.

"THINGS CHANGE. YOU'RE MY FRIEND. IT . . . WASN'T ALWAYS THAT WAY."

As with dystopian fiction, real-life moral understanding is multifaceted. Specifically, van der Ven takes an interactionist perspective on how people come to think and act in morally relevant ways. Characteristics of this perspective include, but are not limited to, foregrounding any analysis of human functioning within an interdependent relationship between persons and their relevant environments and accounting for variability in judgments and actions in consonance with the different ways people may perceive and attribute meaning to real-life situations.[8]

One of the key implications of van der Ven's interactionist perspective for thinking about moral matters pertains to our everyday understandings of a person's character. A person's character is not something that exists prior to and thus outside of the elements within a real-life situation or the meanings they attribute to the situation. Instead, character is a function of interactions with others in the situation. In addition, the person's character is a function of what they consider to be the relevant demands and difficulties of the situation. With this view of character as a baseline, he derives multiple implications, one of which is especially significant here. Virtues and traits do not *belong* to individuals like the clothes they wear belong to them. Unlike the latter, the former is the result of interactions with others; interactions that include an individual's influence on others and vice versa. As a result of this mutual influence, the same virtues and traits can be outputs of certain interactions and inputs in subsequent interactions.[9]

"GOD WILL SAVE ALEXANDRIA . . . BECAUSE GOD HAS GIVEN US THE COURAGE TO SAVE OURSELVES."

An interactive approach to moral understanding implies that moral considerations are often weighed against other considerations. Van der Ven suggests that one aspect of human culture that provides robust opportunities to "see" this kind of interactionism play out is religious beliefs.[10] Religious narratives can potentially inform morally laden social lives in their nuances, ambiguities, tensions, and complexities. One way to think about this relationship is to conceive of religion as sometimes occupying a space "outside" the parameters of human morality. This can be illustrated by the Christian concept of the image of God which views individuals as autonomous and free agents with some degree of inherent moral worth. This conception of the individual, according to van der Ven, precedes human conceptions of morality and is rooted in Genesis 1:26. Another way to view this relationship is whereby religion alters or guides an aspect of human morality. Some examples include the appeal to God's form of justice instead of a human form of justice as implied in the parables regarding compensating laborers (Matt. 20:13–16) and the prodigal son (Luke 15:11–32).

One could also view this relationship with respect to the ways religious narratives, through their use of stories or parables that are both profound and varied in their interpretations, speak to the ambiguities and complexities inherent in many aspects of social life. For van der Ven this is particularly the case with Jesus' parable of the sheep and the goats and more specifically his reference to the "least of these" in verse 45 (Matt. 25: 31–46). Abstract concepts like the "least of these," van der Ven suggests, leave open many possibilities for how people can interpret the text and attempt to apply these meanings to their everyday interactions. Given the possibility that people can attribute different meanings to the same morally relevant events,[11] it seems worthwhile to consider the ways religious beliefs may interact with moral beliefs, particularly in more nuanced or complex situations. This relationship, I contend, is one frequently explored in *TWD*, particularly through Gabriel's journey.

"THE WORD OF GOD IS THE ONLY PROTECTION I NEED."

When we first meet Gabriel, he is sitting on top a rock calling for help as walkers are trying to get him.[12] Rick and his group hear Gabriel's call for help and respond, killing the walkers and saving his life in the process. As will be revealed, Gabriel is a deeply tormented person despite his outward declarations of faith. When, at the start of the apocalypse, he was faced with the choice of opening the church doors so his parishioners could seek safety or keep them closed and allow them to be killed by zombies, he chose the latter.[13] He also lives alone and refuses to kill zombies or people. Five seasons later, we see someone who appears to no longer be tormented by his past and serves as a council member working to maintain a democratically governed community. He is also more violent, and comfortable killing anyone who presents or is perceived as a threat, whether zombie and human.

In between these two versions of Gabriel, and against a backdrop common in dystopian fiction that includes individuals exerting power and authority with the promise to address a societal crisis,[14] we learn about his hopes, fears, and struggles. We also witness a variety of his social interactions, both at the interpersonal and communal levels, that are sometimes cooperative and other times conflictual. Associated with these interactions are the myriad threats he faces to his own well-being and to those he has come to care for. When viewing these phenomena as interrelated (a perspective suggested by van der Ven),[15] we are left pondering the ways these interactions may contribute to his responses to and ambiguities surrounding the morally relevant events he encounters throughout his narrative journey.

"RICK AND CARL TAUGHT ME ABOUT GUNS. OTHER WEAPONS. I AM STILL A PRIEST."

Now that the general arc of Gabriel's narrative journey has been outlined, we can now turn to a few examples that I believe are consistent with the interactionist approach to moral understanding put forth by van der Ven.[16] In some way or another, the examples will speak to Gabriel's apparent understandings of God and grace. I believe these examples are important to consider when thinking about the usefulness of dystopian fiction to explore the nuances and complexities of moral understanding and their relationship to religious beliefs. As so much of *TWD* revolves around the use, prevention, and limits of harm and violence, discussions of both categories will also address Gabriel's orientation towards weapons and violence.

Van der Ven suggests the role of subjective interpretations should be accounted for when thinking about how people may experience morally laden situations and the conflicting moral interpretations that may result.[17] Applied to *TWD*, it is possible for individuals who vary in their assumptions or beliefs about the post-zombie world to interpret the same morally laden act differently. For instance, Rick and his friend Morgan frequently debate the morality of killing and the potential for enemies to change. After joining Rick's group, Gabriel witnessed some of those debates.

Early in the viewers introduction to Gabriel, he responded to questions about killing or self-defense by declaring "the Lord Abhors violence" and "The word of God is the only protection I need."[18] For a character who, from the very beginning links his religious beliefs to his moral beliefs it seems reasonable to assume that Gabriel's diverse social experiences between seasons 5 and 10 have serious implications for how he views this linkage. Two formative experiences occur in Gabriel's church shortly after taking in Rick's group. Gabriel witnesses the group slaughter remaining members from the now-destroyed Terminus once they attacked the church. Afterwards, during a discussion with a group member he is reluctant to take up a weapon to defend himself from future threats and struggles to understand why the group chose to kill them when the leader said they would no longer pose a threat if they could go free. Early on in Gabriel's journey, then, it appears that at least part of him believes that as a man of the cloth, he should avoid harming others to survive.[19]

This perspective appears to change upon forming closer bonds with the group, experiencing more robust threats, and losing more and more people he cares about. Particularly, beginning in season 6 we see Gabriel recalibrate the relationship between his religious and moral beliefs through his changing perspectives on the use of weapons and violence. When their new community Alexandria was overrun by zombies, Gabriel initially volunteered to keep Rick's toddler daughter Judith safe in his church until the horde was driven away; later in the episode he decided to leave Judith with other community members. After leaving Judith, he picked up a machete and joined Rick and others who were killing zombies once their plan to drive them away failed.[20]

When a newly discovered community known as the Saviors was perceived by Rick as an eventual threat to Alexandria, Rick proposes during a community meeting that they attack a Saviors outpost. Gabriel agreed with Rick, despite hearing a heated debate between Rick and Morgan where Morgan voiced his disagreement with pre-emptively killing others. Gabriel does not view the choice to strike in contrast with his present moral values because, while serving as the lookout for those striking the outpost, he assured Tara that he is still a priest. Moments later one of the Saviors escaped the outpost, referred to Gabriel as "Padre," and asked if he was going to kill him. Gabriel recited John 14:1–2 before shooting and killing him. Lastly, the apparent punctuation of Gabriel's recalibration by the end of season 6 is evident when he is put in charge of Alexandria's defenses in the event the remaining Saviors retaliate for the attack on the outpost.[21] Taken together, insofar as Gabriel's changing perspectives on the relationship between his religious and moral beliefs are tied to his changing social interactions and attempts to make sense of them, his narrative journey is consistent with van der Ven's view of character as a function of one's interactions with situations and their varying demands and challenges.[22]

"I'VE SPOKEN TO GOD, HE TOLD ME TO HANG YOU."

In addition to Gabriel's social interactions having a bearing on how he views his religious and moral beliefs, they also inform his criteria for who deserves grace. If the shifts in perspectives on killing can serve as a proxy for his views on the inherent worth of individuals, then these shifts should have implications for his relationship to others, particularly with regards to who deserves grace. Moreover, given Gabriel's role as a priest and his insistence on performing said duties,[23] it is difficult, I contend, to separate his interactions with others from his beliefs about their deservedness of second chances.

If one assumes that individual-environment relationships are reciprocal or mutually influencing,[24] then it follows that the major events contributing to who Gabriel and Rick's group "were" at the time of their initial point of interaction should also be considered. This raises the question: what extent are the initial interactions between Gabriel and Rick and company somewhat "products" of, or at least tangibly influenced by, each party's prior experiences with other groups prior to their meeting? More specifically, how might Gabriel's treatment of his congregation and Terminus' treatment of Rick's group have altered each party's perspectives on retribution, forgiveness, change, and/or the sanctity of human life?

Shortly after meeting them, Gabriel directly witnessed his newfound group being hunted and hunters, victims and perpetrators, kin and killers. How does he make sense of the constant displays of humanity and inhumanity amongst the same group, one that despite learning about how he abandoned his flock, still counted him amongst their family and risked their lives, to keep him alive?[25] These seeming inconsistencies, I contend, are generally in line with an interactive or multifaceted view of character in that they reflect one or more common phenomena in everyday moral decision-making according to van der Ven: competing considerations, interpretations, and ambiguities.[26] In season 5, we see Gabriel oscillating between going out of the way to help the group on the one hand while questioning if he can really trust them on the other. This was particularly apparent when, once they joined the community in Alexandria, he sought out Alexandria's leader Deanna in secret to warn her that she could not trust the group. This was surprising given he was willing to risk his life to make sure Carl and Michonne escaped the church once it was overrun by walkers a few episodes prior.[27]

As with Gabriel's understandings of God, we see notable shifts in Gabriel's relationship to Rick's group after season five, shifts that are also occurring against the backdrop of varying threats and frequent loss of life. Amid presumably the greatest threat and displays of inhumanity he has experienced since the zombie apocalypse,[28] Gabriel solidifies his relationship to and belief in Rick's group in many ways.

When another member, Spencer, questions Rick's leadership in the aftermath of Neegan's retaliation for the outpost attack, which saw Neegan publicly execute two of Rick's group members, Gabriel essentially tells Spencer that Rick inspired him and brings out the good in people. Further, when Spencer responds by questioning Rick's decision to attack the outpost, Gabriel counters by raising the possibility that Rick's arrival to Alexandria was the reason that more people did not die. Later, when Rick is frantically looking for two missing guns so that Neegan does not kill the person responsible for keeping track of the weapons inventory, Gabriel insists that everything will work out. When Rick asks how he can be so certain, he proclaims his faith in Rick and the group ("I have faith in us. I have faith in you") and reminds him that things can change in significant ways and for the better ("You're my friend. It . . . wasn't always that way").[29]

There are also instances of Gabriel showing his faith in the group in a way that has clearer implications for determining who does not deserve to inhabit this better world they are trying to build. When Gabriel finds Rosita in the church and she tells him she is prepared to kill Neegan even if it means she dies too, Gabriel agrees that Neegan deserves to die but insists that she does not. As with his discussion with Rick a few episodes prior, he expresses his faith that things will work out ("We'll win") and that she belongs in the new world when they do (" . . . we need to . . . create it . . . together . . . And you are part of that together").[30] These interactions with Rick and Rosita suggest that in Gabriel's view, the "character" of Rick and his group is such that is deserving of surviving this apocalypse. Thus, he believes in the world they are trying to build together. In contrast, Neegan and the Saviors, through their acts of brutality, control, and intimidation towards Alexandria as well as other surrounding communities, are deserving of death. And given the moral implications of Neegan's and Rick's different governing philosophies, Neegan being more authoritarian and Rick more democratic, Gabriel's faith in Rick and disdain for Neegan suggests that it matters if violence is used for more just ends versus more unjust ends. It is believed that this tension between just and unjust forms of governance or social organization is at the heart of many dystopian narratives.[31]

Gabriel's distinction between those who deserve and do not deserve a second chance is further reflected in the myriad ways that he, now a leader and council member of Alexandria, condones, orders, and perpetrates violence towards perceived enemies and outsiders. Regarding condoning violence, there are a couple of instances where Gabriel looks the other way while members of the Whisperers, a group representing a new type of threat and who killed many people Gabriel cared about, were harmed. In both instances, the Whisperers did not appear to pose an immediate threat. In terms of ordering violence, Gabriel, convinced that their methods of gathering information from Whisperer prisoners is effective, orders Alexandrians to keep any captives alive and torture them by inflicting physical harm. When visiting another Whisperer in prison who ended up infiltrating Alexandria and killing one of the doctors, Gabriel kills him after the prisoner asks if he believes in second chances. Lastly, after encountering someone on a supply run Gabriel is captured by the person who, unbeknownst to Gabriel, was living in the building he was searching for supplies. After learning that the occupant killed his own brother's family after his brother allegedly took his food and attacked him earlier during the apocalypse, Gabriel appeals to change and the possibility of second chances. He convinces the occupant to let him go by telling him that it is not too late for him, and that he can return with them to their community and rebuild his life. As soon as he agrees and frees Gabriel, however, Gabriel kills him. He tells Aaron, who accompanied him on the supply run, that "We couldn't take him with us. He killed his brother's family."[32]

"WE'RE HERE NOW ... AND WE CAN LOOK TO THE FUTURE."

Although by no means am I condoning the actions of Gabriel or anyone else in *TWD*, I think the series provides useful opportunities to grapple with, reflect on, and interrogate morally relevant concepts that help define what it means to be human. Through highlighting a few events from Gabriel's journey, I further hoped to show the usefulness of van der Ven's interactionist approach to moral understanding for thinking about these processes. The above analysis suggests for Christians and non-Christians alike, it may be worth attending to the kinds of questions, alignments, and tensions inherent in the relationship between morality, religion, and society as explored through dystopian narratives. By highlighting different social configurations and applications of morally relevant concepts, dystopian narratives like *TWD* may encourage us to think more deeply about some of the complexities of moral decision-making in our lives, while better appreciating those complexities in the lives of others. If so, then, constantly watching people running from zombies as a means to better understand each other may not be so bad.

NOTES

1. Elliot Turiel, Melanie Killen, and Charles Helwig, "Morality: its Structure, Function, and Vagaries," in *The Emergence of Morality in Young Children*, ed. Jerome Kagan and Sharon Lamb (Chicago: University of Chicago Press, 1987), 155–243.

2. Johannes A. van der Ven, *Formation of the Moral Self* (Grand Rapids, MI: William B. Eerdmans Publishing, 1998).

3. Turiel, Killen, and Helwig, "Morality," 167–86.

4. Each quote comes from an episode discussed later.

5. Erika Gottlieb, *Dystopian Fiction East and West* (Montreal: McGill-Queen's University Press, 2001); David W. Sisk, "Dystopia," in *New Dictionary of the History of Ideas*, ed. Maryanne Cline Horowitz (Farmington Hills, MI: Thomson Gale, 2005), 606–10.

6. Robert Kirkman, *The Walking Dead Vol. 1: Days Gone Bye* (Berkeley, CA: Image Comics, 2010).

7. Gottlieb, *Dystopian Fiction East and West*, 3–4. Regarding religious and secular parallels, for instance, she notes themes such as deity/dictator and damnation/unjust as notable examples.

8. van der Ven, *Formation of the Moral Self*, 28–30, 346–57, 379–80. Many of the ideas discussed were informed by the following works: Paul Ricoeur, "Le problème du fondement de la morale," *Sapienza, Rivista Internazionale di Filosofia e di Teologia* 28, no. 3 (1975): 313; Paul Ricoeur, *Oneself as Another*, trans. Kathleen Blamely (Chicago: University of Chicago Press, 1992); John Dewey, *The Moral Writings of John Dewey*, ed. James Gouinlock, rev. ed. (New York: Prometheus Books, 1994).

9. van der Ven, *Formation of the Moral Self*, 346–57, 379–80. He relies on a three-part structure of character consisting of desires, goods, and reasons based on Platonic and Aristotelian ethics.

10. van der Ven, *Formation of the Moral Self*, 16–19.

11. van der Ven, *Formation of the Moral Self*, 380.

12. *The Walking Dead*, season 5, episode 2, "Strangers," directed by David Boyd, aired October 19, 2014, on AMC (Lions Gate Television, 2015), Blu-ray.

13. *The Walking Dead*, season 5, episode 3, "Four Walls and a Roof," directed by Jefferey F. January, aired October 26, 2014, on AMC (Lions Gate Television, 2015), Blu-ray.

14. Gottlieb, *Dystopian Fiction East and West*, 9.

15. van der Ven, *Formation of the Moral Self*, 354.

16. *The Walking Dead*, season 8, episode 16, "Wrath," directed by Greg Nicotero, aired on April 15, 2018, on AMC (Lions Gate Television, 2018), Blu-ray.

17. van der Ven, *Formation of the Moral Self*, 380.

18. *The Walking Dead*, season 5, episode 2, "Strangers," directed by David Boyd, aired October 19, 2014, on AMC (Lions Gate Television, 2015), Blu-ray; *The Walking Dead*, season 5, episode 16, "Conquer," directed by Greg Nicotero, aired March 29, 2015, on AMC (Lions Gate Television, 2015), Blu-ray.

19. *The Walking Dead*, season 5, episode 3, "Four Walls and a Roof," directed by Jefferey F. January, aired October 26, 2014, on AMC (Lions Gate Television, 2015), Blu-ray; *The Walking Dead*, season 5, episode 7, "Crossed," directed by Billy Gierhart, aired November 23, 2014, on AMC (Lions Gate Television, 2015), Blu-ray. Rick's group met the Terminus community right before escaping and finding Gabriel. The people of Terminus, after welcoming in and helping strangers earlier in the apocalypse, suffered many casualties and sexual assaults at the hands of some of the people they took in. Vowing to never be victimized again, they turned to cannibalism and taking unsuspecting visitors' belongings by the time Rick's group is taken in.

20. *The Walking Dead*, season 6, episode 9, "No Way Out," directed by Greg Nicotero, aired February 14, 2016, on AMC (Lions Gate Television, 2016), Blu-ray.

21. *The Walking Dead*, season 6, episode 12, "Not Tomorrow Yet," directed by Greg Nicotero, aired March 6, 2016, on AMC (Lions Gate Television, 2016), Blu-ray; *The Walking Dead*, season 6, episode 16, "Last Day on Earth," directed by Greg Nicotero, aired April 3, 2016, on AMC (Lions Gate Television, 2016), Blu-ray.

22. van der Ven, *Formation of the Moral Self*, 354.

23. Examples include holding prayer meetings, quoting scripture, eulogizing fallen community members, and providing counsel to community members on spiritual matters.

24. van der Ven, *Formation of the Moral Self*, 30.

25. *The Walking Dead*, season 5, episode 2, "Strangers," directed by David Boyd, aired October 19, 2014, on AMC (Lions Gate Television, 2015), Blu-ray; *The Walking Dead*, season 5, episode 8, "Coda," directed by Ernest R. Dickerson, aired November 30, 2014, on AMC (Lions Gate Television, 2015), Blu-ray.

26. van der Ven, *Formation of the Moral Self*, 171.

27. *The Walking Dead*, season 5, episode 14, "Spend," directed by Jennifer Lynch, aired on March 15, 2015, on AMC (Lions Gate Television, 2015), Blu-ray; *The Walking Dead*, season 5, episode 8, "Coda," directed by Ernest R. Dickerson, aired November 30, 2014, on AMC (Lions Gate Television, 2015), Blu-ray.

28. At the start of season seven, Neegan, the group's most powerful and menacing enemy yet, publicly executes two members from Rick's group in retaliation for the attack on the outpost. He then tells Rick's group that they now work for him, and that the Saviors now own 50% of their (Alexandria's) supplies.

29. *The Walking Dead*, season 7, episode 4, "Service," directed by David Boyd, aired November 13, 2016, on AMC (Lions Gate Television, 2017), Blu-ray; *The Walking Dead*, season 7, episode 7, "Sing Me a Song," directed by Rosemary Rodriguez, aired December 4, 2016, on AMC (Lions Gate Television, 2017), Blu-ray.

30. *The Walking Dead*, season 7, episode 8, "Hearts Still Beating," directed by Michael E. Satrazemis, aired December 11, 2016, on AMC (Lions Gate Television, 2017), Blu-ray.

31. Gottlieb, *Dystopian Fiction East and West*, 13, 21.

32. *The Walking Dead*, season 10, episode 7, "Open Your Eyes," directed by Michael Cudlitz, aired November 17, 2019, on AMC (Lions Gate Television, 2021), Blu-ray; *The Walking Dead*, season 10, episode 8, "The World Before," directed by John Dahl, aired November 24, 2019, on AMC (Lions Gate Television, 2021), Blu-ray; *The Walking Dead*, season 10, episode 10, "Stalker," directed by Bronwen Hughes, aired March 1, 2020, on AMC (Lions Gate Television, 2021), Blu-ray; *The Walking Dead*, season 10, episode 19, "One More," directed by Laura Belsey, aired March 11, 2021, on AMC (Lions Gate Television, 2021), Blu-ray.

BIBLIOGRAPHY

Dewey, John. *The Moral Writings of John Dewey*. Edited by James Gouinlock. Revised edition. New York: Prometheus Books, 1994.

Gottlieb, Erika. *Dystopian Fiction East and West*. Montreal: McGill-Queen's University Press, 2001.

Kirkman, Robert. *The Walking Dead Vol. 1: Days Gone Bye*. Berkeley, CA: Image Comics, 2010.

Ricoeur, Paul. "Le problème du fondement de la morale." *Sapienza, Rivista Internazionale di Filosofia e di Teologia* 28, no. 3 (1975): 313–37.

Ricoeur, Paul. *Oneself as Another*. Translated by Kathleen Blamely. Chicago: University of Chicago Press, 1992.

Sisk, David W. "Dystopia." In *New Dictionary of the History of Ideas*, edited by Maryanne Cline Horowitz, 606–10. Farmington Hills, MI: Thomson Gale, 2005.

Turiel, Elliot, Killen, Melanie, and Charles Helwig. "Morality: its structure, function, and vagaries." In *The Emergence of Morality in Young Children*, edited by Jerome Kagan and Sharon Lamb, 155–243. Chicago: University of Chicago Press, 1987.

van der Ven, Johannes A. *Formation of the Moral Self*. Grand Rapids, MI: William B. Eerdmans Publishing, 1998.

Walking Dead, The. Season 5, episode 2. "Strangers." Directed by David Boyd. Aired October 19, 2014, on AMC. Lions Gate Television, 2015. Blu-Ray.

Walking Dead, The. Season 5, episode 3. "Four Walls and a Roof." Directed by Jefferey F. January. Aired October 26, 2014, on AMC. Lions Gate Television, 2015. Blu-Ray.

Walking Dead, The. Season 5, episode 7. "Crossed." Directed by Billy Gierhart. Aired November 23, 2014, on AMC. Lions Gate Television, 2015. Blu-Ray.

Walking Dead, The. Season 5, episode 8. "Coda." Directed by Ernest R. Dickerson. Aired November 30, 2014, on AMC. Lions Gate Television, 2015. Blu-Ray.

Walking Dead, The. Season 5, episode 14. "Spend." Directed by Jennifer Lynch. Aired March 15, 2015, on AMC. Lions Gate Television, 2015. Blu-Ray.

Walking Dead, The. Season 5, episode 16. "Conquer." Directed by Greg Nicotero. Aired March 29, 2015, on AMC. Lions Gate Television, 2016. Blu-Ray.

Walking Dead, The. Season 6, episode 9. "No Way Out." Directed by Greg Nicotero. Aired February 14, 2016, on AMC. Lions Gate Television, 2016. Blu-Ray.

Walking Dead, The. Season 6, episode 12. "Not Tomorrow Yet." Directed by Greg Nicotero. Aired March 6, 2016, on AMC. Lions Gate Television, 2016. Blu-Ray.

Walking Dead, The. Season 6, episode 16. "Last Day on Earth." Directed by Greg Nicotero. Aired April 3, 2016, on AMC. Lions Gate Television, 2016. Blu-Ray.

Walking Dead, The. Season 7, episode 4. "Service." Directed by David Boyd. Aired November 13, 2016, on AMC. Lions Gate Television, 2017. Blu-Ray.

Walking Dead, The. Season 7, episode 7. "Sing Me a Song." Directed by Rosemary Rodriguez. Aired December 4, 2016, on AMC. Lions Gate Television, 2017. Blu-Ray.

Walking Dead, The. Season 7, episode 8. "Hearts Still Beating." Directed by Michael E. Satrazemis. Aired December 11, 2016, on AMC. Lions Gate Television, 2017. Blu-Ray.

Walking Dead, The. Season 8, episode 16. "Wrath." Directed by Greg Nicotero. Aired April 15, 2018, on AMC. Lions Gate Television, 2018. Blu-Ray.

Walking Dead, The. Season 10, episode 7. "Open Your Eyes." Directed by Michael Cudlitz. Aired November 17, 2019, on AMC. Lions Gate Television, 2021. Blu-Ray.

The Walking Dead, The. Season 10, episode 8. "The World Before." Directed by John Dahl. Aired November 24, 2019, on AMC. Lions Gate Television, 2021. Blu-Ray.

Walking Dead, The. Season 10, episode 10. "Stalker." Directed by Bronwen Hughes. Aired March 1, 2020, on AMC. Lions Gate Television, 2021. Blu-Ray.

Walking Dead, The. Season 10, episode 19. "One More." Directed by Laura Belsey. Aired March 11, 2021, on AMC. Lions Gate Television, 2021. Blu-Ray.

Chapter 6

How NOT to Be a Zombie
The Walking Dead *and* Love for the World

David Penn

We are not, then, done with the banality of evil. We need now to focus on how daily clichés, conventions, and other ways of going on autopilot can actually do the not-so-easy task of disabling our minds, and so our consciences.—Elizabeth Minnich[1]

If we took for granted that divinity . . . means mutuality, bodiliness, diversity, and materiality . . . the implications for our thought and lives would be incalculable.—Grace Jantzen[2]

ETERNITY GHOSTS

There can be little doubt that eternity ghosts haunt pop culture. From Voldemort's—and Dumbledore's—quest for immortality to the werewolves and vampires of *Twilight* and its imitators, to the AI driven science fiction of *Altered Carbon*, *I Robot*, or *Ex Machina*, the specter of eternity will not let us sleep. Still, there are numerous ways in which the modern world, from the State, to religion, and the culture industry itself, *does* encourage the masses to sleep because folks who are not paying attention are easier to exploit or control. Christian Smith and Melinda Denton once identified the prevailing spirituality of America's adolescents as one of "moralistic, therapeutic deism."[3] This spirituality, still prevalent today, is therapeutic in the sense identified by Minnich in the quote that starts off this chapter: it encourages folks to go on autopilot, to shut off thinking, to disengage with the real horror and beauty of the world. Popular culture increasingly bears the burden of exploring questions of eternity, but it is not immune from this therapeutic function; it too can serve as an opiate, an escape from thinking and being in the world as we experience it.

To even name pop culture in such a way suggests a particular kind of worlding process occurring both within and beyond traditional religious institutions. One could cite the recent Gallup poll indicating that, for the first time in recorded American history, fewer than 50% of Americans are active members of a religious congregation.[4] More to the point is the response of undergraduates at a Catholic university with whom I frequently discuss dystopian and religious stories. Many of these students have little or no religious experience, and for many of those who do, the religious ideas to which they have been introduced are experienced as relics frozen in the past that have little bearing on the world. Does this then represent the inevitable decline of Christian theology and perhaps the fulfillment of some version or other of the secularization thesis? Does it mark a move from public to private theology and from religiosity to spirituality? Or is it the sign of a disquiet emerging in the space between modernism and postmodernism, secularism and postsecularism, a disquiet that refuses to let go of the questions of eternity, life, and death, but seeks a broader frame of reference for understanding the human predicament?

To a certain extent, popular culture consumption provides a pluralistic society with shared experience around which cohesion, or at least conversation, may begin. Consider the religious aspects of the practices surrounding pop culture: the liturgy of sitting in one's favorite chair at an appointed time, the feelings of comfort wrought by the weekly or daily practice of vicarious experience through the TV or computer, or, like the doxology, the *ba-dum* sound accompanying Netflix's logo that elicits both a cognitive and embodied response. This shared experience, enfolded as it is within categories of race, class, and gender,[5] is also rapidly changing. Today very few shows are able to achieve the prominence of *Seinfeld* and *ER*, because the proliferation of new channels and streaming services means the shared experience is at least partially one of discernment and (limited) choice.

Nevertheless, the undergraduates I teach are more likely to have the shared experience of seeing the newest dystopian films and shows than of attending religious services. I do not want to suggest that questions of ontology, anthropology, and eschatology have "migrated" from the church to the screen in some axiomatic way; yet what grants dystopia such a prominent place in popular culture is its interrogation of themes that once were more commonly interrogated *primarily* in explicitly religious contexts. As a practical theologian, the question I am haunted by is this: *what sort of moral and spiritual formation* is occurring in people shaped by repeated exposure to dystopias in popular culture? Can such exposure promote *amor mundi,* love of this world, Hannah Arendt's term that serves as the antidote to the banal evils she observed?

The problematic I will work through in this chapter is the tendency of both Christian theology and dystopian fiction to make zombies of us by closing off wonder and engagement with this world. In *The Walking Dead (TWD)*, there are two ways to become a "walker," which is their word for the undead, unthinking masses that roam around the world: be bitten or die, and then convert. Just as Bethany Morrow notes that the fictional worlds she describes are reflections of what is going on in our world, I allege that *TWD* is an apt analogy for how many of us are becoming onto-zombies in our world today through both traditional theology and popular culture consumption.[6] The ways we become zombies are by refusing to ask important questions or unthinkingly accepting simple answers, thus eliminating imagination and wonder, and by maintaining a strict mind/body dualism and thereby devaluing embodied existence and birth. At times, dystopian fiction tends to promote a groundless despair while, at times, theology provides a disembodied hope. Allowing each to haunt the other can point the way toward a spirituality engaged with this world.

In an imaginative essay called "How Not to Be a Religion," John Thatamanil identifies five processes of religionization: textualization, literalization, creedalization, reification, and fetishization.[7] Each of these processes slowly transforms a living, breathing tradition into a shell of itself; Thatamanil calls this shell a religion. These processes name ways in which folks operating within these traditions forget that traditions are porous, malleable, human constructions that are intended to stoke the imagination and provoke wonder. Instead, once a tradition is "religionized," such religions "serve to generate brittle and rigid conceptions of exclusive identity and allegiance . . . they can unleash disruptive and antipluralistic energies into public space that are difficult to call back and to constrain."[8] In short, religionization does to traditions what zombification does to individuals in *TWD*: it destroys wonder, imagination, and creativity, replacing them with little more than a drive for consumption and repetition of the same.

The similarity between John Caputo's insistent, undead God, and the insistent, undead walkers of *TWD* provides a fruitful opening within which zombification can be challenged. One can trace Caputo's thought from the early description of radical hermeneutics to his spectral hermeneutics, to his tongue-in-cheek but nonetheless substantial essay *It Spooks.* In this essay he develops a full hauntology. For Caputo, if God's existence were simply a question of Being, then the theological task would be easy. God either exists or God does not exist. One can then apply some rational thought to the question and determine the truth of the proposition. Either way, certainty puts the discussion to rest.[9] The proposition "God exists," though, turns out to be impossible to pin down. Caputo writes,

> God is that than which there is nothing more perfectly present or even omnipresent—yet is nowhere to be found; nothing is more prestigious than the "word of God"—yet what is more biting than the silence of God when evil surrounds us on every side? Nothing is more luminous than the light of God—yet nothing more hidden; nothing more saving—yet nothing more likely to leave us in the lurch time and again . . . the track record of God coming to the rescue of suffering innocents is so bad you have to wonder why the long robes keep bringing it up.[10]

The history of God is a history of second-guessing, of confusion, of uncertain discernment, of superpresence and no presence. Nevertheless, 100 years after Nietzsche pronounced God dead, God continues to haunt. Caputo writes: "Whoever said God is dead must have been smoking something. God is the most undead of all!"[11] For Caputo, God doesn't exist, God insists. God is almost a shadow, impossible to pin down or simply dismiss. God's promises are like the Jubilee, promised in year 50, while the world seems stuck on 49.[12] Caputo thus refuses to grant—though he perhaps denies—God's ontological status. He prefers to engage God not as pure-Being but as pure-insistence, an event just beyond the reach of human sensibilities. Not unlike the insistent neither-living-nor-dead walkers in *TWD,* the It of *It Spooks* resists simple classification even as it demands response.

Caputo pushes back against a theological complacency that, I believe, makes zombies of many of us. Noting that Christianity under modernism capitulated to an unhealthy spirit/world dualism and that under postmodernism Christianity often became "nothing more than (economic relations, desire for authority, etc.)," Caputo suggests: "Such religion is unbelievable. We don't believe it and there is no need to discredit it as it is making itself unbelievable all by itself."[13] In a response to Caputo in the same volume, Tad DeLay clarifies, "We know an answer does not work, but repetition settles easier than admitting the big farce . . . Our theology does not work and we know it, so we hide in the safety of spaces we have been before. We do this because we know our gods are dying."[14] Any theological perspective that persists despite its unbelievability is doomed to irrelevance. As Grace Jantzen eloquently observes, unless theology explicitly challenges the very directive images and symbolic forms that dominate Western culture, which are based on a violent obsession with other worlds and mastery of this one, it implicitly underwrites them.[15] Ignoring the ways in which traditional theology obfuscates rather than illuminates human embodiment and connection to the material world is the theological analogue to the blind hope many have that climate change will work itself out or the singularity will somehow end human death and suffering. To the extent that theology—in its academic, ecclesial, and popular spheres—refuses to acknowledge its unbelievability and reorient itself to *this* world and to embodied people, it has little to say to a world anesthetized by dystopian literature. Hence Caputo's insistence that God is not a superbeing to be loved as a farmer loves the milk-cow, but a specter inspiring embodied beings to engage with one another.

Similarly, while early dystopian literature and film initially carried a critical or revolutionary tone, dystopia can all too easily slide into simple disaster tourism making a spectacle of despair: "Dystopia used to be a fiction of resistance; it's become a fiction of submission . . . Its only admonition is: despair more."[16] Some dystopian authors, including Octavia Butler and Colson Whitehead, create worlds that Mathias Thaler classifies as *critical dystopias,* dystopias that cut open future realities in ways that maintain some hope for solutions. In Butler's *Parable* series, for example, the main characters construct a utopian reality *within* the dystopian landscape. These are, Thaler explains, the exceptions that prove the rule. As dystopian worlds have exploded in popularity in the last decade, however, dystopian work, like Kierkegaard's knight of infinite resignation, often fails to make the turn from despair to hope. Indeed, Max Brooks, author of the popular zombie book and film *World War Z,* thinks such disaster tourism is the point: "Zombie stories give people the opportunity to witness the end of the world they've been secretly wondering about while, at the same time, allowing themselves to sleep at night because the catalyst of that end is fictional."[17] It is as if the horror of a zombie disaster show inoculates the viewer just enough to minimize actual horrors.

In this chapter, I will explore some ways in which even a dystopian world that Thaler would not classify as *critical* can nonetheless serve a critical function inasmuch as it uncovers "the big farce," that is, the zombifying function of theology. Methodologically I want to avoid a simple correlational perspective: I am not simply saying that dystopia generates questions and theology generates answers. Rather, I am suggesting that dystopia and theology together can help thoughtful viewers move from despair or weak hope toward a more hopeful sense of being-in-the-world. Amy Hollywood argues that "literature—and other works of the imagination—may be the necessary non-place, or place without the limitations of place, for thinking pasts and futures that are literally uninhabitable—and yet whose temporary psychic, imaginative, intellectual, and affective inhabitation is vital for human life."[18] In this sense, both the God who "is neither this nor that" of Caputo's theology and the non-place of dystopia remain unfinished and thus present openings for thinking. Such openings can be productive for the religious imagination of Christians in the twenty-first century if a mutually critical correlation is assumed—in Caputo's words, a hauntology. To make sense of this haunting, I turn to imagination and wonder—the very things the undead, in every iteration, lack.

IMAGINATION

I define imagination in both reproductive and generative terms. Sarah Arthur writes that "the imagination is the image-making faculty of the intellect that helps us discover, process, and creatively express coherent meaning. Or, to state it quite simply, imagination is how we put things together."[19] The imagination is therefore critical to one's ability to create and express meaning. Paul Ricoeur develops a conception of the productive imagination that discloses new dimensions of reality: "putting things together" encompasses not only those things we remember or represent, but is the process whereby newness enters the mind. Since the imagination is always developed in tandem with one's material and cognitive context,

> [The imagination] is, *par excellence,* the instituting and the constituting of what is humanly possible. In imagining his possibilities, man acts as a prophet of his own existence. We can then begin to understand in what sense we may speak of a *redemption through imagination*: by means of dreams of innocence and reconciliation, hope works to the fullest human capacity . . . The imagination, in so far as it has a mytho-poetic function, is also the seat of profound workings which govern the decisive changes in our visions of the world. Every *real* conversion is first a revolution at the level of our directive images.[20]

Ricoeur argues that the Gospel—the directive images at the core of the Christian tradition—became frozen through processes that have repeated many times throughout Christian history. I wish to focus on the consequences of freezing one's directive images and the necessity of engaging imagination to reverse the process. Rubenstein, following Jean-Luc Nancy, argues that closing down or freezing one's imagination by insisting on the priority of oneself as *the* transcendental subject, is the first step toward violence: "It is evil, then, that replaces the inessentiality of existence with the myth of essence."[21] The myth of essence is simply the freezing of identity, whether religious, personal, or national, and the concomitant denial of the relational core of all existence. The way to unwind such myths of essence, like the frozen Gospel, is to expose the imagination to its own limits and allow its directive images to shift.

WONDER

Mary-Jane Rubenstein wonders if it is possible to sustain wonder, particularly in a technological age, or whether wonder always closes itself off by turning into a quest for mastery. Her text *Strange Wonder: The Closure of Metaphysics and the Opening of Awe* traces wonder from its place at the beginning of philosophy in Socrates to its disappearance, or rather, transformation, today. According to Rubenstein, sustaining wonder is difficult because it either tends toward other worlds or it becomes prey to an Enlightenment derived transcendental subject, both of which give wonder over to a will to dominate or master the "objects" of wonder. For Rubenstein, wonder must be sustained because it disrupts conventional ways of thinking: "Without . . . [the danger of unforeseen spirits] thinking is condemned to an identical repetition of the safe, the possible, the Same, all reassuring and ultimately violent structures whose integrity is ensured by the twin edifices of the transcendental subject . . . and a perfect world that hovers over this imperfect one."[22] Rubenstein thus contrasts the modern will toward mastery, which is not wonder at all, with a disposition toward reality that is oriented outward, toward the Other, toward surprise, and toward thinking and openness.

Reading Rubenstein alongside the undead suggests that perhaps the value of the undead dystopia is the very disruption of the autonomous subject's claim of its own wondrousness. Dystopia provides the opportunity for a double movement: the despair generated by extending one's thought to its limit in the world of the undead can be fruitful when theologians and viewers allow such despair to haunt previously congealed theological formations. For Rubenstein, learning to wonder, which is at the heart of religious imagination, means "unsettling these formations [simple identity, otherworldliness] and retying them differently, of welcoming the most troubling houseguests . . . of learning to live with ghosts."[23] These ghosts, I might add, help us begin to see the divine in the everyday, the strange in the mundane. As we will see, the grotesque ontology of *TWD* directly confronts the therapeutic function of theology by flipping it on its head, exposing mastery, simple identity, and stability as myths.

THE WALKING DEAD

There are plenty of shows and movies featuring the undead that one could find. *TWD*, though, has commanded attention like few other shows since 2011.[24] *TWD*, now in its eleventh season, features Rick Grimes, a Georgia sheriff who leads an ever-changing group of survivors in search of sanctuary during a sudden, brutal zombie apocalypse.[25] It is known for its persistent, brutal violence, and its propensity to suddenly end popular characters' lives. A *Time* magazine article in 2014 called it "TV's most relentlessly disturbing and violent drama."[26] Why, though, is the show so popular? Some say it is popular because the show is character-driven and that it is not really about the zombies at all, which is also a critique leveled at it by fans of earlier zombie films and shows. Some say the show is popular because it pushes the limits of the level of violence that can be shown on TV. This may be true, but *TWD* touched on something deeper: it contains its own religious cosmology.

In the first season, the motley band of heroes enters the Centers for Disease Control (CDC) headquarters in Atlanta only to find a single scientist with a secret. He shares the secret with team captain Rick just before the CDC self-immolates. Viewers do not find out the secret until two-thirds of the way through season 2. But the secret is this: you do not have to be bitten by a zombie to be infected because all of humanity is infected. Whoever dies inevitably returns as a zombie. Here is a doctrine of original sin for the twenty-first century.

Humans are cursed. There is no escape; everyone is damned. Life in this dystopia is Hobbesian: nasty, brutish, and short. It finally drives Herschel, the quintessential Bible belt farmer, family man, Christian believer, to say, in the season two finale: "Jesus Christ promised the resurrection of the dead, but I thought he had something a little different in mind."[27] With Herschel, viewers are forced to face our own demons; the living are haunted by the dead, because the dead represent those lost to the past and our own horrifying future.

The question inexorably placed before viewers, then, is this: who are the walking dead? One assumes, fairly enough, that the brainless walkers, prowling in an aimless search for something to bite, are the walking dead. Once it is revealed that this is in fact everyone's destiny, however, a much harsher reality must be faced: we are the walking dead. This point is foreshadowed early in the first season. The heroes/survivors are trapped in central Atlanta, separated from their truck by a huge group of walkers. After wondering why the walkers do not attack each other, the humans decide that it is because the dead can smell the living. They therefore concoct a plan: if they cover themselves with walker parts, they will be camouflaged and can walk to their freedom. To get by in the land of the dead, one must assume the persona of the dead; there is no place for abundant life here. This could probably be read as a critique of exploitative capitalism, but I see it ontologically: with no eschatological horizon, viewers confront the possibility of an existence in which even the goal of simple survival is supplanted by meaninglessness.

Eternity's ghosts simply will not stop haunting *TWD*. It reimagines original sin as a horrific curse stripping the future of meaning and develops a peculiar anthropology. This leads to an eschatology that eschews both life and death, opting instead for undeath. There is no life after death—hell, there is barely life *before* death in this world. The zombies do not take center stage; rather, in the face of a future that is no future, the humans commit ever worse horrors *toward one another* in a futile attempt to fend off despair and death. As viewers work through this horrifying reality, each hope, in the form of the CDC headquarters, an abandoned prison, or a hospital with two functioning floors, is exposed as a false hope. The viewer must confront the possibility, voiced by Beth, that, despite our highest hopes, *"no one's coming!"*[28]

Yet the most poignant scene in *TWD*'s first three seasons was also the most difficult to watch. Partway through season 3, Lori, Carol, Maggie, and Carl are separated from the group in the prison where they have found temporary sanctuary, and Carol and Maggie are forced to perform an emergency C-section on Lori, who sacrifices herself so her baby can survive. The birth obliterates the distance between viewer and scene; its visceral energy suddenly drew me from *TWD*'s fantasy world into the real one. After some twenty episodes focusing on death, the possibility of new life, the quintessentially human moment of birth, shatters the viewer's critical distance, wrenching us inexorably toward hope in the face of unspeakable horror. Eternity's ghosts do not disappear; they remind those who pay attention, like Jacob Marley in *A Christmas Carol,* to embrace the life before us. No one is coming, but we have each other. In a world in which the mundane has disappeared, the mundane itself becomes wondrous: the simple acts of making a garden in season two or listening to a record in season 5 are celebrations of human hope and possibility.

FROM AUTOPILOT TO *AMOR MUNDI*

What formation is happening, then, in the viewing of *TWD*? Initially, it seems that viewers are left either with a fanciful escape from reality or despair, and I fear that many viewers do indeed remain in these places. The ghosts haunting the dystopian horror-scape, though, just might be saying something else: they might be calling for active engagement in the world we *do* live in. As Caputo suggests, "Specters expect to transform lives; they do not expect spectators but deeds. They want to touch afflicted bodies, to disturb lives in easy drift, to provoke action in an indifferent world . . . "[29] Looking *through* the dystopia to the ghosts that haunt allows us to view *TWD* as a call to action. When the survivors cover their bodies with corpses to appear dead to survive, I am haunted by the ways in which the modern world drains life of its vital force, through exploitation, environmental destruction, or the disconnection inherent in our technologies. Just as in Dickens' *A Christmas Carol,* the ghosts that haunt *TWD* are neither good nor evil. Their task is one of revelation, and the response is up to us. When Scrooge awakens after his ghostly encounter, he sees the world anew and marvels at its beauty and wondrousness. His conversion is from autopilot brought about by the therapeutic function of his great wealth to *amor mundi*: "The knocker caught his eye. 'I shall love it as long as I live!' cried Scrooge, patting it with his hand. 'What an honest expression it has! It's a wonderful knocker!'"[30] He suddenly sees the very knocker that initiated his haunt as wonderful—and his entire personality transforms, much to the delight of his family, neighbors, and employees.

The sudden, brutal violence in *TWD* is not an interruption to otherwise flourishing lives; instead, it serves as an ever-present reminder of the fragility of life. It demands a confrontation with the possibility that our lives are truly out of control. This horror jolts thinking out of its comfort zone into a liminal space where it can be properly spooked. If God is undead, as Caputo insists, perhaps it is because *we* are alive, and every new embodied beginning is divinity itself.

NOTES

1. Elizabeth Minnich, *The Evil of Banality* (Lanham, MD: Rowman & Littlefield, 2017), 39.

2. Grace M. Jantzen, *Becoming Divine* (Bloomington, IN: Indiana University Press, 1999), 269.

3. Christian Smith and Melinda Denton, *Soul Searching* (Oxford: Oxford University Press, 2005).

4. Jeffrey M. Jones, "U.S. Church Membership Falls Below Majority for First Time," *Gallup,* March 19, 2021, https://news.gallup.com/poll/341963/church-membership-falls-below-majority-first-time.aspx.

5. I do not want this point to be lost for at least two reasons. First, political commentators could predict one's voting preference with great accuracy depending on whether one viewed *Modern Family* or *Duck Dynasty,* hinting at the very real split between urban/rural watching habits. And second, because surely access to regular TV programming and/or such services as Netflix or Hulu is a sign of at least some economic wealth and/or status.

6. Julia Schifini, "Sirens and Black Voices, with Bethany C. Morrow" June 2, 2021, *Spirits Podcast,* 1:06:25, https://spiritspodcast.com/episodes/sirens-and-black-voices-bethany-c-morrow?rq=Morrow.

7. John Thatamanil, "How Not to Be a Religion," in *Common Goods; Economy, Ecology, and Political Theology,* ed. Melanie Johnson-DeBaufre, Catherine Keller, and Elias Ortega-Aponte (New York: Fordham University Press, 2015), 54–72.

8. Thatamanil, "How Not to Be a Religion," 62.

9. The simplicity of this argument is mirrored in some ways by Jantzen's claim that militant atheists and militant Christian apologists *do* agree on one thing: the male-centered omnipotent nature of the God whose existence is under scrutiny.

10. John Caputo, "Proclaiming the Year of the Jubilee: Thoughts on a Spectral Life," in *It Spooks; Living in Response to an Unheard Call,* ed. Erin Nichole Schendzielos (Rapid City, SD: Shelter50 Publishing Collective, 2015), 25–26.

11. Caputo, "Proclaiming the Year," 26.

12. In this essay and elsewhere Caputo, oddly enough, seems strangely certain of his position, and in doing so, does not emphasize enough his own social location and the ways in which concepts of God function differently for marginalized people and communities. Catherine Keller takes up this discussion in an essay in *It Spooks.*

13. Caputo, "Proclaiming the Year," 18.

14. Tad Delay, "Orthodoxy's Anxiety and Ideas That Fail," in Schendzielos, 60.

15. Jantzen, *Becoming Divine,* 170.

16. Jill Lepore, "A Golden Age for Dystopian Fiction," in *The New Yorker,* May 29, 2017, https://www.newyorker.com/magazine/2017/06/05/a-golden-age-for-dystopian-fiction.

17. Quoted in Nichola Barber, "Why are Zombies so Popular?" *BBC Online,* accessed April 5, 2021, http://www.bbc.com/culture/story/20131025-zombie-nation.

18. Amy Hollywood, "Dystopia, Utopia, Atopia," *Modern Theology* 36, no. 1 (January 2020): 33.

19. Sarah Arthur, *The God-Hungry Imagination: The Art of Storytelling for Postmodern Youth Ministry* (Nashville: Upper Room Books, 2008), 53. This is similar to Richard Osmer's definition of the primary imagination as "*the activity of pattern formation and recognition,*" Osmer, Richard and Ariana Salazar-Newton, "The Practice of Reading and the Formation of the Moral Imagination," *Ecclesial Practices* 1, no. 1 (2014): 55.

20. Paul Ricoeur, *History and Truth* (Evanston, IL: Northwestern University Press, 1965), 127.

21. Mary-Jane Rubenstein, *Strange Wonder* (New York: Columbia University Press, 2008), 193.

22. Rubenstein, *Strange Wonder,* 112.

23. Rubenstein, *Strange Wonder,* 190.

24. See Paul Tassi, "The Walking Dead's Season 8 Premiere Ratings Dropped 33% From Last Year," *Forbes,* October 27, 2017, https://www.forbes.com/sites/insertcoin/2017/10/27/the-walking-deads-season-8-premiere-ratings-dropped-33-from-last-year/#44c2a220298b for a summary of the show's popularity through season 8, which began with a "mere" 11.4 million viewers. That represents nearly 1 in

30 Americans. AMC's second most popular show for some time was a spinoff titled *Fear the Walking Dead.*

25. Oddly, the word "zombie" is never mentioned. The walking dead are typically referred to as "walkers" or "biters."

26. James Poniewozik, "Why The Walking Dead Is So Brutal—and So Popular," accessed April 2, 2018, http://time.com/3506057/why-walking-dead-so-popular-ratings/.

27. *The Walking Dead,* season 2, episode 13, "Beside the Dying Fire," directed by Ernest R. Dickerson, aired March 18, 2021, 22:45.

28. *The Walking Dead,* season 5, episode 4, "Slabtown," directed by Michael E. Satrazemis, aired November 2, 2014, 39:24.

29. John Caputo, "Proclaiming the Year," 39.

30. Charles Dickens, *A Christmas Carol* (Morris Plains, NJ: The Unicorn Publishing House, 1987), 52.

BIBLIOGRAPHY

Arthur, Sarah. *The God-Hungry Imagination: The Art of Storytelling for Postmodern Youth Ministry.* Nashville: Upper Room Books, 2007.

Barber, Nicholas. "Why are Zombies Still so Popular?" *BBC,* October 21, 2014. https://www.bbc.com/culture/article/20131025-zombie-nation.

Caputo, John. "Proclaiming the Year of the Jubilee: Thoughts on a Spectral Life." In Schendzielos, 10–47.

DeLay, Tad. "Orthodoxy's Anxiety and Ideas that Fail." In Schendzielos, 56–63.

Dickens, Charles. *A Christmas Carol.* Morris Plains, NJ: The Unicorn Publishing House, 1987.

Hollywood, Amy. "Dystopia, Utopia, *Atopia.*" *Modern Theology* 36, no. 1 (January 2020): 31–52.

Jantzen, Grace M. *Becoming Divine: Towards a Feminist Philosophy of Religion.* Bloomington, IN: Indiana University Press, 1999.

Jones, Jeffrey M. "U.S. Church Membership Falls Below Majority for First Time." *Gallup.* March 19, 2021. https://news.gallup.com/poll/341963/church-membership-falls-below-majority-first-time.aspx.

Lepore, Jill. "A Golden Age for Dystopian Fiction." *The New Yorker.* May 29, 2017. https://www.newyorker.com/magazine/2017/06/05/a-golden-age-for-dystopian-fiction.

Lief, Jason. *Poetic Youth Ministry: Learning to Love Young People by Letting Them Go.* Eugene, OR: Cascade Books, 2015.

Minnich, Elizabeth. *The Evil of Banality; On the Life and Death Importance of Thinking.* Lanham, MD: Rowman & Littlefield, 2017.

Osmer, Richard and Ariana Salazar-Newton. "The Practice of Reading and the Formation of the Moral Imagination." *Ecclesial Practices* 1, no. 1 (2014): 51–71.

Poniewozik, James. "Why *The Walking Dead* is so Brutal—and so Popular." *Time Online*. October 14, 2014. https://time.com/3506057/why-walking-dead-so-popular-ratings/.

Ricoeur, Paul. *History and Truth*. Evanston, IL: Northwestern University Press, 1965.

Rubenstein, Mary-Jane. *Strange Wonder: The Closure of Metaphysics and the Opening of Awe*. New York: Columbia University Press, 2008.

Schendzielos, Erin Nichole, ed. *It Spooks: Living in Response to an Unheard Call*. Rapid City, SD: Shelter50 Publishing Collective, 2015.

Schifini, Julia, and Amanda McLaughlin. "Episode 234: Sirens and Black Voices (with Bethany C. Morrow)." *Spirits Podcast*. June 2, 2021. Podcast, 1:06:25. https://spiritspodcast.com/episodes/sirens-and-black-voices-bethany-c-morrow?rq=Morrow.

Smith, Christian, and Melinda Lundquist Denton. *Soul Searching: The Religious and Spiritual Lives of American Teenagers*. Oxford: Oxford University Press, 2005.

Tassi, Paul. "The Walking Dead's Season 8 Premiere Ratings Dropped 33% from Last Year." *Forbes*, October 27, 2017. https://www.forbes.com/sites/insertcoin/2017/10/27/the-walking-deads-season-8-premiere-ratings-dropped-33-from-last-year/?sh=71cf13f5298b.

Thaler, Mathias. "Black Dreams, Not Nightmares: Critical Dystopias and the Necessity of Melancholic Hope." *Constellations: An International Journal of Critical & Democratic Theory* 26 (2019): 607–22.

Thatamanil, John. "How Not to be a Religion." In *Common Goods; Economy, Ecology, and Political Theology*, edited by Melanie Johnson-DeBaufre, Catherine Keller, and Elias Ortega-Aponte, 54–72. New York: Fordham University Press, 2015.

The Walking Dead, season 2, episode 13, "Beside the Dying Fire." Directed by Ernest R. Dickerson. Aired March 18, 2021. https://www.netflix.com/watch/70248473?trackId=14170289.

The Walking Dead, season 5, episode 4, "Slabtown." Directed by Michael E. Satrazemis. Aired November 2, 2014. https://www.netflix.com/watch/80010530?trackId=14170289.

Chapter 7

Dystopia in the Apocalypse
Religion and Community in Asimov's Foundation *Universe*

Brandon Simonson

Trantor, the world on which Hari Seldon planned his Foundation, was an exemplar of empire. It was a shining example of human progress, scientific development, and the careful curation of human society, meticulously arranging its people into subterranean neighborhoods that produced for the greater good of the city. Trantor was, after all, one world-sized capital city of an immense empire; a visit to this city-world and heart of the Galactic Empire was the capstone of one's life or career.[1] Yet, the gradual decline of the empire was apparent at different levels of society and Seldon himself was amongst the first to see it. The crux of Isaac Asimov's *Foundation* novels is the fall of the Galactic Empire, the ultimate destruction and rebirth of Trantor, and one man's attempts to preserve the greater cultural memory and scientific advancements of humankind through the eventual dystopian events of the centuries following societal collapse that could potentially last up to a thousand generations. Tasked with the seemingly impossible, that man—Hari Seldon—seemingly functions in a manner similar to the prophets of yore, crafting humankind's lifeline in the form of a breakaway sectarian community at the outermost fringes of society and delivering key messages of secret, insider information to them as they attempt to maintain their way of life until their time of salvation.

When placed in conversation with early Jewish apocalyptic literature, Isaac Asimov's *Foundation* novels serve to illuminate the role and function of divine intercessory communication in these breakaway sectarian communities and offer valuable insight into the work of charismatic leaders and the overall perception of everyday life within these communities. This chapter will explore the parallels between works of early Jewish apocalyptic literature and the example of the breakaway sectarian Foundation established in Asimov's novels. Ultimately, this chapter reads the *Foundation* novels as a work of apocalyptic literature, the character Hari Seldon as a supernatural figure communicating with a human population, and the Foundation's primary task as purveyors of a religion that keeps a sectarian breakaway community together during the dystopian events leading up to and following the fall of the Galactic Empire. In this way, reactions to dystopian elements in Asimov's Foundation help elucidate key relationships between the supernatural and humankind that demonstrate the relative fluidity of terms that have been used to describe apocalyptic texts and communities.

APOCALYPTIC AND DYSTOPIA

As this chapter is part of a volume on the academic study of dystopia, the relationship between the generic categories of apocalyptic and dystopia should be foregrounded. A single key distinction between works of apocalyptic and works of dystopia can be found in the resolution of each: where apocalyptic literature builds to a moment of justice, redemption, or salvation, dystopian literature does not. Amos Wilder notes that most modern apocalyptic literature does not include "the phase of miraculous renovation and that world affirmation which has gone through the experience of world negation . . . [where] the full apocalyptic scenario should include salvation as well as judgment, the new age as well as the old."[2] These modern works of apocalyptic stop short of salvation and redemption that is characteristic of the ancient apocalyptic genre and the divine intercession it brings to the world.

"Apocalyptic" is a term that has been defined and redefined since it was first coined in 1832.[3] It is derived from the Greek *apokalupto* (ἀποκαλύπτω), meaning "to reveal" or "to disclose."[4] The classic definition of apocalypse was established by the Society of Biblical Literature's Genres Project, which defines apocalypse as "a genre of revelatory literature with a narrative framework, in which a revelation is mediated by an otherworldly being to a human recipient, disclosing a transcendent reality which is both temporal, insofar as it envisages eschatological salvation, and spatial insofar as it involves another supernatural world."[5] In apocalyptic literature, the revelation arrives from a divine being or intermediary and often includes secret information that is passed from the divine sphere to the human sphere. The recipient of that secret information is sometimes a prophetic figure. The definition from Semeia was later emended to include that apocalyptic texts were "intended to interpret present, earthly circumstances in light of the supernatural world of the future, and to influence both the understanding and the behavior of the audience by means of divine authority."[6] As a worldview, apocalypticism is dissatisfied with the current state of affairs in the world, and expects divine intervention in the world, sometimes through the imminent arrival of a change-agent, oftentimes known as a "messiah" or chosen figure. Dissatisfaction with the world and the current state of affairs crosses socio-economic boundaries: everyone, from the poor to the rich, the commoner to the elite, could be dissatisfied with society.

There are two types of apocalypses: otherworldly journeys and historical apocalypses. Both of these types can share similar generic elements. In an otherworldly journey, the human recipient tours a world that is not their own in order to glean secret knowledge from the vision that they experience. An example of an otherworldly journey in early Jewish apocalyptic literature is found in the Book of Enoch.[7] In it, Enoch is taken by an angelic guide on a tour of another world that represents conditions in the afterlife. Highlighted in this otherworldly journey are the rewards and punishments that will come to those who were not appropriately rewarded or punished in the present life.[8] In a historical apocalypse, a review of history is central to the revealed information. One example of a historical apocalypse is the book of 4 Ezra, which was written after the destruction of the temple by the Romans in 70 CE.[9] Though it speaks of the present age, the historical apocalypse is grounded in the past that it retells.[10] In the book of 4 Ezra, the title character—Ezra the scribe—is placed in a Neo-Babylonian setting and is wrestling with the difficult issues of theodicy, or divine justice. Ezra argues that throughout history very few of the god of Israel's followers were granted the kind of justice that they deserved. In his lament, we find a retelling of the god of Israel's interactions with humankind. Ezra's lament is heard and addressed by an angelic representative, who reveals to Ezra precisely how justice will be restored. In this way, 4 Ezra functions as a national response to the crisis of the destruction of the temple by the Romans.[11] All works of ancient Jewish apocalyptic respond to a crisis of some kind, whether grounded in the human sphere or the divine sphere.

Apocalyptic is primarily concerned with transition and the end of time. Eschatology, or the study of the end of time, is therefore directly related to the apocalyptic genre. There are two types of eschatology present in the Hebrew Bible and early Jewish literature—or, in other words, two ways to envision redemption, salvation, and justice as it would come about at the end times—and they include prophetic eschatology and apocalyptic eschatology. According to Paul Hanson, prophetic eschatology is "a religious perspective that focuses on the prophetic announcement to the nation of the divine plans for Israel and the world which the prophet has witnessed unfolding in the divine council and which he translates into the terms of plain history, real politics, and human instrumentality."[12] According to this view of the end times, redemption, salvation, or justice will happen within the scope of contemporaneous reality and according to the standards of justice in this same reality.[13] In this case, rewards and punishments will be realized in the here and now, and in this world. Opposite prophetic eschatology is apocalyptic eschatology, which Hanson defines as:

> a religious perspective that focuses on the disclosure (usually esoteric in nature) to the elect of the cosmic vision of [YHWH]'s sovereignty—usually as it relates to God's acting to deliver the faithful—which disclosure the visionaries have largely ceased to translate into the terms of plain history, real politics, and human instrumentality due to a pessimistic view of reality growing out of the bleak post-exilic conditions within which the visionaries and those associated with them found themselves. Those conditions seemed insurmountably unsuitable as a context for the magnificent, envisioned restoration of [YHWH]'s people.[14]

For the people of ancient Israel, apocalyptic eschatology provided a kind of hope in times when redemption, salvation, or justice were not possible in the world that they inhabited. According to an apocalyptic eschatology, rewards and punishments will be distributed in the next world, under new circumstances and not necessarily in this time, not this world, and certainly not with these actors.

The term "dystopia," on the other hand, is derived from the Greek *dus* (δυσ) and *topos* (τοπος), meaning "bad place."[15] Dystopia often stands in contrast to "utopia," which is defined as "good place" or "no place" depending on its usage.[16] While the use of the term utopia traces its origins to a sixteenth century work by Sir Thomas More, popular usage of the term dystopia is much more recent.[17] Tom Moylan suggests that "dystopian narrative is largely the product of the terrors of the twentieth century. A hundred years of exploitation, presession, state violence, war, genocide, disease, famine, ecocide, depression, debt, and the steady depletion of humanity through the buying and selling of everyday life provided more than enough fertile ground."[18] Dystopian works often feature images of misery and suffering, and take place during a time of transition in a community, society, or world.

Dystopian literature does not contain images of misery and suffering just for the sake of displaying images of misery and suffering; instead, most forms of dystopian literature are meant to invoke a sense of urgency for change on behalf of the reader or viewer.[19] Gregory Claeys writes that "the task of literary dystopia, then, is to warn us against and educate us about real-life dystopias. It need not furnish a happy ending to do so: pessimism has its place. But it may envision rational and collective solutions where irrationality and panic loom."[20] Here, then, is where we return to the primary difference between apocalyptic and dystopian literature: apocalyptic comes to a conclusion as a moment of justice, redemption, or salvation where dystopian literature does not.

Still, apocalyptic works can contain dystopian settings, events, and themes. In his biblical commentary *Asimov's Guide to the Bible,* Isaac Asimov himself acknowledges the dystopian circumstances that brought about apocalyptic writing and its meteoric rise to popularity during and following the Seleucid period. His commentary on the Apocalypse of Isaiah (Isa. 24–27) explores the dystopian dimension of society that leads to the demand for texts in the apocalyptic genre:

> After 200 BC apocalyptic writing became very common among the Jews. The situation seemed to call for it. Before that time, there had been a tendency to consider the return from the Exile a sort of happy ending of the Biblical story. The Old Testament, as we have it, almost makes it seem so for the latest of the authentic historical books in the Jewish canon is Nehemiah, featuring the restoration of the walls of Jerusalem. And yet the happy ending seemed to dissolve into nothing; into worse than nothing, for the persecution under the Seleucid Empire rose to a high pitch after 200 BC and the condition of the Jews was suddenly more miserable than it had been even in the days of Nebuchadnezzar. The frustration was the greater since the new miseries seemed to be without cause.[21]

These populations were yearning for justice, and apocalyptic literature provided the ancient people with the promise of justice that they needed. Apocalyptic literature was the answer to the prayers of the dystopian experience as these texts offered a new conception of justice that was not otherwise possible in the world that the ancient people inhabited.

Redemption, salvation, and justice are not key aspects of the greater structure of a dystopian narrative, but both apocalyptic and dystopian literature bring about an urgency in the reader to make some kind of real-world societal change. In this way, dystopian literature could be read as demythologized apocalyptic.[22] Apocalyptic texts certainly feature a dystopian element, whereas dystopian texts are not necessarily apocalyptic.

APOCALYPTIC AND DYSTOPIA IN THE *FOUNDATION* UNIVERSE

In the greater Foundation universe, we find two concrete examples of dystopian themes. The first is found in the earlier novels *The Caves of Steel* and *Pebble in the Sky*, part of Asimov's extended reading list on his novels portraying the rise and fall of the Galactic Empire.[23] These novels take place on an irradiated Earth about three thousand years into our future. The eponymous "Caves of Steel" are the cities in which the inhabitants of the overpopulated Earth dwell, sending the wealthy "Spacers" of society to one of fifty or so inhabited worlds out amongst the stars.[24] In this way, Asimov approaches concepts of social and economic inequality. The second key dystopian theme is outlined in the two prequel novels of the *Foundation* series and the first *Foundation* novel itself, though dystopian experiences are peppered throughout all of the *Foundation* novels.[25] The setting of this dystopia is even further into the future, when "Earth" is but a mere mythic memory.[26] In these three books, Asimov's chief protagonist Hari Seldon develops and executes his plan to rebuild society after the inevitable fall of the Galactic Empire.

The process of predicting this fall and the steps necessary to rebuild after its fruition is the result of a new field of academic inquiry: psychohistory. The "Encyclopedia Galactica" defines psychohistory, in part, as "that branch of mathematics which deals with the reactions of human conglomerates to fixed social and economic stimuli."[27] Studying these conglomerates allowed the mathematicians known as psychohistorians to track the ebbs and flows of human society and progress over the course of millennia, therefore predicting with relative accuracy the course of human events. There are two axioms of psychohistory: first, that the population sample must be sufficiently large, and second, that the population should be ignorant of psychohistory because awareness might change group behavior.[28]

But to what end did they predict human events? To some, Seldon's psychohistory seemed to provide the answers that they needed to remain in power and control.[29] But to Seldon and those who engaged in the academic discipline, history could not be controlled in such a manner. Rather, psychohistory allowed Seldon and his team to track the major movements in history in a way that allowed future generations to avoid the major pitfalls that would lead humanity to those thousands of years of suffering. For the most part, individual choice was inconsequential to the greater ebbs and flows of human society and progress, as the discipline favored tracking massive groups of people.

From Asimov's first *Foundation* novella, Seldon's stated overarching goal throughout the *Foundation* novels was to avoid the suffering that would come about as a result of the societal collapse.[30] In a trial in one of the few scenes where a living Seldon appears outside the prequel novels, he is asked to respond to what the imperial representative calls "the so-called fall of the Empire" and the inevitable destruction of the capital city planet of Trantor. Seldon responds:

> I do not say now that we can prevent the fall. But it is not yet too late to shorten the interregnum which will follow. It is possible, gentlemen, to reduce the

duration of anarchy to a single millennium, if my group is allowed to act now. We are at a delicate moment in history. The huge, onrushing mass of events must be deflected just a little,—just a little—It cannot be much, but it may be enough to remove twenty-nine thousand years of misery from human history.[31]

The primary goal of Seldon's work, therefore, was to assuage the impact of the dystopian events that could follow the collapse of society. Seldon would become a guide that had the potential to lead humankind away from the additional suffering and misery promised by these dystopian events. The eerie resemblance between the warning in Seldon's speech and the warnings about climate change that we have heard in recent decades should be noted. In both cases, the damage might be mitigated but not reversed.

Seldon's speech before the imperial court sets in motion events that would lead to his group's exile to Terminus—a planet on the far edges of the galaxy and farthest away from the imperial capital of Trantor. After this point, the reader no longer sees a living Hari Seldon; instead, Seldon takes on an immortal and almost divine quality, transcending time and space as his words, his image, and his memory made an impact in the thousand years to come. Also coming to a halt after Seldon's lifetime was the formative work on psychohistory as the practitioners of psychohistory in *Forward the Foundation* and *Foundation* are replaced by the Foundation's first imperative: the compilation of the Encyclopedia Galactica.

What followed was known as Seldon's plan. Because the process of societal collapse had already started, Seldon focused on mitigating the damage by creating two Foundations that preserved human advancement and scientific progress that would function as the cornerstones of a new empire.[32] Over the course of the next millennium, ten distinct events would define humankind's path to salvation, which in the *Foundation* novels is defined as life on a new, better world.[33]

THE SELDON CRISIS AS APOCALYPTIC EVENT

Moments of revelation occurred early in the history of the Foundation, following a major social, political, or other turning point that was known as a "Seldon crisis." Following each Seldon crisis, a holographic Hari Seldon would appear in a vault on Terminus and reveal secret insider information to the community explaining what the Foundation had been through and how it impacted the trajectory of human history. The recorded holographic image of Seldon itself represents an otherworldly being—otherworldly in the sense that Seldon had recorded his instruction and explanation to the people of the Foundation and they were played long after his death. The recipients were also humans in the community, awaiting instruction and explanation for what they experienced and what they had yet to encounter. Seldon crises and the revelations that followed meet many of the criteria that define the generic category of apocalyptic.

The first Seldon crisis occurred about fifty years after the creation of the Foundation and was specifically related to the location of Terminus at the periphery of the galaxy. Asimov uses language of "barbarism" to describe the kingdoms and principalities located on planets surrounding Terminus. These "barbarian" kingdoms, unaided by atomic technology, would vie for power in the outer periphery of the galaxy. This Seldon event marked the first stage of the Foundation's separation from Empire. Though the primary work of the Foundation until that point had been to write a vast encyclopedia of human knowledge, the changing nature of the empire's fall prompted Seldon crises that would lead to subtle changes ensuring the Foundation's survival.

Though Seldon crises were never known in advance, Seldon's messages were especially temporal. Using psychohistory, Seldon was able to speak to specific circumstances at the time the crisis would occur. Seldon's messages were also spatial, and existed in the same supernatural world—a vault that enabled his hologram to appear and instruct the masses. Seldon's messages were also directly related to the eschatological salvation of the community. In this case, "salvation" occurs both in immediate and nonimmediate senses; the community was able to understand the impact of the Seldon crisis for their immediate present and their distant future.

Like a historical apocalypse, an historical narrative is often repeated at the time of a Seldon crisis. About 300 years after the creation of the Foundation, a citizen of the Foundation repeats the history of the Seldon plan and her interpretation of it while she is visiting family on another world:

> It seems to me that the whole essence of Seldon's plan was to create a world better than the ancient one of the Galactic Empire. It was falling apart, that world, three centuries ago, when Seldon first established the Foundation—and if history speaks truly, it was falling apart of the triple disease of inertia, despotism, and the maldistribution of goods in the universe . . . If the story of Seldon is true, he foresaw the complete collapse of the Empire through his laws of psychohistory, and was able to predict the necessary thirty-thousand years of barbarism before the establishment of a new second empire to restore civilization and culture to humanity. It was the whole aim of his life-work to set up such conditions as would insure a speedier rejuvenation.[34]

Characteristic of a historical apocalypse, this specific retelling happened just before the fifth Seldon crisis.[35] This act of retelling squarely places the events surrounding the Seldon crisis into the parlance of a historical apocalypse.

The question of the type of eschatology present in the narrative now arises. Effectively, Seldon's hologram occupies a supernatural status on Terminus. Seldon, bringing secret knowledge about the future, arrives at appointed times in order to shape human reaction to and understanding of current events. Although both prophetic eschatology and apocalyptic eschatology might equally define the revelatory nature of the *Foundation* series, Seldon's role as supernatural advisor speaking to specific human actors is perhaps the most telling clue in identifying Foundation as a work of apocalyptic eschatology.

FOUNDATION AND RELIGION

Throughout this exploration of the apocalyptic features of Seldon's interactions in Asimov's *Foundation* universe, I have ventured to compare elements of Hari Seldon's plan with traditional components of early Jewish apocalyptic literature. It was determined that Seldon's interactions with the Foundation after his death and as the Seldon plan commences mirror works of early Jewish apocalyptic literature, especially historical apocalypses and works of apocalyptic eschatology. One major question remains: to what degree is "religion" present in the *Foundation* universe?

At one point in the first *Foundation* novel, specifically in the second Seldon crisis, the solution to the crisis was to develop a religious tradition around the technology that the Foundation supplied its neighbors.[36] As the systems neighboring Terminus grew in military strength, the Foundation's technology-based religion also grew in influence; when one neighbor, the Anacreonians, decided to invade, the Foundation's priesthood kept them at bay.[37] This religion was somewhat similar to the classic definition of a "cargo cult," where lesser developed societies develop a new religious practice in hopes that more advanced societies will distribute new and advanced technologies.[38] The result of this decision to foster a religious tradition on Terminus led to the next appearance of Seldon, but he warned of the limitations of such kinds of spiritual warfare.[39] Of course, the Foundation's priesthood winnowed over the course of the next century, but this is not the only time we might find religion in Asimov's Foundation.

The Foundation and their reliance on science and psychohistory might be best understood through the field of religious studies.[40] Bronislaw Malinowski argued that religion can function to help those who could not fully predict situations outside of their control, reducing stress in the community.[41] Every society, no matter how "primitive," Malinowski contends, has at least a cursory grasp on the concepts of magic, science, and religion.[42] Religion and ritual can, therefore, have a functional use in the society. In the absence of science, magic or religion might take precedence though all three exist in all societies to some extent. As an academic discipline on Terminus, psychohistory was not the same as it was on Trantor. None of the new generations of scholars learned the methods of psychohistory that were used by Hari Seldon or Yugo Amaryl.[43] Understanding religion through Malinowski's definition, "psychohistory" might make a good candidate as a nonexplicit form of "religion" on Terminus: Seldon's use of psychohistory is inherently moral, ritual takes precedence when humankind is unsure of how to proceed, and Seldon's regular appearances following crisis events brought hope to the people of the Foundation. By the time the people of the Foundation are living on Terminus, "psychohistory," while a respected discipline, takes on the quality of a religion—it is no longer practiced in the same way as a science, and faith in Seldon's wisdom places the psychohistorical enterprise firmly within the category of religion nearly 300 years after the beginning of the Foundation.[44]

SECTARIAN COMMUNITIES IN APOCALYPTIC LITERATURE AND ASIMOV'S *FOUNDATION*

While the ultimate symbol of human progress and scientific advancement, Asimov's Galactic Empire was also corrupted from within as it was clear during the fall of the empire.[45] In the beginning, the Foundation functioned as a representative of the empire, but before too long—and save for the mythical "Second Foundation" at that point—Terminus was alone in the galaxy. A common theme found in some postapocalyptic dystopian fiction is the collection of human survivors into microsocieties that function to preserve one or more elements or ideals of the previous pre-apocalyptic world. These societies appear in apocalyptic texts as the main audience of the text and secret knowledge is granted to them.

Just like Trantor, Jerusalem in the Hellenistic and Roman eras bore some resemblance as an important city of a great empire. In the first century before the common era, the community at Qumran might have resembled Terminus in *Foundation*: a fringe, breakaway sectarian community led by its principles to retreat to the farthest reaches of the territory in order to live according to their laws and values. Qumran is best known as the settlement next to the caves where the Dead Sea Scrolls were discovered at the beginning of the twentieth century. While the relationship between the community and the scrolls is debated, there is strong evidence to suggest that the sectarian documents found in the caves were in some way related to the community living at Qumran. The archaeological site reveals a number of miqvaot, or ritual baths. This is significant because the sectarian documents are especially concerned with ritual purity, which would require frequent immersion in miqvaot.

The parallels between the Foundation and Qumran are strong: if Qumran was made up of sectarian Essence separatists, then it is possible that they were fleeing persecution by the empire in Jerusalem. Similar to the Foundation, one might draw insight from the community at one site to inform an interpretation of the other. If psychohistory and the revelations that result from the Seldon crises make up a sort of religious tradition for the inhabitants of the Foundation, then we can understand the breakaway sectarian community located on Terminus as a sort of Qumran——a small group of like-minded believers living together to avoid empire and believe in a similar cause.

CONCLUSION

In this chapter, I identified Asimov's *Foundation* novels as a work of apocalyptic literature by comparing them to the generic features of early Jewish apocalyptic literature. It was determined that Hari Seldon's character functioned as a supernatural being that mediated a revelation to a human recipient. During this mediation, a transcendent reality (one of limited dystopian suffering and misery) was revealed in time and space. Eschatological salvation was also revealed through this series of mediations. Seldon's appearances were meant to interpret the present, earthly circumstances in light of the greater Seldon plan, ultimately influencing the understanding and behavior of the audience by means of his supernatural authority. I also suggested that although the Foundation crafts its own technological religion early on in its lifespan, Seldon's revelatory behavior effectively helps the reader identify psychohistory as a "religion" of its own. The community that arises based on adherence to this religion bears a striking resemblance to breakaway sectarian communities like that at Qumran.

NOTES

1. Isaac Asimov, *Foundation* (New York: Bantam, 2004), 12. The first description of Trantor is found in the narrative of a young academic Gaal Dornick, who travels to Trantor in order to join Seldon's endeavors. To Dornick, the trip to meet Seldon on Trantor is described as "the undoubted climax of his young, scholarly life." Asimov, *Foundation*, 4.

2. Amos Wilder, "The Rhetoric of Ancient and Modern Apocalyptic," *Interpretation* 25, no. 4 (1971): 451–52.

3. For a concise treatment of the term "apocalyptic" and its role as a generic term, see: John J. Collins, "What Is Apocalyptic Literature?" in *The Oxford Handbook*

of Apocalyptic Literature, ed. John J. Collins (Oxford: Oxford University Press, 2014), 1–16.

4. Henry George Liddell and Robert Scott, *A Greek-English Lexicon* (Oxford: Oxford University Press, 1996), 701.

5. John J. Collins, ed., *Apocalypse: The Morphology of a Genre*, Semeia 14 (Missoula, MT: Scholars Press, 1979).

6. Adela Yarbro Collins, *Cosmology and Eschatology in Jewish and Christian Apocalypticism*, Supplements to the Journal for the Study of Judaism 50 (Leiden: Brill, 1996), 7.

7. George W.E. Nickelsburg and James C. VanderKam, *1 Enoch: The Hermeneia Translation*, Hermeneia (Minneapolis, MN: Fortress Press, 2012); and John J. Collins, *The Apocalyptic Imagination: An Introduction to Jewish Apocalyptic Literature*, Third Edition (Grand Rapids, MI: Eerdmans, 2016), 61–75.

8. Rewards and punishments appear as Enoch is guided on his otherworldly journey. Cf., Nickelsburg and VanderKam, *1 Enoch: The Hermeneia Translation*, 38–49.

9. 4 Ezra appears in the deuterocanonical book of 2 Esdras 3–14. Though this book does not appear in Jewish or Christian canons of the biblical text, it is preserved in the Apocrypha. Collins, *Apocalyptic Imagination*, 242–46.

10. Cf., 2 Esdras 3:1–36. In this passage Ezra retells a version of ancient Israel's past focusing on major events that lead to rewards and punishments. Even though the people were committing iniquities, for example, the god of Israel still chose one whom he loved: "When those who lived on earth began to multiply, they produced children and peoples and many nations, and again they began to be more ungodly than were their ancestors. And when they were committing iniquity in your sight, you chose for yourself one of them, whose name was Abraham; you loved him, and to him alone you revealed the end of the times, secretly by night" (2 Esdras 3:12–14, NRSV).

11. Collins interprets 4 Ezra, 2 Baruch, and the Apocalypse of Abraham as a cluster of responses that might be considered ancient Judaism's only extant national response to the destruction of the temple. Collins, *Apocalyptic Imagination*, 241.

12. Paul Hanson, *The Dawn of Apocalyptic: The Historical and Sociological Roots of Jewish Apocalyptic Eschatology* (Philadelphia: Fortress Press, 1979), 11.

13. For ancient Israel, this was rooted in the doctrine of retribution, which, according to the Torah, would allow blessings for those who have acted righteously and curses for those who have acted wickedly.

14. Hanson, *The Dawn of Apocalyptic*, 11–12. The name YHWH, known as the tetragrammaton, is the transliteration of the proper name of the god of Israel. It is standard for the name to be written without vowels in Hebrew and English transliteration and, therefore, not pronounceable.

15. Liddell and Scott, *A Greek-English Lexicon*, 1806. For a more comprehensive definition of dystopia, utopia, and apocalyptic, see chapter 1 of this volume ("Dystopia as Demythologized Apocalyptic") and Gregory Claeys, *Dystopia: A Natural History* (Oxford: Oxford University Press, 2017), 3–18.

16. A more thorough definition and discussion of utopia is available in chapter 1 of this volume. Cf., Liddell and Scott, *A Greek-English Lexicon*, 704, 1266–67, and 1806.

17. Thomas More, *Utopia*, trans. Clarence H. Miller (New Haven, CT: Yale University Press, 2001).

18. Tom Moylan, Scraps of the Untainted Sky: *Science Fiction, Utopia, Dystopia* (New York: Routledge, 2018), xi. In the preface and first chapter of this volume the editors also attribute the recent rise in popularity of the dystopian genre as related to important world events, including Hurricane Katrina in 2005 and the COVID-19 pandemic in 2020.

19. Claeys, *Dystopia: A Natural History*, 501. This is also known as "critical dystopia," which some authors distinguish from dystopia more generally construed. Cf., Moylan, *Scraps of the Untainted Sky*, 188.

20. Claeys, *Dystopia: A Natural History*, 501.

21. Isaac Asimov, *Asimov's Guide to the Bible*, Two Volumes in One: The Old and New Testaments (New York: Avenel Books, 1981), 541.

22. For more on this concept, see the first chapter of this volume.

23. In an Author's Note in *Prelude to Foundation*, Asimov offered readers an extended reading list of all the novels documenting the development of the Galactic Empire. *The Caves of Steel* (1954) was the second on that list. Isaac Asimov, *Prelude to Foundation* (New York: Bantam, 2004), xiii-xv. Cf., Isaac Asimov, *Caves of Steel* (New York: Bantam, 1991); Isaac Asimov, *Pebble in the Sky* (New York: Orb, 2010).

24. Asimov, *Caves of Steel*.

25. Asimov, *Prelude to Foundation*; Isaac Asimov, *Forward the Foundation* (New York: Bantam, 2004); and Asimov, *Foundation*.

26. The fate of Earth is itself the subject of the seventh and final novel set in the Foundation universe, one in which Asimov brings his epic narrative to a conclusion, reintroducing a key character introduced in *The Caves of Steel*. Isaac Asimov, *Foundation and Earth* (New York: Bantam, 2004).

27. Asimov, *Foundation*, 19.

28. Other Axioms were added later—Ebling Mis added two that were the subject of *Foundation and Empire* and Golan Trevize another that was the subject of *Foundation and Earth*. The two listed above were the original axioms created by Hari Seldon.

29. This is especially the case for Emperor Cleon I who, in the two prequel novels, took an interest in Seldon's work so that he might benefit from advanced knowledge of future events.

30. The first novella of the Foundation universe is "The Psychohistorians," which was published as "Foundation" in the May 1942 edition of *Astounding Science Fiction*. Asimov, *Foundation*, 3–96.

31. Asimov, *Foundation*, 37.

32. This historical narrative is often retold, again and again, in the *Foundation* novels. While it is likely this was Asimov's way of reminding the reader of necessary backstory, the repeated retelling of history is precisely what appears in a historical apocalypse. See, for example, Asimov, *Foundation and Empire*, 111–12 for a retelling of this historical narrative.

33. Asimov, *Foundation and Empire*, 111.

34. Asimov, *Foundation and Empire*, 111.

35. This was the first crisis that Seldon was unable to predict with any accuracy. The difficulty in predicting this crisis was due to an external, nonhuman actor known as the Mule, who was capable of changing the emotions of those around him. Seldon's work with the first *Foundation* did not account for the emotional manipulation. The work of the second *Foundation*, however, helped account for this discrepancy and, therefore, the crisis of the Mule was still averted. Asimov, *Foundation and Empire*, 103–282.

36. Asimov, *Foundation*, 97–170.

37. Asimov, *Foundation*, 161–64.

38. Peter Worsley, *The Trumpet Shall Sound: A Study of "Cargo Cults" in Melanesia* (New York: Schocken, 1957), 17–30; for some difficulties and nuance of the term, cf. Doug Dalton, "Cargo Cults and Discursive Madness," *Oceania* 70, no. 4 (2000): 346–49.

39. Asimov, *Foundation*, 167–68.

40. Following J.Z. Smith, "religion" itself is best defined as a scholarly construct, a second order term that allows for the disciplined study of phenomena. J.Z. Smith, "Religion, Religions, Religious," in *Critical Terms for Religious Studies*, ed. Mark C. Taylor (Chicago: University of Chicago Press, 1998), 281–82.

41. Bronislaw Malinowski, *Magic, Science, and Religion and Other Essays* (Long Grove, IL: Waveland Press, 1992).

42. Malinowski, *Magic, Science, and Religion*, 17.

43. Hari Seldon and Yugo Amaryl were perhaps the two most integral psychohistorians on the project in *Forward the Foundation*.

44. "I have faith in the wisdom of Seldon yet!" a defiant Bayta proclaimed. Asimov, *Foundation and Empire*, 281–82.

45. Asimov expounds on the deteriorating conditions within the empire in the prequel novels, *Prelude to Foundation* and *Forward the Foundation*. It is not necessary to delve into these details in this chapter, but it is worth mentioning that one of the roadblocks that Seldon encounters in *Forward the Foundation* is the lack of proper access to library resources (Asimov, *Forward the Foundation*, 345–48). Academics working during the COVID-19 pandemic knew this reality all too well, and the detail with which Asimov describes this difficulty seems to suggest Asimov knew it once, too.

BIBLIOGRAPHY

Asimov, Isaac. *Asimov's Guide to the Bible*. Two Volumes in One: The Old and New Testaments. New York: Avenel Books, 1981.
———. *Caves of Steel*. New York: Bantam, 1991.
———. *Forward the Foundation*. New York: Bantam, 2004.
———. *Foundation*. New York: Bantam, 2004.
———. *Foundation and Empire*. New York: Bantam, 2004.
———. *Pebble in the Sky*. New York: Orb, 2010.
———. *Prelude to Foundation*. New York: Bantam, 2004.

Claeys, Gregory. *Dystopia: A Natural History*. Oxford: Oxford University Press, 2016.

Collins, John J. *The Apocalyptic Imagination: An Introduction to Jewish Apocalyptic Literature*. Third Edition. Grand Rapids, MI: Eerdmans, 2016.

———. "What Is Apocalyptic Literature?" In *The Oxford Handbook of Apocalyptic Literature*, edited by John J. Collins, 1–16. Oxford: Oxford University Press, 2014.

Dalton, Doug. "Cargo Cults and Discursive Madness." *Oceania* 70, no. 4 (2000): 345–61.

Liddell, Henry George, and Robert Scott. *A Greek-English Lexicon*. Oxford: Oxford University Press, 1996.

More, Thomas. *Utopia*. Translated by Clarence H. Miller. New Haven, CT: Yale University Press, 2001.

Moylan, Tom. *Scraps of the Untainted Sky: Science Fiction, Utopia, Dystopia*. New York: Routledge, 2018.

Nickelsburg, George W.E., and James C. VanderKam. *1 Enoch: The Hermeneia Translation*, Hermeneia. Minneapolis, MN: Fortress Press, 2012.

Smith, Jonathan Z. "Religion, Religions, Religious." In *Critical Terms for Religious Studies*, edited by Mark C. Taylor, 269–84. Chicago: University of Chicago Press, 1998.

Wilder, Amos. "The Rhetoric of Ancient and Modern Apocalyptic." *Interpretation* 25, no. 4 (1971): 436–53.

Worsley, Peter. *The Trumpet Shall Sound: A Study of "Cargo Cults" in Melanesia*. New York: Schocken, 1957.

Yarbro Collins, Adela. *Cosmology and Eschatology in Jewish and Christian Apocalypticism*. Supplements to the *Journal for the Study of Judaism* 50. Leiden: Brill, 1996.

Chapter 8

Katniss, Christos

Sacrifice and Salvation in Scripture and Young Adult Dystopian Novels

Shayna Sheinfeld

Roman rule of Judaea in the first century CE was fraught with violence.[1] Many Jews rejected not only the Romans, but also any Jewish collaborators with Rome, including the Herodian rulers and some of the priestly class who were responsible for proper temple function. For some Jews, the corruption of temple priests and Roman imperial rule were harbingers of the end times, when, they imagined, these corrupt authority structures would be overthrown through an act of self-sacrifice, which would then lead to liberation and salvation. This trope—self-sacrifice leading to salvation—is ubiquitous in ancient Jewish writings, from Moses to the Maccabees to the Mishnah. It is equally ubiquitous in contemporary English-language dystopian fiction, where visions of overthrowing the current political powers to catalyze an era of justice is widespread. This chapter argues that in certain ancient and modern dystopian narratives, willing self-sacrifice is a path to salvation, not just for the individual(s) sacrificing themselves, but for the larger population. The discourse of this self-sacrifice is used to encourage an identification between the audience and the promoted ideology. To examine this argument, we will consider two contemporary young adult dystopian trilogies, *The Hunger Games* and *Divergent*, alongside two first-century CE texts, the *Testament of Moses* and *Hebrews*.

Sacrifice is a loaded term. Its contemporary connotations are complex, and range in meaning from positive to negative. For example, the sacrifice of a soldier in order to protect the freedom of many is often seen favorably. It can also be used negatively, such as in accusations of sacrificing other people's lives or well-being for selfish, political, or financial gain. In antiquity, too, its meaning and function were complex and could also be ambiguous. Take, for example, the unnamed mother of seven sons in 2 Maccabees 7 who willingly sacrifices her sons and herself to the tortures of a tyrant rather than succumb to his demands that they halt Torah observance. In this narrative she encourages her sons to hold true to their Jewish observance in the face of persecution, even while she watches as each one is tortured and killed, before she herself is murdered. The author uses this story to, among other things, construct the mother as a role model, with her unwavering commitment to Torah in the face of death.[2] Another positive example of sacrifice is the near-sacrifice of Isaac in Genesis 22, as it is used to make Abraham a positive role model of loyalty and obedience to God. Not all sacrifices in antiquity, however, were depicted as good. For instance, the portrayals of human sacrifice in Judges 11 with Jephthah's daughter or the (staged) sacrifice of the protagonist Leucippe in the second-century CE Hellenistic novel *Leucippe and Clitophon,* are ambiguous at best.

What these examples, positive and negative, ancient or contemporary, have in common is that the audiences' understanding of what a particular sacrifice means is derived from the narrative context: Abraham is commanded by God to offer his son as a sacrifice, so this is an acceptable (near-)sacrifice (Gen. 22), while Jephthah makes a sloppily phrased vow to offer as sacrifice the next thing that walks out of his front door, which ends up being his only child (Judg. 11). The narrative framing of Jephthah's sacrifice of his daughter works to portrays the vow and its outcome (her death) negatively.[3] In other words, as James Watts argues, the language used to talk about the sacrifice shapes its meaning and interpretation.[4] In the case of the four texts we will explore in this chapter, their shared cultural understanding of sacrifice is inevitably built upon paradigmatic scriptural narratives, such as the near-sacrifice of Isaac in Genesis 22 and its parallels in Islam, and the crucifixion of Jesus as described in the New Testament. These ancient sacrificial narratives are foundational even when the text under analysis is itself not religious in nature or content.[5]

Like sacrifice, salvation is a loaded term. In contemporary Western settings, where Christian interpretations of salvation form the cultural understanding of the word, salvation may refer to a rescue from original sin and its eternal consequences. It can also mean saving from something more generally, such as any preservation from some sort of harm: "Getting an air conditioner was my salvation this summer." This is not so very different from the range of meaning in the ancient understanding of salvation (Hebrew ישועה, Greek σωτηρία, Latin *salus*), which also ranged from a focus on saving from troubles related to the here and now (e.g., health, finances, and love),[6] to more metaphorical meanings such as atoning for past sin to save the people from divine anger (e.g., 2 Macc.).[7] In the ancient and contemporary texts under analysis in this paper, it is with the former definition—saving from some sort of imminent, tangible trouble—that the narratives approach the perceived problems and solutions. What this exploration of the words "sacrifice" and "salvation" highlights is that in contemporary English, just as in antiquity, the words had a range of meaning that, while sometimes used, build upon paradigmatic narratives that are reused in ancient Jewish and Christian texts and in contemporary YA literature.

JUDAEA IN THE FIRST CENTURY CE

While the trope of salvation through self-sacrifice can be found in many Jewish and Christian texts from many different periods of time, the first century CE is especially ripe for exploration. Judaea in the first century was marked by pockets of discontent with Roman rule, resentment by average Jews toward elites who benefited from collaboration with Roman authority, poor leadership from both elite Jews and Romans, threat of (and actual) violation of Jewish law, and high taxes, all of which affected the lower classes acutely.[8] This situation, coupled with a literary tradition that viewed political independence as a sign of divine blessing, created an atmosphere where many Jews hoped to gain freedom from Roman rule. The decades between the death of Herod the Great in 4 BCE to the beginning of the first Jewish revolt against Rome in 66 CE saw repeated protests, which frequently turned into riots followed by violent suppression by the Roman authority.[9] While some Jews benefited from and worked to support Roman rule, including many of the priests who were running the Jerusalem Temple, others worked to overturn the status quo, often gathering followers. Some of these groups were violent; many others were not; however, since these groups gathered in a social context in which civil unrest was common, the Roman authorities suppressed any hints of rebellion with swift and violent responses.[10] Jews across the Roman Empire, including those who came to believe in the resurrected Christ, were affected by this tumultuous period. It is in this socio-political context that the Testament of Moses and Hebrews, which both highlight how willing self-sacrifice can lead to salvation, were written.

TESTAMENT OF MOSES

The Testament of Moses is a pseudepigraphon, that is, a text with an unknown author attributed to a famous person from the past. It claims to be written by the biblical Moses but was written by an anonymous first century Jew in response to Roman imperialism and its influence on the priestly class.[11] The narrative reports Moses's deathbed discourse to his chosen successor, Joshua. In that liminal space between life and death, Moses is granted access to secret knowledge and visions of God's future salvation for Israel. Like other testamentary literature, Moses's visions are of Israel from his present until the eschaton, that is, the end of days, which would conveniently occur just after the time that the actual author is writing.

In Moses's telling, right before the eschaton, the world will descend into terrible times. For example, monarchs will persecute Torah-abiding Jews, forcing them to offer animal sacrifices to other gods and to cease following their ancestral customs. These events are depicted by the author as predictions that the end times are imminent, although of course they are really the author's own description of contemporaneous society. At that time of oppression, a Jewish man from the Tribe of Levi named Taxo, together with his seven sons, will fast for three days and then they will ensconce themselves in a cave to offer themselves up as willing bodily sacrifices. Taxo says:

> Which nation or which province or which people, who have all done many crimes against the Lord, have suffered such evils as have covered us? Now, therefore, sons, heed me. If you investigate, you will surely know that never did our fathers nor their ancestors tempt God by transgressing his commandments. Yea, you will surely know that this is our strength. Here is what we shall do. We shall fast for a three-day period and on the fourth day we shall go into a cave, which is in the open country. There let us die rather than transgress the commandments of the Lord of Lords, the God of our fathers. For if we do this, and do die, our blood will be avenged before the Lord. (9:3–7)[12]

Taxo understands that the bodily sacrifice of his seven sons and himself will be the impetus for their God to intercede on behalf of the Jewish people.[13] That is, this willing self-sacrifice will trigger salvation for all Jews, saving them from the socio-political nightmare in which they live. According to the rest of the Testament of Moses, Taxo's sacrifice works: the foreign overlords are destroyed, the devil is done away with, God will wreak vengeance upon the idolatrous nations, and Israel will be raised into the heavens.[14]

In this text, salvation is achieved by God's direct involvement in the world. But God only becomes aware of the terrible extent of things when innocent blood cries out; this is what Taxo accomplishes in his passive self-sacrifice. The author of the Testament of Moses lived in Judaea in the first century under Roman domination. The Jewish monarchy was now Roman-appointed rather than independent, and the Temple priesthood was a pay-to-play position, which according to some corrupted the temple sacrifices offered to God.[15] This text offered the hope of salvation, through the willing self-sacrifice of the innocent blood of Taxo and his sons, as a way to respond to contemporaneous power dynamics and political oppression.

HEBREWS

Following ideas from early Jewish texts such as 2 Maccabees, some of Jesus's followers understood the crucified Christ as an expiatory self-sacrifice, that is, as a sacrifice that atones for sins. The crucified Christ was understood to be a sacrifice effective in place of the (now corrupted) temple atonement sacrifice. Except, by the time of the writing of Hebrews, some began to see Jesus as not only atoning for recent sins in order to turn God's face toward people for salvation from tyrannical rule, he also atoned permanently: no other sacrifice was needed in the future as long as one believed him to be the ultimate sacrifice. And this atonement was not just about the expiation of sins, but also about attaining a more metaphorical salvation: in this theology, which survives in much of Christianity to this day, Christ's crucifixion acts as a willing bodily self-sacrifice to atone for the sins of believers in this life *in order that* they may attain salvation in the next life. Salvation, according to parts of the early Jesus movement, is not temporary atonement of sins, but an ultimate defeat of death.

This is nowhere clearer than in the New Testament text called Hebrews.[16] Written in the second half of the first century of the Common Era, Hebrews presents Jesus as an alternative high priest, but an eternal, incorruptible, heavenly one, drawing direct connections between Jesus and the Jewish sacrificial cult.[17] In making this connection, Hebrews is critical of temple rituals, calling them "ineffective (7:11, 18–19; 10:4), endlessly repetitious (7:23; 10:1), impermanent (8:13; 9:9–10), and tainted by the sin of the priests who offered them (5:3; 7:27; 9:7)."[18] Hebrews' critique of the sacrificial cult does not invalidate the process, but instead shows that the ultimate temple is the heavenly temple, and that Jesus is both its priest and its definitive sacrifice:[19]

> Furthermore, the former priests were many in number, because they were prevented by death from continuing in office; but [Jesus] holds his priesthood permanently, because he continues forever. Consequently he is able for all time to save those who approach God through him, since he always lives to make intercession for them. For it was fitting that we should have such a high priest, holy, blameless, undefiled, separated from sinners, and exalted above the heavens. Unlike the other high priests, he has no need to offer sacrifices day after day, first for his own sins, and then for those of the people; this he did once for all when he offered himself. For the law appoints as high priests those who are

subject to weakness, but the word of the oath, which came later than the law, appoints a Son who has been made perfect forever. (7:23–28 NRSV)

This excerpt highlights a dichotomous comparison between earthly and heavenly realms, with earth representing imperfect worship and sacrifice, and heaven representing the ideal.[20] The author of Hebrews is making the argument that the earthly temple cult is imperfect, with priests who must continuously offer sacrifices for themselves and for the people, and who die because they are, after all, human. Jesus is the ultimate priest because he has defeated death with his resurrection. Even more relevant, however, is that Hebrews points out that Jesus has willingly *offered himself*: in this text, Jesus's crucifixion is an act of bodily self-sacrifice that eliminates the current "world order" as it was understood by some first century Jews, and instead offers salvation through the sacrifice and subsequent resurrection of Jesus.

For many Jews in antiquity, including those who participated in the early Jesus movement, certain acts of self-sacrifice that atoned for past sins of the nation could bring about salvation for their people. In the case of the Testament of Moses, the terrible treatment of Jews by their foreign rulers led to the willing self-sacrifice of Taxo and his sons, which then brings about the end days: after an expiatory sacrifice is given, God turns from punishing Israel via its enemies, and instead punishes the enemies, after which all of Israel will be delivered. In Hebrews, the crisis at hand is not foreign rulers, but sin and death. Jesus's self-sacrifice, made on behalf of the people just as Taxo's was, eliminates both sin and death—in this case, only for those who believe.

YOUNG ADULT (YA) DYSTOPIAS

Dystopian literature, defined as works of fiction which are "primarily concerned to portray societies where a substantial majority suffer slavery and/or oppression as a result of human action," has taken off as a genre in the past century, building on the previous popularity of utopian literature.[21] More recently we have seen the growth of dystopian literature geared toward a YA audience, which has exploded in popularity after 9/11.[22] While there are many possible reasons why YA dystopian literature has surged in popularity, one reason may be the perceived lack of control in the lives of young adults, especially as to whether their futures hold the promise of disaster, from climate disasters to economic ruin to extremist violence. The protagonists in YA dystopias can take action, gain control, and have an impact on their worlds, offering their (young) readers a vicarious sense of control and hope they themselves may lack.[23]

In part, dystopian writing serves to critique existing social conditions or political systems. Young adult dystopian fiction generally does this, as M. Keith Booker states, through the "imaginative extension of those conditions and systems into different contexts that more clearly reveal their flaws and contradictions."[24] The points of contact between YA dystopia and ancient literature become clearer: ancient texts such as the Testament of Moses and Hebrews provide socio-political critique while also providing access to the promise of salvation, often through willing self-sacrifice. Similarly, although an array of alternate salvific vehicles could conceivably be narrative choices, it is often willing self-sacrifice that leads to the attainment of salvation in dystopian fiction as well.[25] Two young adult dystopias, *The Hunger Games* and the *Divergent* trilogies, will serve as examples of how this genre represents the ancient Jewish literary trope of salvific self-sacrifice of a protagonist. For these novels, just like for our ancient communities, a corrupt political order must be overcome in order for salvation to be attained.

DIVERGENT TRILOGY

Veronica Roth's *Divergent* trilogy (*Divergent, Insurgent, Allegiant*) provides a good example of salvation through self-sacrifice.[26] Taking place in a postapocalyptic Chicago, all citizens are split into one of five factions based on one dominant trait—Erudite, Abnegation, Dauntless, Amity, and Candor. The main character, Tris, learns that she is "divergent"—that is, inclined toward more than one trait—and thus a threat to the political system. But it is her divergence that allows her to figure out and disrupt a government plot for control. In book two, Tris and her community are eventually able to watch the video that shows the community's origins: their community was started by an outside group to increase the number of divergents. The third book has Tris and some other people moving outside of their Chicago community to a world that suffers from its own issues related to socio-economic status, violence, and obsession with genetic purity, with those who are genetically pure being those who are divergent, and therefore superior to everyone else.

The Bureau that set up the Chicago experiment plans to save it by wiping the memories of everyone in Chicago and starting anew. While some of Tris's friends take an antidote back to Chicago to try to prevent this, Tris develops a plan to release the memory-wiping serum at the Bureau headquarters to erase the societal conflict based on genetics. Knowing it is likely a suicide mission, Tris breaks in and releases the serum, saving her Chicago community and erasing the conflict from the memories of those working at the Bureau. She is caught by the head of the organization and killed.

After successfully releasing the serum, before she is killed, Tris reflects about what she learned from her murdered mother:[27]

> [My mother] taught me all about real sacrifice. That it should be done from love not misplaced disgust for another person's genetics. That it should be done from necessity, not without exhausting all other options. That it should be done for people who need your strength because they don't have enough of their own. That's why I need to stop you from "sacrificing" all those people and their memories. Why I need to rid the world of you once and for all.[28]

Tris goes knowingly to her death, choosing to sacrifice herself strategically and effectively to save her remaining family, friends, *and* the larger world. Her death ultimately brings the larger world salvation by stopping the genetics war. Tris consciously links her death, her sacrifice, to stopping the corrupt political powers "once and for all." Her sacrifice is necessary to save not only her Chicago community but also the rest of the world from war and class discrimination. As with the self-sacrifices of Taxo in the Testament of Moses and of Jesus in Hebrews, Tris recognizes the power of self-sacrifice, which she learned about from her mother. The purpose here is not just to save oneself, which is the kind of "sacrificing" she is rallying against in her final speech here to the head of the Bureau, but to sacrifice oneself for a larger population and ideologies beyond herself in order to save the larger population—in this case, her community in Chicago as well as those concerned with genetic purity/impurity outside the city.

THE HUNGER GAMES TRILOGY

In *The Hunger Games* trilogy, the postapocalyptic nation of Panem is run by a decadent elite supported by the forced labor of twelve districts.[29] To punish the districts for a previous revolt, the Capitol requires each district to send two children as "tributes" to compete in the annual televised "Hunger Games." The tributes are chosen by lottery, and must fight to the death, leaving only one victor. The first book follows protagonist Katniss Everdeen to the Hunger Games. Katniss has volunteered as tribute in place of her little sister, Prim, knowing this self-sacrifice will mean her own death. But she and her district partner, Peeta Mellark, win the games.

The district rebellions hinted at in the first book are further emphasized in the second, when Katniss and Peeta are punished for thwarting the system by being forced to participate in the games once again. Rather than attempt to win, Katniss chooses to do whatever is in her power, including sacrificing herself, to ensure that Peeta returns home victorious. Some of the other tributes sacrifice themselves for Peeta as well, by extension protecting Katniss who has unknowingly become the face of the rebellion against the Capitol. The final book traces Katniss's reluctant acceptance of her role as the face of the uprising led by the previously unknown district 13. She eventually infiltrates the Capitol and sees its defeat, only also to witness the senseless death of her sister Prim, the person she originally sacrificed herself to save in book one. With the current political orders gone—both the president of the Capitol and the leader of district 13 are dead—the political status quo that Katniss and the districts have rebelled against is overthrown and a new government is established, one that is not built upon the sacrifice of children.[30] For Katniss, the salvation of the greater good is personal and painful as she mourns her sister's death.

Sacrifice and salvation are connected in a personal way throughout *The Hunger Games* trilogy.[31] Katniss's self-sacrifice is initially meant just to save one person: her sister. In the second book Katniss wavers between wanting to sacrifice herself for individuals—for her hunting partner and sometimes love interest Gale, while she is in her district, and for her fellow tribute and sometimes love interest Peeta, once they are both tributes in the next Hunger Games—and for the larger rebellion. She struggles with the idea of committing herself to a larger ideology if it may put her loved ones as risk. Even in the final book, Katniss agrees to be the Mockingjay, the figurehead of the rebellion, mainly because it will give her an opportunity to kill President Snow for personal revenge. However, even while Katniss agrees with the intention of killing Snow, she realizes that her self-sacrifice can also serve others, a realization that comes from a conversation with her sister.[32] It is only with the death of her sister and the realization that she is being lied to by the rebel leader that Katniss realizes her own power to bring about salvation for all the districts: she embraces her death with the final (she thinks) act of killing the president of the rebels. This act, alongside the death of the Capitol's original president, paves the way for salvation—a new society not burdened with the old regime. Unlike in the other texts discussed in this chapter, however, Katniss's self-sacrifice does not end in her expected death but in a different kind of personal salvation, one where she is able to raise children in a world free from the problems of the previous regime.

CONCLUSION

In the first book of *The Hunger Games* trilogy, a single slip of paper with the name of Katniss's sister, Primrose Everdeen, is chosen during the lottery out of the thousands of names. As Prim walks to the stage, Katniss stops her and rushes to take Prim's place, calling out: "I volunteer! . . . I volunteer as tribute!"[33] Rather than letting her younger sister suffer the fate of most of the tributes—that is, eventual death by starvation or combat—Katniss willingly submits herself as tribute. While she is aware this means almost certain death, more importantly for her is that it means her sister will live. This scene is paradigmatic of the texts under analysis in this chapter in that it reflects the trope of salvation that is brought about through willing self-sacrifice.

Although only four texts have been discussed here, many examples exist of the ways that narratives employ self-sacrifice as a way of moving an audience toward sympathy with a given ideology, often one that construes the contemporaneous context as one of injustice or corruption. In both ancient Jewish literature and in modern English-language YA dystopias, self-sacrifice, while complex, is presented as a constructive act that, done under the right conditions, can lead to salvation. What is consistent amongst these texts is that the individual must choose self-sacrifice of their own free will. This choice, then, leads to the salvation of the group to which the sacrificed individual belongs, whether family, the religious group, or the whole world.

NOTES

1. This chapter was first presented as a talk at the inauguration of the Embodied Religion Research Theme in the Sheffield Institute of Interdisciplinary Biblical Studies, Sheffield University, England, June 2016 and later at the Midwest American Academy of Religion Annual Meeting (virtual) April 2021.

2. On the fluidity of definitions of Torah in early Jewish and early Christian periods, see Shayna Sheinfeld, "From *Nomos* to *Logos*: Torah in First-Century Jewish Texts," in *The Message of Paul the Apostle within Second Temple Judaism*, ed. František Ábel (Lanham, MD: Lexington Books/Fortress Press, 2020), 61–74.

3. Interestingly, in the rewriting of Judges 11 in the first century text, Liber antiquitatum biblicarum, by Pseudo-Philo, Jephthah's daughter (here named Seila) acknowledges that if she does not go to her death willingly, it will not be an acceptable sacrifice to God (40.3).

4. James W. Watts, "The Rhetoric of Sacrifice," in *Ritual and Metaphor: Sacrifice in the Bible*, ed. Christian A. Eberhart (Atlanta: Society of Biblical Literature, 2011), 3–16.

5. As Northrop Frye famously argues in *The Great Code: The Bible and Literature* (San Diego: Harvest, 1983).

6. See, for instance, Mary Beard, John North, and Simon Price, *Religions of Rome*, vol. 1 (Cambridge: Cambridge University Press, 2017), 287n119 and Water Burkert, *Ancient Mystery Cults* (Cambridge, MA: Harvard University Press, 1987), 12–29.

7. So, classically, martyrologist Jan Willem Van Henten, *Maccabean Martyrs as Saviours of the Jewish People: A Study of 2 & 4 Maccabees* (Leiden: Brill, 1997). For a catalog showcasing the wide semantic range of messianic deliverance for ancient

Judaism, see Gerbern S. Oegema, *The Anointed and His People: Messianic Expectations from the Maccabees to Bar Kochba* (Sheffield: Sheffield Academic, 1998), and more recently Matthew Novenson, *The Grammar of Messianism: An Ancient Jewish Political Idiom and Its Users* (Oxford: Oxford University Press, 2017).

8. For more on life in first century Judaea, see: Helen K. Bond, "The Social and Political Milieu," in *The Cambridge Companion to the New Testament*, ed. Patrick Gray (Cambridge: Cambridge University Press, 2021), 3–24.

9. Richard A. Horsley, *Bandits, Prophets & Messiahs: Popular Movements in the Time of Jesus* (Harrisburg, PA: Trinity Press International, 2007), 34–43.

10. David M. Rhoads, *Israel in Revolution, 6–74 C.E.: A Political History Based on the Writings of Josephus* (Philadelphia: Fortress Press, 1979), 80–84.

11. Fiona Grierson, "The Testament of Moses," *JSP* 17, no. 4 (2008): 275–76.

12. Translations from John Priest, "Testament of Moses: A New Translation and Introduction," in *The Old Testament Pseudepigrapha*, ed. James H. Charlesworth (Peabody, MA: Hendrickson Publishers, 1983), 1.919–34.

13. Shmuel Shepkaru, "To Die For: The Evolution of Early Jewish Martyrdom," in *Martyrdom, Self-Sacrifice, and Self-Immolation: Religious Perspectives on Suicide*, ed. Margo Kitts (Oxford: Oxford University Press: 2018), 30–31, and John J. Collins, "Some Remaining Traditio-Historical Problems in the Testament of Moses," in *Studies on the Testament of Moses: Seminar Papers*, ed. George W E. Nickelsburg, SBLSCS 4 (Cambridge, MA: Society of Biblical Literature, 1973), 42.

14. David P. Moessner, "Suffering, Intercession and Eschatological Atonement: An Uncommon Common View in the Testament of Moses and in Luke-Acts," in *The Pseudepigrapha and Early Biblical Interpretation*, ed. James H. Charlesworth and Craig A. Evans, JSPSup 14 (Sheffield: Sheffield Academic Press, 1993), 201–15.

15. On the parallels in the Testament of Moses and the politics of first century Judaea, see Kenneth Atikinson, "Taxo's Martyrdom and the Role of the Nuntius in the *Testament of Moses*: Implications for Understanding the Role of Other Intermediary Figures," *Journal of Biblical Literature* 125, no. 3 (2006): 457–67.

16. Eisenbaum notes that Hebrews "stands out from other New Testament literature" as "the only document that contains a sustained argument on the nature of Christ." Pamela Eisenbaum, "The Letter to the Hebrews," *The Jewish Annotated New Testament 2nd Edition NRSV*, ed. A.-J. Levine and Marc Zvi Brettler (Oxford: Oxford University Press, 2017), 460.

17. The dating of Hebrews is challenging, but most scholars date between 60–100 CE. Harold W. Attridge, *The Epistle to the Hebrews: A Commentary on the Epistle to the Hebrews*, Hermeneia (Philadelphia: Fortress, 1989), 9.

18. Richard D. Nelson, "'He Offered Himself': Sacrifices in Hebrews," *Interpretation* 57, no. 3 (2003): 251. Hebrews is not the only ancient Jewish text that is critical of the priests at the Jerusalem Temple. Some Dead Sea Scrolls are critical of the priesthood, for example, 4Q390, which describes the defilement of the temple by the priests. Some scholars such as Atkinson also link Testament of Moses to a critical view of priests.

19. Nelson, "'He Offered Himself,'" 251. See also Ra'anan S. Boustan, "Confounding Blood: Jewish Narratives of Sacrifice and Violence in Late Antiquity," in

Ancient Mediterranean Sacrifice, ed. Jennifer Wright Knust and Zsuzsanna Varhelji (Oxford: Oxford University Press, 2011), 265–98, especially: "It would be misleading . . . to characterize the so-called end of sacrifice as the progressive spiritualization of religion. Indeed, sacrificial cult continued to serve throughout late antiquity as the dominant paradigm for ritual action and religious piety, even in the 'post-sacrificial' forms of Judaism, Christianity, and indeed paganism that emerged in this period. If anything, sacrifice—and specifically, the symbolic function of sacrificial blood—provided an increasingly charged domain of contact and competition across the full spectrum of religious groups in the Mediterranean world" (265).

20. Georg Gäbel, *Die Kulttheologie des Hebräerbriefes: Eine exegetisch-religionsgeschichtliche Studie*, WUNT 2/212 (Tübingen: Mohr Siebeck, 2006), 17, 476.

21. Gregory Claeys, *Dystopia: A Natural History* (Oxford: Oxford University Press, 2017), 290.

22. Rebekah Fitzsimmons, "Exploring the Genre Conventions of the YA Dystopian Trilogy as Twenty-First Century Utopian Dreaming," in *Beyond the Blockbusters: Themes and Trends in Contemporary Young Adult Fiction*, ed. Rebekah Fitzsimmons and Casey Alane Wilson (Jackson, MS: University of Mississippi Press, 2020), 14.

23. Shayna Sheinfeld, "Scenes from the End of the World in American Popular Culture," in *The Oxford Handbook of the Bible and American Popular Culture*, ed. Dan W. Clanton, Jr. and Terry Ray Clark (Oxford: Oxford University Press, 2020), 210–11.

24. M. Keith Booker, *Dystopian Literature: A Theory and Research Guide* (Westport, CT: Greenwood Press, 1994), 3.

25. While I do not address gender in this chapter, there is a clear connection between modern conceptions of self-sacrifice and ideas of femininity. Along with attributes like passivity, weakness, and silence, self-sacrifice is often associated with the feminine. Both Tris and Katniss disrupt these traditional societal standards of the feminine. Tris is a fighter, while Katniss is a hunter. Both women also kill and seek out violence as a solution. Maria Nikolajeva, *Power, Voice and Subjectivity in Literature for Young Readers* (New York: Routledge, 2010), 103, 133.

26. Veronica Roth, *Divergent* (New York: Tegen, 2011), *Insurgent* (New York: Tegen, 2012), *Allegiant* (New York: Tegen, 2013).

27. Self-sacrifice plays an explicit role in this trilogy, and not only with Tris's decision to release the serum even though she expects it to result in her death. In the first book, Tris's mother runs at guards who are looking for insurgents, sacrificing her own life so that Tris can get away and complete the salvific mission. Her father, too, sacrifices himself by leading rebel Dauntless fighters away from Tris so she can stop the Erudite simulation that is causing the attack. Their self-sacrifice rests heavily on Tris, and throughout the second book she continuously places herself into dangerous situations as a way to try to die as they died, through self-sacrifice.

28. Roth, *Allegiant*, 473–74.

29. Suzanne Collins, *The Hunger Games* (New York: Scholastic, 2008), *Catching Fire* (New York: Scholastic, 2009), *Mockingjay* (New York, Scholastic, 2010).

30. Gretchen Koenig, "Communal Spectacle: Reshaping History and Memory through Violence," in *Of Bread, Blood, and the Hunger Games: Critical Essays on*

the Suzanne Collins Trilogy, ed. Mary F. Pharr and Leisa A. Clark (Jefferson, NC: McFarland, 2012), 47.

31. Emily McAvan explores the variety of sacrifices and sacrificial meaning found in *The Hunger Games* trilogy in "'May the Odds Be Ever in Your Favor': The Sacrificial Logic of The Hunger Games," *Bible and Critical Theory* 13, no. 2 (2017): 49–62.

32. Collins, *Mockingjay*, 33–35.

33. Collins, *The Hunger Games*, 22.

BIBLIOGRAPHY

Atkinson, Kenneth. "Taxo's Martyrdom and the Role of the Nuntius in the *Testament of Moses*: Implications for Understanding the Role of Other Intermediary Figures." *Journal of Biblical Literature* 125, no. 3 (2006): 453–76.

Attridge, Harold W. *The Epistle to the Hebrews: A Commentary on the Epistle to the Hebrews*. Hermeneia. Philadelphia: Fortress, 1989.

Beard, Mary, John North, and Simon Price. *Religions of Rome. Volume 1*. Cambridge: Cambridge University Press, 2017.

Bond, Helen K. "The Social and Political Milieu." In *The Cambridge Companion to the New Testament*, edited by Patrick Gray, 3–24. Cambridge Companions to Religion. Cambridge: Cambridge University Press, 2021.

Booker, M. Keith. *Dystopian Literature: A Theory and Research Guide*. Westport, CT: Greenwood Press, 1994.

Boustan, Ra'anan S. "Confounding Blood: Jewish Narratives of Sacrifice and Violence in Late Antiquity." In *Ancient Mediterranean Sacrifice*, edited by Jennifer Wright Knust and Zsuzsanna Varhelji, 265–98. Oxford: Oxford University Press, 2011.

Burkert, Walter. *Ancient Mystery Cults*. Cambridge, MA: Harvard University Press, 1987.

Claeys, Gregory. *Dystopia: A Natural History*. Oxford: Oxford University Press, 2017.

Collins, John J. "Some Remaining Traditio-Historical Problems in the Testament of Moses." In *Studies on the Testament of Moses*, edited by George W.E. Nickelsburg, 38–43. SBLSCS 4. Missoula, MT: Society of Biblical Literature, 1973.

Collins, Suzanne. *The Hunger Games*. New York: Scholastic, 2008.

———. *Catching Fire*. New York: Scholastic, 2009.

———. *Mockingjay*. New York, Scholastic, 2010.

Eisenbaum, Pamela. "The Letter to the Hebrews." In *The Jewish Annotated New Testament 2nd Edition NRSV*, edited by A.-J. Levine and Marc Zvi Brettler, 460–62. Oxford: Oxford University Press, 2017.

Fitzsimmons, Rebekah. "Exploring the Genre Conventions of the YA Dystopian Trilogy as Twenty-First Century Utopian Dreaming." In *Beyond the Blockbusters: Themes and Trends in Contemporary Young Adult Fiction*, edited by Rebekah Fitzsimmons and Casey Alane Wilson, 3–19. Jackson, MS: University of Mississippi Press, 2020.

Frye, Northrop. *The Great Code: The Bible and Literature*. San Diego: Harvest, 1983.

Gäbel, Georg. *Die Kulttheologie des Hebräerbriefes: Eine exegetisch-religionsgeschichtliche Studie*. WUNT 2/212. Tübingen: Mohr Siebeck, 2006.
Grierson, Fiona. "The Testament of Moses." *Journal for the Study of the Pseudepigrapha* 17, no. 4 (2008): 256–80.
Horsley, Richard A. *Bandits, Prophets & Messiahs: Popular Movements in the Time of Jesus*. Harrisburg, PA: Trinity Press International, 2007.
Koenig, Gretchen. "Communal Spectacle: Reshaping History and Memory through Violence." In *Of Bread, Blood, and the Hunger Games: Critical Essays on the Suzanne Collins Trilogy*, edited by Mary F. Pharr and Leisa A. Clark, 39–48. Jefferson, NC: McFarland, 2012.
McAvan, Emily. "'May the Odds Be Ever in Your Favor': The Sacrificial Logic of The Hunger Games." *Bible and Critical Theory* 13, no. 2 (2017): 49–62.
Moessner, David P. "Suffering, Intercession and Eschatological Atonement: An Uncommon Common View in the Testament of Moses and in Luke-Acts." In *The Pseudepigrapha and Early Biblical Interpretation*, edited by James H. Charlesworth and Craig A. Evans, 201–15. JSPSup 14. Sheffield: Sheffield Academic Press, 1993.
Nelson, Richard D. "'He Offered Himself': Sacrifices in Hebrews." *Interpretation* 57, no. 3 (2003): 251–65.
Nikolajeva, Maria. *Power, Voice and Subjectivity in Literature for Young Readers*. New York: Routledge, 2010.
Novenson, Matthew. *The Grammar of Messianism: An Ancient Jewish Political Idiom and Its Users*. Oxford: Oxford University Press, 2017.
Oegema, Gerbern S. *The Anointed and His People: Messianic Expectations from the Maccabees to Bar Kochba*. Sheffield: Sheffield Academic, 1998.
Priest, John. "Testament of Moses: A New Translation and Introduction." In *The Old Testament Pseudepigrapha*, vol. 1, edited by James H. Charlesworth, 919–34. Peabody, MA: Hendrickson Publishers, 1983.
Rhoads, David M. *Israel in Revolution, 6–74 C.E.: A Political History Based on the Writings of Josephus*. Philadelphia: Fortress, 1979.
Roth, Veronica. *Divergent*. New York: Tegen, 2011.
———. *Insurgent*. New York: Tegen, 2012.
———. *Allegiant*. New York: Tegen, 2013.
Sheinfeld, Shayna. "From *Nomos* to *Logos*: Torah in First-Century Jewish Texts." In *The Message of Paul the Apostle within Second Temple Judaism*, edited by František Ábel, 61–74. Lanham, MD: Lexington Books/Fortress Academic, 2020.
———. "Scenes from the End of the World in American Popular Culture." In *Oxford Handbook of the Bible and American Popular Culture*, edited by Dan W. Clanton, Jr. and Terry Ray Clark, 201–18. Oxford: Oxford University Press, 2020.
Shepkaru, Shmuel. "To Die For: The Evolution of Early Jewish Martyrdom." In *Martyrdom, Self-Sacrifice, and Self-Immolation: Religious Perspectives on Suicide*, edited by Margo Kitts, 18–39. Oxford: Oxford University Press: 2018.
Van Henten, Jan Willem. *Maccabean Martyrs as Saviours of the Jewish People: A Study of 2 & 4 Maccabees*. Leiden: Brill, 1997.

Watts, James W. "The Rhetoric of Sacrifice." In *Ritual and Metaphor: Sacrifice in the Bible*, edited by Christian A. Eberhart, 3–16. Atlanta: Society of Biblical Literature, 2011.

Chapter 9

Dystopian Festivals, Utopian Fictions

Sovereignty, Sacrifice, and Sanctity in Biblical Jubilee and **The Purge**

C. J. McCrary

In great festivals, one spends and one spends oneself.—Jacques Gernet, *Buddhism in Chinese Society* (1995), 241

Homo ludens' evergreen longing for the carnival or fête shines perhaps nowhere more brightly than in dystopian fiction.[1] Despite, or maybe because of, the political tumult and economic scarcity typical of societies in the dystopic imagination, festivals, games, and feast days are not uncommon features in dystopian fiction. Indeed, they are often large, perhaps even nationwide, events and unfathomably expensive. On the occasions when such celebrations do appear in dystopian fiction, they frequently serve as a narrative linchpin, and the more extravagant the celebratory display, the more likely its centrality to the tale. This chapter will consider one of the most recent examples of such an extravagant festival in dystopian fiction: *The Purge* saga.

The Purge franchise is comprised of five films and two seasons of a television show, which appeared in U.S. theaters and on American TV between 2013 and 2021. It cobbles together a sprawling, fascist, twenty-first-century American dystopia out of the disparate stories of dozens of individual characters from up and down the socioeconomic ladder, all of which converge on the night of the eponymous Purge. The Purge is an annual holiday organized around an explosive release of public violence. Although it is framed from the beginning as a patriotic holiday, not unlike Independence Day or Memorial

Day, the Purge can also be seen as a profoundly religious festival, analogous in many respects to Carnival, the Feast of Fools, or even the biblical Jubilee. Each of these holidays stages a reversal of the social order in one way or another—the Feast of Fools by crowning a pauper a "king-for-the-day" and the biblical Jubilee by forbidding planting or harvesting for a time and proposing a return of property. The Purge too stages a reversal, a return to the state of nature, by temporarily suspending criminal law (or "legalizing all crime," as the Purge night emergency broadcast system puts it). These highly circumscribed ritual reversals bring us tantalizingly close to understanding the sovereign, lawgiving power, which they simultaneously suspend and shore up by way of that suspension. Within the dystopian fiction of the Purge specifically, the sacred, literally "set apart," quality of sovereignty rises close to the surface.

Festivals, and especially those festivals like the biblical Jubilee and the Purge, are the skilled hands that pry off the watch face of society to reveal those subterranean machinations, powering it totally unseen. This chapter will make a case that sacrifice opens the window onto the interior workings of society. By looking closely at the ways in which sacrifice operates in the rituals of the Purge and holidays like it, especially the biblical Jubilee and the Sabbath, this chapter will address a handful of questions. What, if anything, is being sacrificed in these festivals? What does festive ritual sacrifice accomplish—that is, what do the celebrants in these festivals get out of their sacrifices? What does the suspension of law in these festivals say about or do for the sovereign lawgiver behind it? In what ways are economic factors like labor and consumption related to the sacred? And how might the sacred be connected to sovereign power? I will argue that the sacrificial rituals of the Purge and Jubilee/the Sabbatical construct a fiction. Together, they tell a story about sovereign power's necessity and holiness, a story that not only serves to legitimize the power of the lawgiver and the existing order she has put in place, but which comes to comprise the very fabric of sovereignty itself. I will demonstrate how sacrifice in these festivals renders sovereign power sacred, or rather, draws our attention to the sacredness of sovereign power through rituals of conspicuous consumption.

DYSTOPIA AND SOVEREIGNTY

Before showing what *The Purge* saga has to say about sovereign power, it is necessary to define dystopia and sovereignty. For the purposes of this chapter, there are three main qualities of dystopias. The first is that dystopias are generally fantastical. That is to say, dystopias are the product of an anxious cultural imagination. They may take place in the "distant" future of George

Orwell's *1984*, or in the distant past of Philip K. Dick's *The Man in the High Castle*, or as *The Purge* suggests, even in the present. This is connected to the second quality of dystopia. Unlike much utopian fiction, which is generally aspirational, dystopias are typically cautionary. Like the Ghost of Christmas Yet to Come from Charles Dickens' famous *A Christmas Carol*, the authors of dystopian fiction paint for us bleak visions of what the future holds for society as we know it, if nothing is done to address catastrophic climate change (*The Drowned World*), Christian nationalism (*A Handmaid's Tale*), our relationship to technology (*Ready Player One*), the growing threat of global pandemic (*Station Eleven*), or any of the other multitude of problems that trouble our reality in the present. Specifically, these fictions warn us about the state of society, which underscores the third main quality of dystopia within this chapter: dystopias are socially oriented. That is to say, dystopian fictions, like utopian ones, are interested in the ways society is organized and regulated to ensure resilience, equality, justice, and prosperity—or not—for that society's members. This is, perhaps, why we see an overwhelming preponderance of dystopian fictions concerned with unchecked authoritarianism and the societies that it produces (*Brave New World*, *The Man in the High Castle*, *We*, *The Handmaid's Tale*, *The Purge*, etc.).

Dystopian fiction's interest in the organization of society suggests to us the nature of dystopia's relationship to sovereignty. However, it does not answer the question: what precisely is sovereignty? The question is a challenging one because sovereignty requires the sovereign to be, in some significant way, "outside" of, or rather above, society and the laws that govern it. Like a king or queen, the sovereign's power is supreme, not only over her subjects, but over the law itself. The father of political theology, Carl Schmitt, once wrote "sovereign is he who decides on the exception"; that is to say, the real sovereign is the person or the political body who, standing "above" the law as it were, gets to decide when the law no longer applies and when certain laws might be suspended.[2] In his analysis of Schmitt's *Political Theology*, Giorgio Agamben argued that it is the very existence of such "states of exception" to the regular legislative order that bring "to light in a parodic form the anomie [or 'lawlessness'] within the law," and ultimately serve to *reinforce* sovereign power.[3] The sovereign not only gets to decide on how to regulate the social order through the law, but also when, to what extent, and in what circumstances. Each decision, exemption, and suspension represent yet another demonstration of the sovereign's complete power over the rule of law.

Holidays like the biblical Jubilee or even the Purge are just the sort of "anomic explosions within well-ordered societies,"[4] which Agamben pointed to as the narrow point where "law and anomie show their distance and, at the same time, their secret solidarity."[5] In a stroke of irony, the "temporary reversal of the human to the nonhuman, the cultural to the natural," which occurs in both celebrations is quite strictly circumscribed—Jubilee by Levitical law, the Purge by the U.S. Constitution.[6] Therefore, both represent a pure exercise of sovereign power in Schmitt's sense of the term; however, the Purge in particular displays an even more nuanced concept of sovereignty, one that would appear slightly more in keeping with Georges Bataille than with Schmitt.

For Bataille, "sovereignty" (*souveraineté*) was another name for the sacred, a quality that he located "in moments of violence, eroticism, or excretion, in behaviors marked by excess, exuberance, consumption or waste, when the body may be penetrated or conversely, exude outside its boundaries and either perpetrate or experience transgression that is simultaneously moral and physical."[7] Bataille thought that sovereignty was sacred insofar as the possession of sovereign power sets an individual or an institution apart from the transactionalism that defines ordinary life. He writes, "What distinguishes sovereignty is the consumption of wealth, as against labor and servitude, which produce wealth without consuming it . . . We may call sovereign the enjoyment of possibilities that utility doesn't justify . . . Beyond need, the object of desire is *humanly*, the *miracle*; it is sovereign life, beyond the necessary that suffering defines."[8] The excesses on display in the Purge constitute a naked display of sovereignty in Bataille's sense of the word; ergo, the Purge cannot escape the airs of religiosity, of sanctity, that accompany Bataille's notion of sovereignty. A closer examination of the specific ritual excesses of the Purge promises to yield a clearer picture of this sacred core at the heart of sovereign power.

THE PURGE

What immediately stands out about *The Purge* as a piece of dystopian fiction is its near-sightedness. If most dystopian fiction locates dystopia in the distant future, while a select few project it into fantasies of a dystopic past, *The Purge* does not see past the present decade. Beginning with the first film in the summer of 2013 and ending with the franchise's final installment in the summer of 2021, *The Purge* films and television series have built a disturbing alternative timeline of current U.S. events. Following a catastrophic economic downturn in 2013—not coincidentally, the same year the first *Purge* film debuted in U.S. theaters—*The Purge*'s America spirals into a period of intense social unrest and skyrocketing crime. The public response in the presidential election cycle to follow is dramatic: the U.S. elects a new fascist party's candidate into the White House in 2016, and a year later the first annual Purge is held. What begins as a government social experiment on Staten Island metastasizes into an annual holiday, enshrined within a 28th amendment to the U.S. Constitution and complete with its own religious and market economies, the size of which could rival Christmas in dollars spent (albeit, on security systems and weapons rather than on candy and toys) and in popular religious importance.

While preparations for the annual Purge may require every one of the 364 days preceding it, the actual event lasts only twelve hours. During this twelve-hour period, all criminal law is suspended within U.S. borders, transforming the nation utterly into a "zone in which life's maximum subjection to the law is reversed into freedom and license."[9] One can imagine the outrageous perils to which such a suspension exposes civil society; however, this risky, annual break in the legal order is more than just a wanton celebration of violence for violence's sake. The Purge ostensibly serves a single purpose: to reduce crime, which it does quite effectively. The fascist party responsible for implementing the Purge, the New Founding Fathers of America (NFFA), boasts of historically low crime rates and unemployment below 1% following the institution of the annual Purge. The NFFA attributes this nigh miraculous reduction entirely to the efficacy of the new holiday. By providing a legal outlet for the public ire threatening to boil over in the United States, the Purge does what it says on the box: it *purges* one of all her feelings of dissatisfaction, hatred, and powerlessness, freeing her to be a law-abiding citizen and reliable worker during the other 364 days in the year. Participation in the Purge is key, therefore, to the Purge's overall effectiveness. Such high stakes render participation a matter of patriotic and moral obligation. Participation, specifically in violent crime, on Purge night becomes a boon and a duty, a chance at personal catharsis, which makes one a better worker, a better citizen, and a wealthier and safer American.

At least, that is the official line from the NFFA and the media outlets that it controls. The reality that plays out on the street is far different than the violent catharsis theory propped up by the fascist ruling party. Season 2 of the USA Network's *Purge* television series reveals that the violent urges, which the Purge supposedly slakes, are not purged through violence. Brain scans, psychological evaluations, and other evidence demonstrate quite the opposite, that in fact the Purge makes people *addicted* to violence, and actually increases off-Purge crime. Such psychological evidence exposes the government's utopic crime rate to be entirely fabricated. That the state is able to monitor and cover up this year-over-year increase in violent crime is a testament to the strength and reach of the NFFA's surveillance and news media apparatus.

However, even if the Purge does not quite do what it says on the box, its dramatic impact on unemployment and, by extension, on the U.S. economy, remains legitimate. The booming U.S. employment statistics of which the

NFFA boasts are indeed the result of the annual Purge, only not for the reason the government gives. While the Purge does create jobs, it cannot create enough of them or "vacate" enough jobs via Purge night culling to bring unemployment below 1%. Instead, it relies upon a far simpler, more brutal premise: eliminating the unemployed. Suspending the law, and by extension its protections for society's most vulnerable, directly facilitates this project. The wealthy are able to afford the most weapons and ammunition, the most sophisticated home defense systems, perhaps even guards; for the homeless, the unemployed, the disabled, the impoverished, the most protection they may be able to afford is plyboard over the windows, if they are fortunate to have shelter at all. This has the effect of eliminating the most vulnerable "noncontributors" from the economy, reducing the burden on federal social safety nets and the number of unemployed overall.

It is plain to see that the dangers of Purge night are by no means distributed equally. Indeed, class is perhaps the single most important factor in determining who lives and who dies on Purge night. The antagonizing, catalyzing presence of the U.S. caste system is ubiquitous; one might even be tempted to call it the true antagonist of the franchise. Class determines who is the most armed, who is the best protected, and therefore, who can most afford to risk a so-called "hunting expedition" on the night of the Purge. Consequently, a permeating sense of entitlement to the lives of the poor and the disadvantaged prevails, particularly in college-aged youth like the gang of young adults who break into the Sandins' home in pursuit of a homeless man in the first *Purge* film. So too do the Sandins' jealous, vengeful neighbors express a sense of entitlement over the Sandins' lives, even going so far as to kill the Sandins' home invaders when they begin to kill members of the family, "robbing" the neighbors of their right to purge the Sandins themselves. Above all else, the Sandins' neighbors believe in their right to purge their envy and hatred; that then entitles them to the lives of the family that provoked such feelings. The Sandins' wealthy neighbors making designs upon the even wealthier Sandins is, however, something of an anomaly in *The Purge* franchise. Even the well-spoken ringleader of the home invaders, who first prey on the Sandin family, admits that the Sandins' obvious wealth ought to insulate them against violence from people like him—that is, from their socioeconomic peers. Purging is a right owed to the wealthiest, most privileged Americans, a right they exact, by and large, upon the bodies of those they judge their socioeconomic inferiors.

Indeed, on the Purge night, class takes on the misty aura of the numinous. Those with the means are obliged to participate in Purge night crime; the continuing existence of the prosperous, crime-free America that so enriches them depends on the wealthy and well-armed doing so. The mirror side of this obligation is that demanded of the poor and disadvantaged. They are expected to joyfully submit to the violence of their betters, to gladly sacrifice their lives for the good of their country. But these obligations are not merely patriotic. When the Sandins' neighbors join hands and pray over the surviving Sandin family members like they would over a Thanksgiving turkey, it is because they believe their right to the Sandins' lives is a God-given one. Similarly, the first season of the *The Purge* television series introduces the existence of a Purge death cult, a small, insular religious group largely comprised of vulnerable young people, who willingly offer their lives up in a blaze of glorious Purge night martyrdom. What the government positions as a secular, utilitarian holiday, the cultists see as a sacred time of purification and spiritual cleansing by fire, although not for the cult's devotees. By willingly offering themselves to be killed on Purge night, the cult's members believe their souls are already guaranteed paradise. The true beneficiary of each individual's sacrifice is not them, but their killer(s). Those out roaming, seeking to do violence on Purge night, are those most in need of purging their hostility, so the cultists think. It is to them that the cult's members render the greatest service, for it is they who are truly transformed by the devotees' sacrifice.

The explosive release of violence in the Purge, figured in the highly sacral language of "sacrifice," serves as an empowering fiction for the NFFA. Citizens are obliged to participate in violent crime on the night of the Purge, and yet the hideous sights and sounds of their dutiful participation will appear on cable news as a tacit affirmation that American civil society is full to bursting with violence and that nothing short of the strict authoritarian control of the NFFA can restrain it. By tying the hands of criminal law for a night, the NFFA not only demonstrates its power over the law, but legitimizes its own invasive and brutal use of sovereign power, ensuring that like the return of the sun, the restoration of their total authority will be welcomed with the dawn. But this elaborate dystopian theater is only half of the equation. Festivals similar to the Purge such as the biblical Jubilee and the Sabbatical year crack open society in the same way, theatricalizing the same "what if" of sovereign absence, but not in quite such dystopic terms. In fact, Jubilee and the Sabbatical imagine not lawless chaos, but a utopic state of nature in the absence of sovereign power. By understanding some of the similarities between the sacrificial rituals common to both the dystopian Purge and the utopian Sabbatical/Jubilee, we can get a fuller picture of the sovereign power that each sustains, sanctifies, and unveils.

JUBILEE AND THE SABBATICAL YEAR

Debate still swirls today around accounts of the biblical Jubilee and the related Sabbatical year found in the Hebrew Bible. So startling are they in their communitarian aspirations that one may very well doubt that they actually occurred at all. Both the Sabbatical and Jubilee proscribed "organized tilling, planting and harvesting every seventh year in the case of the Sabbatical and every forty-ninth or fiftieth year in the case of the Jubilee"; but despite the relative infrequency of the events, particularly in the case of the Jubilee, these "commanded abstentions constituted a very severe burden on an agricultural economy in which many individuals were involved in subsistence farming."[10] The rules of these agricultural sabbaths are comprehensive and had far reaching consequences for ancient Israelite society even beyond agriculture. The most detailed descriptions of the rules of the Jubilee and the Sabbatical year can be found in two places in the Hebrew Bible. The lengthier of the two passages, found in the book of Leviticus, is the most descriptive:

> Six years you shall sow your field, and six years you shall prune your vineyard, and gather in their yield; but in the seventh year there shall be a sabbath for the Lord: you shall not sow your field or prune your vineyard. You shall not reap the aftergrowth of your harvest or gather the grapes of your unpruned vine: it shall be a year of complete rest for the land. You may eat what the land yields during its sabbath—you, your male and female slaves, your hired and your bound laborers who live with you; for your livestock also, and for the wild animals in your land all its yield shall be for food . . . That fiftieth year shall be a jubilee for you: you shall not sow or reap the aftergrowth or harvest the unpruned vines. For it is a jubilee; it shall be holy to you: you shall eat only what the field itself produces. (Lev. 25:3–7, 11–12, NRSV)

The threat such abstentions posed to Israel's subsistence farmers was only mitigated by one key, divine intervention: a miraculously large harvest in the year prior to the appointed fallow period.[11]

Not unlike the Purge, the Sabbatical and Jubilee both represent major disruptions to the social order, if not an outright threat to its survival. All three festivals expose the nakedly "un- or even antieconomical dimensions of religion," but that does not mean they do not serve a purpose.[12] Indeed, many scholars have speculated about what purpose the Sabbatical year and the Jubilee may have served in ancient Israel. What social good, economic advantage, or agricultural benefit could have been so attractive, so valuable, that it was worth such dramatic disruptions to an already pressed agrarian economy? One explanation emphasizes the sacredness of the land during Jubilee and the Sabbatical year: the Jewish philosopher Hava Tirosh-Samuelson has used the mandatory resting of farmland enshrined within the Sabbatical/Jubilee to argue for the existence of a uniquely Jewish environmental ethic. She draws on the language of property and private ownership to talk about the theological and social import of the Sabbatical year rest: "By *returning* the earth to God, nature's vitality is restored and protected from human use and abuse."[13]

Although Robert Yelle dismisses Tirosh-Samuelson's argument for a Jewish environmental ethic as an anachronism, her understanding of the rest as a "return" of land to its rightful owner, God, is tremendously useful and hardly unique to her argument.[14]

PROPERTY, SACRIFICE, AND THE ECONOMY

Key to understanding the Sabbatical/Jubilee and the Purge is understanding the connection between the sacred, private property and the religious economy, and it is precisely to this connection that Tirosh-Samuelson's argument gestures when she speaks of "returning" land. While several eminent thinkers like Sigmund Freud and W. Robertson Smith have associated the holy with blessedness, virtue, or some other intrinsic good quality, holiness or sacredness has far more to do with ownership and property than with goodness or value. Even the language(s) we use to describe holiness betrays this meaning. As Yelle observed, "the Latin *sacer* and Hebrew *qadosh* (n. *qodesh*), both of which may be translated as 'sacred,' refer to things that are set apart or restricted, not to things that possess some inherent degree of goodness ... The opposite of holy is not impure, but rather profane or common (Hebrew *hol*)."[15]

The restriction from public use tacit in the concept of holiness is essentially ambiguous; sacred things are often set apart not for being uniquely good, but for being unclean or even dangerous. Cathedrals and corpses alike are sacred things, not because they share some mysterious "holy" quality but because neither belong to the world of human use. Rather, sacred things belong to the deity either by virtue of natural right or by sacrifice. Thomas Hobbes famously described this proprietary relationship between God and the holy in *Leviathan*:

> Out of this literal interpretation of the Kingdom of God ariseth also the true interpretation of the word HOLY. For it is a word which in God's kingdom answereth to that which men in their kingdoms use to call *public*, or the *king*'s ... For by holy is always understood, either by God himself or that which is God's in propriety ... And wheresoever the word Holy is taken properly, there is still something signified of property gotten by consent.[16]

Hobbes' provocative, if incomplete, definition of the holy as "property gotten by consent" ushers us right to the threshold of the sacrifice issue. All holy things, apart from the deity themself, are *made* holy by the act of surrendering or sacrificing them. To sacrifice is literally "to make [something] sacred," to remove it from common, profane use and give it over to the gods' use. In practice this often means removing the sacrifice from the human economy by destroying its use value: killing and immolating people, livestock, or crops; spilling oil or wine. However, all sacrifices do not necessarily result in the destruction of the offering itself. Bataille emphasized this economic aspect of destruction via ritual sacrifice:

> Sacrifice destroys that which it consecrates. It does not have to destroy as fire does; only the tie that connected the offering to the world of profitable activity is severed, but this separation has the sense of a definitive consumption; the consecrated offering cannot be restored to the real order. This principle opens the way to passionate release; it liberates violence while marking off the domain in which violence reigns absolutely.[17]

From Bataille's perspective, the Purge and the Jubilee/Sabbatical are festivals of extravagant sacrifice, ones whose dimensions are as economic as they are religious. Indeed, the material, economic expenses of the Purge and its religious importance are more connected than they may at first appear. From the flowers that are customarily displayed outside the home on Purge night as a sign of support for the holiday to the elaborate and often garish costumes that Purge night hopefuls wear out on their hunting expeditions, the Purge is rife with the kind of consumable "ceremonial paraphernalia . . . items of conspicuous waste," that Thorstein Veblen considers an essential feature of religious observances.[18] Human and physical capital alike are sacrificed (broken, stolen, killed, etc.), ostensibly for the sake of achieving some nationwide, cathartic emotional release. However, the true beneficiaries of the wanton Purge night destruction are not those who participate in the supposedly purifying violence, but rather the NFFA whose sovereignty is shored up by the Purge's extravagant display of waste.

Much of what has been said about the economic dimensions of sacrifice in the Purge also apply to the Jubilee and the Sabbatical year. While the Sabbatical sacrifice may not "destroy as fire does," it still sacrifices, or makes sacred, all cultivated lands by setting it apart from the human agrarian economy for a season, thereby destroying its potential yield for the year. In this way the Sabbatical/Jubilee too indulges in conspicuous waste and thereby reflects a vision of Bataille's "sovereign life, beyond the necessary." However, the vision of sovereign life that is staged and performed within the Sabbatical sacrifice is quite unlike the dystopian, fascist sovereignty, which the Purge sacrifice sustains. The state of nature dreamed to life in the Jubilee and Sabbatical year legislation is a vision of communitarianism in which cultivated lands are reclaimed by wild overgrowth. From the wealthiest and most privileged in Jewish society to "the poor of your people,"[19] "your male and female slaves, your hired and your bound laborers who live with you," and even livestock and wild animals, all living things subsist on what each can individually glean from the land's natural yield.[20] Gustavo Benavides saw quite lucidly the utopian nature of the Jubilee and Sabbatical's labor laws: "In the Babylonian, the Israelite and countless other cases, divinely instituted reversals remind us of an aspect of religion . . . that which involves dismantling hierarchies, erasing distinctions, leaving behind all forms. Should one be surprised to find that most of these utopian dreams have to do with leaving work behind?"[21] But unlike the communitarian state of nature to which the Sabbatical sacrifice seeks to return Jewish society, the Purge seeks to return to a state of total anomie in which only the fittest survive and primal violence spreads unchecked like wildfire. This return to primordial chaos delivers the greatest benefit, not to the poor or even to wealthy Americans like the Sandin family, but to the most politically influential in the NFFA. The NFFA writes the Purge into an amendment of the U.S. Constitution as a demonstration of its own sovereignty, tacitly echoing Schmitt's words: "Sovereign is he who decides on the exception."

The Purge and the Jubilee reveal competing ideas about the state of nature, the one violent and lawless, the other communitarian and utopic. However, both of these festivals and the fantasies of lawlessness or communitarianism that they respectively perform ultimately serve the same purpose. Both produce fictions that come to comprise the very fabric of sovereign power; both represent a naked display of the sovereign's power over the law; and both finally sanctify, or rather *reveal* the sacredness of the sovereignty, which they perform and reinforce via their performance. Through sacrificial rituals of conspicuous waste, each becomes a tableau of "sovereign life, beyond the necessary." But where Jubilee and the Sabbatical are utopic and aspirational, the Purge is cautionary. *The Purge* franchise remains fundamentally skeptical about the sacredness of sovereign power. Within the films, nationalism and American exceptionalism are destructive symptoms of a devout reverence for sovereign power, but these are not threats that lie in a far-off future. In *The Purge*, as in reality, it is the present that is at greatest risk. While the Purge's revelation of sovereign power serves to uphold the authority of the NFFA in the context of the narrative, for the audience it is an exposure. The Purge pulls back the curtain on how sovereign power, especially in an American context, is masked in ideology, reinforced through ritual, and ultimately how it might be resisted. Whether we, its audience, receive its warning in time remains to be seen.

NOTES

1. *Homo ludens*, literally "man, the player" was the allegorical name for human beings coined by Johan Huizinga in his 1949 book by the same name. Like other allegorical names for humans, such as *Homo sapiens* "wise man" or *Homo faber* "man, the maker," *Homo ludens* purports to describe an essential function of being human. Huizinga argues that like thinking or making, recreational play is behavior all humans exhibit from a young age, and which stems from human beings' efforts to transform and adapt the world around them (transforming it through the fabrication of tools to alter its topography, or transforming it as a child does through games of make-believe, for example).
2. Carl Schmitt, *Political Theology: Four Chapters on the Concept of Sovereignty*, trans. George Schwab (Chicago: University of Chicago Press, 2005), 5.
3. Giorgio Agamben, *State of Exception*, trans. Kevin Attell (Chicago: University of Chicago Press, 2005), 72.
4. Agamben, *State of Exception*, 71.
5. Agamben, *State of Exception*, 73.
6. Agamben, *State of Exception*, 66.
7. Robert Yelle, *Sovereignty and the Sacred: Secularism and the Political Economy of Religion* (Chicago: University of Chicago Press, 2019), 11.
8. Georges Bataille, *Accursed Share*, trans. Robert Hurley (New York: Zone Books, 1991), 3:198–99.
9. Agamben, *State of Exception*, 72.
10. Yelle, *Sovereignty and the Sacred*, 130.
11. Lev. 25:20–22.
12. Yelle, *Sovereignty and the Sacred*, 132.
13. Hava Tirosh-Samuelson, "Nature in the Sources of Judaism," *Daedalus* 130 (2001): 110. Emphasis mine.
14. Yelle, *Sovereignty and the Sacred*, 133.
15. Yelle, *Sovereignty and the Sacred*, 81.
16. Thomas Hobbes, *Leviathan*, ed. Edwin Curley (Indianapolis, IN: Hackett, 1994), chap. 35, §§14–16.
17. Bataille, *Accursed Share*, 1:57–58.
18. Thorstein Veblen, *The Theory of the Leisure Class: An Economic Study of Institutions* (New York: Macmillan, 1912), 307.
19. Ex. 23:11, NRSV.
20. Lev. 25:6–7, NRSV.
21. Gustavo Benavides, "Towards a Natural History of Religion," *Religion* 30 (2000): 237.

BIBLIOGRAPHY

Agamben, Giorgio. *State of Exception*. Translated by Kevin Attell. Chicago: University of Chicago Press, 2005.

Bataille, Georges. *The Accursed Share*. Translated by Robert Hurley. 3 vols. New York: Zone Books, 1991–1993.
Benavides, Gustavo. "Towards a Natural History of Religion." *Religion* 30 (2000): 229–44.
Gernet, Jacques. *Buddhism in Chinese Society*. Translated by Franciscus Verellen. New York: Columbia University Press, 1995.
Hobbes, Thomas. *Leviathan*. Edited by Edwin Curley. Indianapolis, IN: Hackett, 1994.
Schmitt, Carl. *Political Theology: Four Chapters on the Concept of Sovereignty*. Translated by George Schwab. Chicago: University of Chicago Press, 2005.
Tirosh-Samuelson, Hava. "Nature in the Sources of Judaism." *Daedalus* 130 (2001): 99–124.
Veblen, Thorstein. *The Theory of the Leisure Class: An Economic Study of Institutions*. New York: Macmillan, 1912.
Yelle, Robert. *Sovereignty and the Sacred: Secularism and the Political Economy of Religion*. Chicago: University of Chicago Press, 2019.

Chapter 10

The Ability or Inability to Change by the Presence or Absence of *Deus ex Machina*

Beáta Gombkötő

Dystopian tragedies encompass a surprisingly wide range of literary works, centering around the suffering of an imagined society.[1] Like classical tragedies, where the purpose is to aid the spectator to confront and process difficult emotions, and to bring forth emotional catharsis, a sort of mental purification, dystopias also generate sympathy for the suffering dystopian protagonists. However, some dystopias appear to lack the purpose of a cathartic experience. A dystopian storyline usually does not offer any alternative or a way out of the conditions that cause the suffering. For large portions of the works, dystopia portrays its protagonists as emotionally paralyzed without any hope of ever overcoming their difficulties. This observation concerning emotional paralysis and a general sense of hopelessness, not the pain itself, is what elicits sympathy in the spectator, while the lack of emotional resolve leaves behind feelings of great concern and emotional agitation. In many dystopian works, readers experience unresolved emotional frustration rather than catharsis at the end of the novel. In the following paragraphs, I will examine how *Deus ex Machina*, a key element in classical tragedies that functions to aid towards catharsis, operates in dystopias, and what purpose it may serve for the reader in its apparent failure to deliver catharsis to the protagonists.

The word catharsis, originally a medical term, took on the meaning of spiritual purification and elevation through the experience of tragic events.[2] According to Aristotle, catharsis is the central element of a tragedy, which is most easily reached by arousing "fear and pity" in the spectators. Experiencing continual distress could eventually culminate in a crisis point, where no solution seems available, leaving the sufferer feeling helpless. At such point, *Deus ex Machina* can appear. The *Deus ex Machina* provides a turning point in the form of divine intervention, followed by the diffusion of the crisis and the characters, and possibly the spectators as well, reaching catharsis. Thus, *Deus ex Machina* serves the purpose of dissolving an impossible crisis, where the protagonist is either emotionally or even physically lifted away, which ends their suffering and aids the sufferer in catharsis. *Deus ex Machina* can be anything or anyone who changes the situation: a royal messenger who saves everyone from destruction with a letter, a magical device that comes up from below a physical stage, or the sudden appearance of an extraterrestrial being. In fact, anything or anyone can play the role of *Deus ex Machina*, especially when the tableau seems insoluble. In the conventional sense, divine intervention is inserted to liberate from a crisis; however, in this chapter, I will explore how a crisis itself could take the role of *Deus ex Machina*, specifically in dystopian writings.

Crisis itself can become *Deus ex Machina* and lead to catharsis. Crisis infuses the entire world of the sufferer, both external and internal, to the core with no escape until a breaking point is reached, which either permanently destroys or liberates the sufferer. Crisis as *Deus ex Machina* in form of human sacrifice is a frequenty used method to reach catharsis in mythologies. This form of cathartic experience through human sacrifice forms the basis of Christian ideology, where Jesus, the ultimate *Deus ex Machina*, is sacrificed for the transformation of the whole of Creation to the core. Thus, it is possible to see how crisis as divine intervention can lead to a kind of rebirth, lifting one from an unjust or hopeless situation that was otherwise impossible to overcome. However, divine intervention in dystopias, especially in a totalitarian environment, has different dynamics. It is the oppressor who often takes on a divine character. The oppressor appears out of reach, indestructible, and all-powerful. This character frequently demands its subjects fully surrender body and soul. Meanwhile, the oppressed experiences a consistent and unescapable existential crisis. Within a dystopian milieu, the protagonists become human sacrifices through their continual agony or death, providing the opportunity for the desired emotional transformation: catharsis. Yet, catharsis frequently remains unachieved. Instead of leading to catharsis, the continual torture and human sacrifice has the opposite effect, further sinking individuals into desolation. Why does this happen? Why is catharsis not reached by the dystopian protagonists?

In this chapter I search for answers to such questions in two Hungarian dystopian novels: *The White King (A Fehér Király)* by György Dragomán and *The Shortest Ice Age (A Legkisebb Jégkorszak)* by János Térey. These authors grew up at the tail end of a totalitarian regime in Central and Eastern Europe, experiencing both an oppressive political environment and the subsequent liberation. The experience of political oppression and liberation are focal points for both writers, often mixing reality with dystopia. This study focuses on the dystopian characters, specifically on their (in)ability to experience emotional transformation, and takes a close look at how *Deus ex Machina* operate in these dystopias.

CRISIS AS THE *DEUS EX MACHINA*

We already examined the conventional meaning of *Deus ex Machina* in the introduction, where it is described as an external factor, a constructive intervention to liberate the protagonist(s) from a crisis. The word crisis literally means "turning point."[3] It is the crisis preceding catharsis, more specifically how the characters respond to a crisis, that marks the real turning point in a drama. A classic example is Euripides' *Medea*, where it is not the divine intervention but the characters' reaction to the crisis that marks the turning point in the story. In this interpretation, the crisis itself can play the role of *Deus ex Machina*, which only provides the opportunity for change, and it is the sufferers' response that brings about the real turning point. Mihály Kornis writes that these crisis events are ways of communication from *life*: "The turn of fate—love letters from *life*—speak to me. . . . Everything in the world speaks to you, really speaks. It wants you to understand. It believes that you will understand. . . . Sighing for an answer."[4] Kornis points out that turning points are *life*'s messages that people should listen to, understand, and answer. Is it possible to perceive crisis as *life*'s message? In dystopias, at least in the ones examined in this study, crisis does not necessarily lead the dystopian characters to a positive change, thus reaching catharsis is never certain. Can crisis as *Deus ex Machina* be effective in dystopias?

THIS WAS THE WORLD I KNEW

Crisis does not necessarily work as a functional *Deus ex Machina* in dystopias. The characters' attitudes fall into apathy and their responses often do not go beyond survival. What happens when fear becomes unbearable? Hungarian writer György Dragomán was born in 1973 in Romania, which was governed by a totalitarian regime at the time. He illustrates this unbearable pain in his dystopian novel, *The White King*, projecting his own experiences:

> He slapped Janika across the face with the gloves, then he stepped back and kneed the ball right into Janika's stomach who doubled over. As the ball snapped back, I saw that Coach Gica was about to kick it again, but this time he kneed

Janika's face. I heard something crack, and Janika fell onto the coat rack and skid across the floor.[5]

The film adaption of György Dragomán's book, *The White King*, depicts a grim fascist dystopian future. It can be considered as such because it feels so Orwellian and universal. But for a reader who lived behind the Iron Curtain, this is a not-so-distant past and feels like a realistic experience in a socialist-communist dictatorship. Anna T. Szabó considers Orwell's book, *1984*, life-changing after escaping the Romanian communist dictatorship.[6] Orwell explicitly described the horrors of totalitarianism, what it felt like to be a prisoner and to be afraid. This was the world she knew, the demand for uniformity, censorship, bans, imprisonment, and samizdat. For her, *1984* was accurate and realistic.

In Dragomán's *White King*, the torture of people, including children, is beyond description. The protagonist is Djata, a twelve-year-old boy whose father is taken away in front of him by the secret police. There are various kinds of miseries. This type of crisis and suffering decreases one to a mum-chance. Soelle says that "Extreme suffering turns a person in on himself completely, it destroys his ability to communicate."[7]

> The guard holding the chain yanked at it and then Father gradually looked up, and that is when I saw his face and felt my belly bunch up. His face was gray with stubble and he'd lost so much weight, but that's not what scared me, no. It was his eyes, his completely blank stare.... It wasn't Father I was seeing, no, it was no longer him. He didn't remember me or Mother anymore. He didn't remember a thing, and he didn't even know himself anymore.[8]

People who experienced such a deep fear by a totalitarian system were surviving rather than living. It is not easy for others to reach such a person. According to Soelle, it is cynicism to create a theology around such misery.[9] Does such a pain entirely exclude the chance for change, learning, and development? How deep should the trauma be to make a person numb? In *The White King*, Djata's father, mother, and Djata himself are unable to speak when they finally meet. They only wince like animals. Soelle also says that when a situation completely controls us, our lament sounds more like a cry of an animal.[10] However, at the highest point of the crisis, when Djata's father suddenly appears at a funeral, they begin to run towards each other despite a large group of people trying to stop them. This running bares the vision of power. Physical running may not make any difference in the political system, but this act symbolizes much on a personal level. It is a first step away from mute helplessness. In this very moment, regardless of their wretchedness, Djata and his parents feel there is hope for change. And hope is fundamental for catharsis. Djata did "what Christ did, that plays the role of God in conditions of helplessness."[11] Imagine a society where at one point people wake up to the realization that they possess the power to change the world around them, they find a way to stand in defiance against evil even at the cost of personal risks, similar to actions of Christ. For freedom, resurrection, and new life, people must risk their lives. Is it really a must? What comes afterward? What does freedom look like?

"THE GODS ARE ANGRY WITH US FOR THE LAST HUNDRED YEARS"

János Térey's novel, *The Shortest Ice Age*, is both a climate fiction and a dystopia, first published in 2015.[12] It is a Hungarian social satire built around a plausible yet shocking natural disaster: a drastic cooling during the winter of 2019/20 that throws the entire European continent, including Hungary, into an ice age. The center of the novel is the response of the Hungarian society. Preceding the ice age is one hundred years of continual global warming, which is not directly discussed in the novel. Responses are superfluous and ineffectual as they lack true motivation or effort to make real changes. Instead, people seem to accept and adjust to the climate change and allow it to progress into a real crisis. The human-caused global warming threatens survival, yet it is met with societal apathy. The most depressing feature in dystopias is when the characters remain unaware of their catastrophic conditions. Even if they do assess their own dire condition with clarity, their opinions do not go beyond empty platitudes and their actions remain inconsequential. Térey describes Europe as culturally and spiritually dead. That is the primary crisis.

> Europe is dead, Europe is sick.
> Since for a hundred years now.
> Its Youngs lack culture, lasting poetry is absent.
> There is no recovery from this.
> Everyone is tragically and irreversibly left to fend for themselves.
> Every goal is too far and unreachable.[13]

And Hungary is no exception to this, where Hungarian society is doomed by its politics, getting lost in bipartisan fighting and forgetting to stay relevant in the international context. In Térey's opinion, it is now pointless for Hungary to catch up internationally, since "our ally, the Western democracy is dying; on the other hand, the Eastern autocracies remain suspicious."[14] It rather seems that humanity needs to be rescued not from the global warming, but rather from its own apathy.

To this social climate arrives a new and even more devastating natural disaster, the ice age, as a result of serial volcanic eruptions from many European volcanoes. Atmospheric accumulation of volcanic fumes and ash blocks much of the sunlight for months, plunging the region into an ice age. The arrival of an ice age amid global warming is a crisis within a crisis. This crisis within a crisis can be a *Deus ex Machina* because it presents an opportunity for people to wake up from the last hundred years of societal apathy. The disastrous events do not escape attention, yet once again people do not, or chose not to, understand the weight of the situation and fail to react appropriately. The novel's characters become normalized to the new standards of life posed by the ice age, quickly returning to the concerns of everyday life while the disaster looms in the background. Térey laments about the crisis of societal apathy in a form of a funeral dirge, ending the complaint with lines resembling Psalm 137: "The violins are set aside, hanging on willow trees, as if they were already in exile, sitting by the waters of Babylon, banned from Sion. The cries of their psalms remain without voice."[15] Térey draws parallel between the dire political climate of Hungary and the exile of the Jews in Babylon. He emphasizes how in both cases the outcries of the sufferers remain unheard, as if the cries were mute. The story ends how it began, with societal apathy. No resolution is reached despite a multitude of threats to survival. What leads to such impenetrable apathy, where humans resign to their fate without a real fight?

I hypothesize that this apathy in face of danger is the consequence of the past political oppression that many of these people have endured, illustrated in Dragoman's *The White King*. People who have experienced the oppressive communist dictatorship are likely conditioned to feel powerless in face of societal danger and will default to the learned survival mechanism of quiet retreat.

> The dividing line between the generations after the change of regime was mainly defined by the relationship with the past. Continuity can be seen in the passive, distanced relationship with the high levels of the political system. Despite the fact that today politics has become part of our everyday life, this kind of dichotomy persists (even if less sharply). The individual subjectively experiences politics as something outside him or her, distant and in which he or she has little to say. But the weight of the legacy of the past weighs least on young people.[16]

Even if they chose to act, they try to do so without ruffling feathers. The younger generation born after the regime-change are portrayed in Térey's dystopia as inconsequential trouble makers, whose only purpose is to blow off steam in the name of upholding the legacy of Hungary's past. The rebellion of this young extremist group against apathy by carrying out outrageous acts is in appearance only. Their motivation is not to inspire real change, but rather to cause outrage for the sake of attention. Nobody takes them seriously, not even the extremists themselves. "The only opposition is the fundamentalists—but this group is not a political force, it is just a few obsessed idiots, and they quickly roll-up."[17] The superfluous behavior defines all layers of society, including the very top. The prime minister seems unmoved and his attitude is cynical, manifested by his indifferent manner of discussing such horrific events while showing off his brand-new veranda to his lover. The finale of the novel is neither a tragedy nor a cathartic turn. Snow covers everything, and everybody is frozen, numb, and apathetic.

Dante describes the lowest circles of hell, the place for traitors whose punishment is freezing, a figurative ice age of souls. Thus, according to Dante, there is no deeper hell than a frozen soul, when one falls into apathy and resigns to the status quo. László F. Földényi describes the souls in Dante's hell as being hazy and transparent like frozen glass fragments trapped under ice. He draws a clear parallel between Dante's *Inferno* and Térey's *The Shortest Ice Age*:

> Térey's novel is also about frozen souls. However, the people are not in the depths of the Earth, but on the surface, residing on the icy crust. Hell has moved to the surface, to the land of the living and seems as eternal as Dante's hell. . . . Everyone is busy maintaining a frozen state to survive, creating their own hell while still alive, which is all the more hellish. . . . He [Térey] gives an enlightening portrayal of a world that has reached a dead end.[18]

According to Soelle, a frozen soul is numb and cannot feel pain, and has only apathy towards suffering. She connects this apathy with the middle-class notion of avoiding suffering. Térey's upper-middle-class characters illustrate that a suffering-free state that is not capable of suffering is also incapable of change or experience real happiness. Does anything have the power to shake up an apathetic soul frozen into complacency? Rabbi Hanokh writes that "The real exile of Israel in Egypt was that they had learned to endure it."[19] When God inspired Moses to have the strength and charisma to lead the Jewish people out of Egypt, it acted as a *Deus ex Machina* that managed to wake them from generations of complacency and motivate them to face the grueling challenges it took to break from enslavement. Thus, religious faith, inspiration from God, or spiritual awakening could provide the needed motivation for liberation. However, it is so often not the case. Roger Philip Abbott conducted research among the Haitian earthquake survivors. He found only a few among the survivors "for whom their theology provided, beyond lament, any motivation or direction when it came to addressing these deeply embedded structural evils."[20] The survivors, many of whom confessed to be religious, did not blame God. They were able to identify the real factors responsible for high death tolls in the earthquakes, poverty, corruption, and absence of earthquake preparedness. Yet their religious sentiment did not seem to inspire them to take steps against the flaws of the system. His research participants often lacked any theology that motivated a protest for social justice.

Térey's dystopia is disturbing because the catharsis after the crisis and the resolution is absent. The Hungarians in Térey's novel are unhappy and paralyzed and the *Deus ex Machina* is unable to wake them from their emotional slumber. The upper-middle-class protagonists, while educated and self-aware, consider their knowledge as cliché and remain unmotivated. Education, money, power, or social status seem inadequate to empower for action. Is anyone responsible for this? What causes such apathy? Disasters are often interpreted as deserved divine punishment that needs to be endured and not corrected. Dorothee Soelle illustrates this in her book, *Suffering*, with a citation from Calvin's theology: "the scriptures teach us that Pestilence, War, and other calamities of this kind are chastisements of God, which he inflicts on our sins."[21] Soelle calls such a theology sadistic, which can develop into Christian masochism. A masochistic Christian resigns him/herself to the whims of a sadistic God, but what makes it truly masochistic is the growing belief that this punishment is good, serves an important purpose, and brings one closer to God. Thus, the sufferer not only resigns to their fate, but welcomes it as an opportunity to please God. "The gods have been angry with us for the last hundred years."[22] This statement sounds like the gods are sadistic torturers and the disasters are their punishments humans must endure.

Térey often brings a crisis into association with God or gods in his novel. This is well illustrated in a highly symbolic scene in the novel, when experts from different disciplines—a chief meteorologist, a climate historian, and an astrologist—are brought together in a TV interview to discuss the climate crisis. The perception that the climate crisis is a punishment from the gods is voiced by the astrologist, whom Térey caustically portrays as a charlatan and a con artist. Thus, Térey removes the idea of "crisis is a divine punishment" from Christian ideology and portrays it as nothing more than a fraudulent opinion. This is a bold and provocative move by Térey. He wants to distance Christian ideology from such masochism and offers a different direction instead:

> God does not seem to propose that we should run away from our problems:

> He rather wants us to learn from them, to discover what we can do.
> If we call God in our difficult moments, He has the power to take us
> to the scene of our failures, and hand us our success there.[23]

This is very similar to the interpretation of Mihály Kornis, who states that "everything in the world speaks to you, really speaks. It wants you to understand. It believes that you will understand."[24] In other words, crisis can be seen as an opportunity, from which one should not run away before examining it and understand if anything can be learnt from it. Such examination and delving into a crisis can be followed by a breakthrough success, similar to the experience of catharsis and spiritual enlightenment.

It might appear perverted to consider suffering as anything divine, yet this perspective, that suffering provides an opportunity towards something better, has deep ancient roots. This ideology is older than Christianity itself. In Greek mythology, Oedipus has to penetrate into the heart of his greatest pains and fears, into the home of Erinyes, before finding eternal peace. There are scientific research efforts studying how crisis effects the human body, and whether it can elicit any positive personality changes. Tedeschi and Calhoun claim that positive effect of stress exists and gave it the term Post-Traumatic Growth (PTG). According to them, beyond the obvious negative consequences of suffering on the human psyche, it can also trigger personal growth. However, they do not suggest that trauma is good.

> Posttraumatic growth is neither universal nor inevitable. Although a majority of individuals experiencing a wide array of highly challenging life circumstances experience posttraumatic growth, there are also a significant number of people who experience little or no growth in their struggle with trauma.[25]

Thus, despite how masochistic it seems to consider suffering as a potential source of catharsis, it does provide such an opportunity, and for this alone it should be examined more closely.

Dorothee Soelle's effort to distance Christian theology from what she considers as masochistic appears futile exactly for the reason of her efforts to find meaning in human suffering. This is most apparent in her chapter, "The Pain of Birth," in which she gives suffering a feminist undertone.[26] Soelle describes labor pains as the combination of two separate processes, both sources of physical pain: the contractions and the need to push. She only considers the latter as a constructive and meaningful form of pain, one that results in the birth of something new. The woman is an active participant in the labor of pushing; thus, the painful process appears to be under the control of the woman with a foreseeable and fruitful end. It is not only physically productive, but also provides a meaningful personal experience. It teaches the woman that some pain can be constructive and fruitful as it brings about something new and better, for which it is worth submitting to the pain. In *The Shortest Ice Age*, Térey describes childbirth in very similar terms:

> "Childbirth without a doubt is a source of horrific pain,
> But it needs to be said that it is neither bestial nor inhumane.
> Rather, I say, it is the most attractive out of all the suffering that exists."
> "It is gratifyingly cataclysmic, isn't it!?" said Pispek.
> "And unimaginably painful." "Great fear, great pain, even greater catharsis."[27]

In the beginning of his novel, Térey used the word cataclysm to describe the volcanic eruptions. This association is interesting in light of our central question, which asks whether any new and good can be born from the pain and devastation of a disaster. We can perhaps find some answers by examining the manner of Christ's death. The circumstances of his death could be considered partially dystopian, since he had the power to escape his fate, yet he chose not to. Should we conclude that his death is the constructive kind of disaster, from which something positive sprouts? The next question that follows is whether we also live like that? Can we recognize if our choices bring about destructive or constructive pain? Do we choose to leave our pain behind or do we choose to embrace it in hopes of gaining salvation? Which direction do we take when the choice is presented to us?

"Get your feet, faithful servants of God, to avoid Satan's venomous spittle!,"[28] implying that humans have little free will reduces human existence to nothing more than survival and obedience. On the other hand, this statement can also be interpreted as a call for "servants of God" to rise up against "Satan's venomous spittle." What does it mean to be "servants of God"? It implies that as servants on Earth we have a close link to God, whose duty is to act and protect against disasters and oppression, as Soelle imagines that "we too, play God for one another."[29]

According to Dianne Oliver, "disasters are not accidents or acts of God ... Disaster is made inevitable by the historically produced pattern of vulnerability, evidenced in the location, infrastructure, socio-political structure, production patterns, and ideology that characterizes a society."[30] Thus, as "servants of God," we must bear the responsibility to circumvent such disasters, which can also be achieved by a radical act of playing the role of God for one another.

CONCLUSION

Recognizing a *Deus ex Machina*, deciding to respond to it and bearing the consequences does not necessarily mean that peace will follow. If anything, such acts generate newer conflicts, which can only be endured if we believe that we have the power to change the world we live in. The instinctive and brave run of Djata in Dragoman's *The White King*, while an act without concrete outcome, is the first step towards overcoming oppression and, therefore, suffering. The battle against powerlessness may at first only consist of the recognition that oppression can be changed; taking on this battle has the potential to change even the embedded societal structures. Totalitarianism is one of the most problematic crises because people are forced to endure oppression long enough that eventually it becomes an accepted way of life. But there is no good reason to be in it. The force that holds their world together is fear. Djata's father is a person who is trying to change things, but he is taken away to a labor camp. His sacrifice seems to bring the worst of outcomes, appearing at the end of the novel not as a free man but as a mentally broken prisoner. The twelve-year-old Djata has an appropriate, instinctive, and childish reaction at the highest point of the crisis, namely his running, which does not liberate him immediately. However, as Jesus said about children: "the kingdom of God belongs to such as these" (Mark 10:14, NIV). In this interpretation, Djata plays the role of God, the liberator in the face of helplessness. While oppression often appears unbreakable, people are not powerless. This is what Djata proves.

Amongst the many types of human suffering, there are ones that are clearly destructive, ones that humans cannot overcome. Such overwhelming pain produces nothing but emotional paralysis and apathy as it is illustrated in Dragoman's novel. The source of suffering can stem from systematic oppression, which people relate to as something beyond their reach to solve and thus unchangeable, becoming destructive suffering. To overcome such destructiveness requires the sufferer to make a conscious decision to risk one's life and livelihood, which comes with its own set of horrors. Yet this self-sacrificial risk is worth taking if it provides a way out of destructive apathy. The question the sufferer needs to answer is which direction to choose if all possible options lead to pain. Which option is constructive? Which one is comparable to Christ-like sacrifice or to the pains of childbirth labor, at the end of which there is a promise of a new life? The tension that stems from the task of a dystopian hero to choose between impossible options is ever present in dystopias.

According to Soelle "the first step towards overcoming suffering is to find a language that at least says what the situation is."[31] In Térey's novel,

The Shortest Ice Age, this language is not missing; however, people come to different conclusions about what they must do. It is apparent that language, freedom, education or power cannot by themselves ensure that the disaster and its message will be understood. Their apathy is possibly a result of their prior experience with political oppression, where they learnt that it was better to remain silent for the sake of survival; otherwise, they were punished. Their apathy is connected with the middle-class notion of avoiding suffering. It is the life that Soelle calls "death by bread alone":

> We can change the social conditions under which people experience suffering. We can change ourselves and learn in suffering instead of becoming worse. We can gradually beat back and abolish the suffering that still today is produced for the profit of a few. But on all these paths we come up against boundaries that cannot be crossed. Death is not the only such barrier.[32]

Térey recognizes the flaws of his society; however, it is not in his repertoire to provide a solution. His novel is an accurate societal mirror, however without the much-desired catharsis, leading the reader to feel the pressure and urgency of a solution more than ever. His dystopian protagonists possess such commonplace character flaws, which the readers can easily discover within themselves, thus unable to create a convenient emotional distance. The feeling of "this could be me" further intensifies the frustration, and exactly this frustration is what could inspire the reader to act decidedly and differently from their dystopian counterpart. Thus, this unresolved tension and frustration in dystopias harbors the possibility for change: not for its protagonists, but for its readers. For this, the dystopian tragedies themselves can be considered as *Deus ex Machinas*.

In conclusion, we should maintain not only hope in general, but also hope in the format of dystopia itself, which can be a powerful way of communication, a psalm, a cautionary tale holding up a true and accurate mirror to contemporary societies. The dystopia is a form of communication and help to analyze the status quo. Dystopia is a genre that gives voice to people in their fears and pain. Our process of recognition is frequently painful, but this pain is like the pain of a woman in labor, carrying the potential of new life. The factors that cause the suffering of a society and its individuals are clearly portrayed in dystopias. Thus, dystopia can be our source of a turning point, a *Deus ex Machina* itself, from where our liberation can be organized and catharsis reached.

NOTES

1. A sincere thank-you to Hajnalka Nyitrai for her diligent copyediting of this chapter.
2. κάθαρσις = (Greek), 1. purification, purgation of the body, 2. cleansing from guilt or defilement. Henry George Liddell and Robert Scott, *A Greek-English Lexicon* (Oxford: Clarendon Press, 1940).
3. κρίση = (Greek), 1. decision or opinion, 2. critical point in illness where the life of the patient is determined, 3. absence of established criteria for undertaking and signifying an action. ΚΡΙΣΗ: Biannual Scientific Review, accessed 9 May 2022, https://e-krisi.gr/en/krisi-judgement-and-crisis.
4. Mihály Kornis is a Hungarian writer, director, and teacher. He uses the word *life* for the divine in place of religious terms for nonreligious readers in his book, *Lehetőségek könyve* (*Book of Possibilities*) (Pozsony: Kalligram, 2007). Unless otherwise specified, all English translations are from the Hungarian original by the author of this paper. Kornis, *Lehetőségek könyve,* 224.
5. György Dragomán, *The White King,* trans. Paul Olchváry (Boston: Houghton Mifflin, 2019), 32. Kindle.
6. Anna T. Szabó is a Hungarian poet, born in Romania, wife of György Dragomán.
7. Dorothee Soelle, *Suffering* (London: Darton, Longman & Todd, 1975), 70.
8. Dragomán, *The White King,* 257.
9. Soelle, *Suffering,* 69.
10. Soelle, *Suffering,* 70.
11. Dianne L. Oliver, "The Christological Vision of Dorothee Soelle," in *The Theology of Dorothee Soelle,* ed. Sarah K. Pinnock (Harrisburg, PA: Trinity Press International, 2003), 115.
12. János Térey, *A Legkisebb Jégkorszak* (Budapest: Libri Kiadó 2015), 36.
13. Térey, *A Legkisebb Jégkorszak,* 86.
14. Térey, *A Legkisebb Jégkorszak,* 540.
15. Térey, *A Legkisebb Jégkorszak,* 88.
16. Rita Csőzik, "Átalakult lázadás," in *Racionálisan lázadó hallgatók 2012,* ed. Andrea Szabó (Szeged: Belvedere Meridionale, 2012), 48.
17. László F. Földényi, *Befagyott Lelkek,* Magyar Narancs, November 22, 2015.
18. Földényi, *Befagyott Lelkek.*
19. Soelle, *Suffering,* 33.
20. Roger Philip Abott, "I Will Show You My Faith by My Works: Addressing the Nexus between Philosophical Theodicy and Human Suffering and Loss in Contexts of 'Natural' Disaster," *Religions* 213, no. 10 (2019): 13.
21. Soelle, *Suffering,* 24.
22. Térey, *A Legkisebb Jégkorszak,* 36.
23. Térey, *A Legkisebb Jégkorszak,* 174.
24. Kornis, *Lehetőségek könyve,* 224.
25. Lawrence G. Calhoun and Richard G. Tedeschi, "The Foundations of Posttraumatic Growth: An Expanded Framework," in *The Handbook of Posttraumatic*

Growth, ed. Lawrence G. Calhoun and Richard G. Tedeschi (New York: Psychology Press, 2014), 3.
26. Dorothee Soelle, *Against the Wind: Memoir of a Radical Christian* (Minneapolis: Fortress Press, 1999), 73–79.
27. Térey, *A Legkisebb Jégkorszak,* 510.
28. Térey, *A Legkisebb Jégkorszak,* 37.
29. Oliver, "The Christological Vision of Dorothee Soelle," 100–115.
30. Abott, "I Will Show You," 13.
31. Soelle, *Suffering*, 70.
32. Soelle, *Suffering*, 178.

BIBLIOGRAPHY

Abott, Roger Philip. "I Will Show You My Faith by My Works: Addressing the Nexus between Philosophical Theodicy and Human Suffering and Loss in Contexts of 'Natural' Disaster," *Religions* 213, no. 10 (March 2019): 1–17.
Calhoun, Lawrence G., and Richard G. Tedeschi. "The foundations of Posttraumatic Growth: An expanded Framework." In *The Handbook of Posttraumatic Growth*, edited by Lawrence G. Calhoun and Richard G. Tedeschi, 3–21. New York: Psychology Press, 2014.
Dragomán, György. *The White King*. Translated by Paul Olchváry. Boston, New York: Houghton Mifflin Harcourt Publishing Company, 2019.
Földényi, László F. "Befagyott Lelkek." *Magyar Narancs,* November 22, 2015.
Kornis, Mihály. *Lehetőségek Könyve.* Pozsony: Kalligram, 2007.
Liddell, Henry George and Robert Scott. *A Greek-English Lexicon.* Oxford: Clarendon Press, 1940.
Oliver, Dianne L. "The Christological Vision of Dorothee Soelle." In *The Theology of Dorothee Soelle*, edited by Sarah K. Pinnock, 109–28. Harrisburg, PA: Trinity Press International, 2003.
Rita, Csőzik. "Átalakult lázadás." In *Racionálisan lázadó hallgatók 2012,* edited by Andrea Szabó, 45–64. Szeged: Belvedere Meridionale, 2012.
Soelle, Dorothee. *Against the Wind*. Minneapolis: Fortress Press, 1995.
———. *Suffering.* London: Darton, Longman and Todd, 1975.
Takács, Ferenc. "Télvég-Játék." *Mozgó Világ* 42, no. 5 (January-June 2016): 111–14.
Térey, János. *Legkisebb Jégkorszak*. Budapest: Libri Kiadó, 2015.

Chapter 11

The Spectacle of Hope beyond Capital's Dehumanizing Violence

Reading George Lucas's Dystopian THX 1138

John C. McDowell

In a year of three studio-made dystopian films, George Lucas's largely independent "message" movie *THX 1138* (1971) depicted a *dus topos*, a diseased or faulty place. Yet, while his low-budget arthouse framing of the dystopia may have been set in some unspecified future society, what it reflected on was not far from home.[1] Accordingly, he declared that it was "an abstraction of [America in] 1970."[2] "The places are real," Lucas proclaimed, "and the people are more or less like that."[3] The figures uncompromisingly generated for this austere dystopian environment were framed onscreen in quite distinctive fashion. The filmmaker's critical gaze focused on the way life is reduced, in the words of the influential critical theorist Herbert Marcuse, to the kind of "administered living" that is characteristic of the "one dimensional man" produced and conditioned by "advanced industrial society."[4] Lucas's biographer Dale Pollock contended that "*THX* is Lucas's most complex film . . . that he hoped would induce people to take some measure of their own lives."[5] However, this observation is insufficient. It would be better to say that Lucas's visual dramatization engaged its audience in reflection on the very motors that drive social life and provide the conditions for shaping consciousness, thought, and agency. In other words, it provided a critical perspective "on problematic social and political practices that might otherwise be taken for granted or considered natural and inevitable."[6] As Raffaella Baccolini and Tom Moylan maintain, the dystopian imagination has served as a prophetic vehicle, the canary in the cage, for writers with an ethical and political concern for warning us of terrible socio-political tendencies that could, if continued, turn our contemporary world into the iron cages portrayed in the realm of utopia's underside.[7]

This chapter asks how *THX 1138* imagines hope since, Marcuse claims, critique has a distinctive purpose in that it serves to analyze "society in the light of its used and unused or abused capabilities for improving the human condition."[8] The argument is that *THX 1138* functions as a "critical dystopia" when it radically refuses to provide the possibility of a cathartic resolution that could mitigate the impact of critique.[9] George Orwell once admitted that "I do not believe that the kind of society I describe [in *1984*] necessarily will arrive, but I believe . . . that something resembling it could arrive."[10] Critical dystopian fiction signals a warning by drawing attention to the dystopian logic of key social and political values and actions.[11] After all, Lucas observed in an interview in 1974, "I'm very interested in America and why it is what it is."[12]

To make this case regarding *THX 1138*, the chapter takes four main steps. The first, and briefest, section provides reader-orientation through the film's plot. Where the chapter's second section reflects on the nature of the person or subject within Lucas's imagined world, the third asks what the systematic disciplining of persons involves. The last section explicitly addresses the issues of hope, arguing that the movie is most critically interesting when the possibility of any resolution is denied, and hopeful agency is rendered ambiguous.

FADING IN WITH THE DÉCOR: THE PLOT

Lucas's debut feature film is heavily stylized and metaphorical, an unconventional tone-poem composed of abstract image and sound. The plot is distinctly basic and the characters it portrays are psychologically thin. This is quite deliberate given the way the movie critically develops "stylized and two-dimensional" symbolism when depicting the "one dimensional man."[13]

Without contextualizing exposition, the film casts the viewer into the middle of a city that, only late on, is revealed to have been located underground in the aftermath of an otherwise unexplained ecological disaster. This subterranean metropolis is constructed on the twin pillars of industry production and consumption. Social order is maintained through state-provided sedation of citizens that both suppresses desire and manages anxiety, constant surveillance, an android police force, and a civil religion that articulates glib consumerist messages. The environment's stark and monochromatic white aesthetic may well owe something to Kubrick's *2001: A Space Odyssey*, but in *THX 1138* it provides a distinctive visual metaphor. In his review of the film, Vincent Canby observes that "actors are, intentionally, almost but not quite indistinguishable from the décor."[14] The import of this is observed by J.P. Telotte when he claims that the film depicts "a sterile and lifeless world" in which "individuality and individuation simply have no place."[15] All individuality is denied, including sexual activity. Fetuses are grown in jars. Exclusively white citizens are known not by name but instead by a three-letter prefix followed by four numbers made visible on an identity badge, have had their heads shaved, and wear indistinctive white garments.

Michael Pye and Lynda Myles recognize that "only two [sic, four] individuals are presented, because anonymity is the essence of the underground world."[16] The central protagonist, THX 1138, is a worker with the fissile materials that power the security androids. The drama begins when THX's roommate, LUH 3417, substitutes her pills for his, thereby causing him to discover both sexual desire for her and an awareness of himself. Because of the ever-present surveillance system, their sensual liaison is monitored, and it leads to their arrest and imprisonment. On escaping his incarceration with a city monitor SEN 5241 and a black hologram SRT 5752, THX comes to discover that his pregnant mate had been "consumed" and therefore destroyed. A motor chase ensues with the conclusion being that THX successfully escapes from his android pursuers up to the surface world where he stands watching the sun setting.

"AN ORDINARY, NORMAL HUMAN BEING": THE MINIMIZED SELF

The movie's visually antiseptic aesthetic is remarkably consistent throughout except for two markers that frame it, the opening and the closing scenes. Prefacing even the American Zoetrope production logo is an advertisement for episode two of a 1939 *Buck Rogers* adventure serial, *Tragedy on Saturn*. The voiceover begins significantly with "Buck Rogers in the twentieth century."[17] Given that the drama takes place five centuries after Buck and Buddy Wade have been revived from suspended animation, this temporal marker makes matters more immanent to the audience. A second theme that will be equally significant in marking out what is to come in *THX 1138* is announced with the language of "the wonderful world of the future."[18] This is described as "a world that sees a lot of our scientific and mechanical dreams come true." The ethos here is distinctly progressivist, and such a sensibility is further accentuated by a combination of kaleidoscopically moving imagery and an energetic score played triumphantly by trumpets. A third theme is one that is singled out for comment by Lucas in the DVD commentary Director's Cut of *THX 1138*, is that of the ordinariness of Buck. The serial's advertising voiceover declares that "He's just an ordinary, normal human being who keeps his wits about him." This is representative heroism, the everyman acting with valor.

The screen turns black, and an audible low rumble signals an atmospheric mood shift. An ominously somber, gently paced, and wordless choral score is accompanied by radioactively colored titles that unconventionally drop from above into the base of the screen. The implication is that things are out of kilter. Within the next few moments, a disorienting set of quick-fire images appear that only become intelligible with fuller contextualization later in the piece: state-sanctioned sedation, the bureaucracy of numbers on a computer printout, surveillance intrusion into even private spaces, police brutality, an education system conditioning students for production and consumption, and the evisceration of language with incessant platitudinous sloganizing and a frequent meaningless conjoining of words. Even at the movie's early stage an important question is audible: "Are you now or have you ever been?" The evocation is of the activities of the House Committee on Un-American Activities popularly associated with the anticommunist investigations of the late 1940s and 1950s. The moment of interrogative voiceover comes significantly with a surveillance image of police brutality, and it trains Lucas's critical filmic lens on the United States. Lucas mentions that later "There is real doubletalk in the film [used by SEN 5241] like, 'We need dissent but creative dissent.' Nixon said that."[19]

One soon learns that the enigmatic title is a *name* designating a laborer who manufactures police androids, the source of maintaining the social order, a metaphor for labor's alienation from the products of that labor. The identification of persons by letters-numbers denotes a reductionistic bureaucratization of personhood, and it performs two main functions. Firstly, the nomenclature denies ways of distinguishing persons through names that link them to histories, particularly the complex histories of families of one kind or another, including tribes and nations. Critical theorists such as Theodor Adorno, Max Horkheimer, Erich Fromm, and Herbert Marcuse were concerned with the way that, despite the array of messages that marketed *individualism* to Americans, this was very much a manufactured and disciplined individualism. The modes for expressing one's individuality, such as through consumer choices, were little more than expressions of a *massified* society. "It was capitalism," Terry Eagleton explains, "that standardized people, not socialism. . . . It is consumer capitalism that decks out its citizens in uniforms known as tracksuits and trainers."[20] Lucas's movie presses this individuating logic in terms of persons' alienation from others and from themselves, with the result being minimized selves, or the "vanishing" of the individual.[21] Persons are relationally isolated from each other, including from sexual encounters;

and they make the most trivial of consumer choices, such as deciding what to watch on their holographic projectors or in making purchases of indistinct items that are subsequently simply destroyed and recycled without any use whatsoever. The reason the movie is dramatically thin is precisely because it involves thinned out or diminished agents for whom "the activity of choosing matters more than what is being chosen."[22]

This, then, is an individualism of a socially solipsistic variety of persons who "peacefully coexist in indifference."[23] And yet the movie provides a range of visual metaphors that *massify* the collection of individuals. For instance, all the characters have shaved heads and are uniformly garbed in indistinctive white apparel. The visual aesthetic of the whiteness of the people's flesh and clothes makes them, in Karl Marx and Friedrich Engel's term, "melt" into the austerely sterile and vividly lit background, thereby producing a depthlessness to the characters.[24] As the film later reveals, this homogeneous society is literally manufactured given that almost all the people are designed and produced. People are grown in jars like those in *Brave New World*'s predestination centers.[25] Lucas drew on this again in *Attack of the Clones* (2002) with the Kaminoan bioproduction cloning process. In fact, with their black uniforms, only the police androids provide a visual marker of difference.

The second thing the impersonal letter-number naming sequence does is contribute to the reduction of the persons to their roles of producing and consuming. Adorno and Horkheimer draw on Max Weber's earlier talk of "instrumental rationality" to describe the totalitarian logic of the Enlightenment as instrumentalizing, as modeling all human existence on the factory. This involves the reduction of all things through "the calculation of effects."[26] Accordingly, all things are bound up in a "structural necessity" of "generated slavery" and disposability.[27] Given this, the consumptive need to dispense, displace, dispose, discard, and replace things has a particularly ominous capacity for rendering all lives expendable. The chilling way *THX 1138* gestures towards this is in the revelation of "the harvesting of organs, the ultimate reduction of the human to a commodity," a revelation that includes that LUH has been "consumed" and her name reassigned to bottled fetus 66691.[28] In the words of Henry Giroux, this is "a society of throwaways of both goods and people."[29] Significantly, when the surveillants of THX at work identify a "sedation depletion," one of them authorizes and inflicts a control overriding "mind-block" that almost has dire destructive consequences due to the radioactive materials he had been in the midst of working with. Moreover, at one point in THX's imprisonment, a pair of voices of surveillants discuss the technical mechanics of operating the "cortical bond" with a similar emotional detachment to those referring to a malfunctioning police droid earlier in one of the corridors. This discussion occurs while utterly ignoring THX's squirming pain and discomfort.

Racially marked figures are voyeuristically proffered for violent comedy and sexual self-gratification. On one of the channels on which THX alights, only for his roommate LUH 3417 to switch over, catharsis and "an ethical tranquilization" occurs through spectating a random act of violence in which a security android simply beats a floored man with a police baton.[30] An equally effective depiction of the instrumentalization logic sees, via surveillance monitors, a similar production line to the one THX himself works on explode from a radiation overload. A screen displays several bloody bodies being dragged out, followed soon after by an announcement proclaiming that "that accident over in Red Sector L destroyed another sixty-three personnel, giving them a total of two hundred and forty-two lost to our one hundred and ninety-five. Keep up the good work and prevent accidents."

There are two things that are important to observe in this regard. The first is the way that the culture industry pacifies persons, reducing them to docile consumers whose only agency is to choose which channel to spectate. Consequently, there is an evident absence of artistic creativity in this agency-sterilized environment other than the banal forms of holographic entertainment. This is art reduced by capitalism to a "mechanical reproduction" fabricated to be "uncritically enjoyed."[31] Persons are a reflection of their minimized capacity for exercising agency in their chemically and ideologically somnolent state. An amusing scene shows two people continuing to stand in a lift even with the repeated announcement that "this elevator has been removed from service. Please use the next elevator on your right."

The second is the linguistic reduction. According to Slavoj Žižek, under late capitalism "we 'feel' free [only] because we lack the very language to articulate our unfreedom."[32] There is a lack of the very language through which to identify and articulate real distress. In the light of this, it is important to note how the art of language functions in *THX 1138*. While the movie is particularly light on conversation, it is nonetheless pervaded by words. Predominantly, the words are mediated technologically by those monitoring the situations. This linguistic meaning-depletion, then, exhaustively functionalizes communication by rendering speech monological and directive. Accordingly, the language conditions subjects and social arrangements that are thereby incapacitated from communicating with each other in ways other than through the production/consumption system, and this contributes to the subject's "complicity with the prevailing ... trends."[33] There is considerable use of language that is a meaningless conjunction of seemingly random sentences and even words combined in an even more fragmented way.

"WE ARE THE DRUGGED SOCIETY": THE HAPPINESS OF THE MECHANIZED SELF

THX 1138 is replete with images of surveillance, the factory, policing, state-manufactured and administered consumerism, religiosity, the detention room, and state-provided sedation all as forms of control within this disciplinary society. This is a deep state, of totalizing power so that even what might be considered one's "private" life or private spaces are nonexistent. A range of Soviet-style clichés and the design of uniforms based, screenplay cowriter Walter Murch in the DVD's commentary claims, on the People's Revolution in China, would resonate with anti-Communist sentiment during the Vietnam War. It is evident, however, that this is not a Soviet city, or even America under Communist rule. Rather, it is the massification of persons within late modern industrialization, in spite of all manner of claims that America is the 'free world' in which people are individuals capable of self-realization. Lucas locates a range of socio-political pressures that are conducive to making quiescent people in a society that is, in its own way, homogenous and utterly bureaucratized. In fact, a voice is heard on several occasions announcing that "for greater efficiency, consumption is being standardized."

The state may be deep in its disciplinary provision, but the ethos of Lucas's movie resonates more with the state's provision of satisfaction that appears in *Brave New World* rather than in the totalitarian governance built principally on fear in *1984*. As THX briefly switches channels, one character proclaims, "Never before have we been so contented." The society is not built on the anxiety and dread induced by the manufacture of "the other." As Marcuse recognizes, "'totalitarian' is not only a terroristic political coordination of society, but also a nonterroristic economic-technical coordination which operates through the manipulation of needs by vested interests. It thus precludes the emergence of an effective opposition against the whole."[34] After all, even *THX 1138*'s stylization provides vibrantly bright lighting, and a conspicuously clean manufactured reality. Governance generally has a light touch, and it is the state that narcoticizes its citizens apparently to enhance their ability to cope with stressful demands. This contributes to social order, life, and health, in contrast to the deathliness of the natural environment that has suffered a catastrophe that the movie otherwise never explains, and the dehumanizing devolution that is on view with the Shell-Dwellers who live nearer the surface. Within its massified equity, there is an absence of the kind of brutal competitiveness that is a feature of capitalism and its "predatory individualism," or the "uninhibited self-preservation that always ends up in destruction."[35] Even the automated voice from the medicine cabinet offers direction and aid. Moreover, apart from a couple of instances, the policing too is benign and not primarily characterized by what Judith Butler calls "forcible handling."[36] An early scene depicts a police android walking down a corridor holding the hand of a child while another has an officer hand his baton to a group of children at their request. The androids' voices are polite, relaxed, comforting, and reassuring. The watchers are themselves watched so that within this automated and administered society no *person* governs and benefits at others' expense. Within this society, it is OMM 0000, a computer system, that manages matters rather than some self-aggrandizing dictator or oligarchy profiting from the use of others-as-instruments.

Lucas on occasions has made it clear that there is a sense in which this society is a *utopia*, an imagined no-place, *eu-topos*, in which needs are provided for. "I never said the society was oppressive. Nobody was having any fun, but no one was unhappy. A lot of people live that way now. . . . We are the drugged society."[37] Crucially, talk of happiness occurs on several occasions. For instance, THX, when suffering the effects of drug-withdrawal, explains to LUH that he had been "happy." Notably the masses of frenetically paced people shuffle through the hallways rather than stagger as in Fritz Lang's image of the labor-slaves in *Metropolis* (1927).

Nonetheless, this form of happiness is more a thin solipsistic form of happiness, or chemically induced hedonistic affectivity, than of thick social flourishing or well-being. As Lucas admits, "pleasure's fun, but just accept the fact that it's here and gone. . . . Pleasure's purely self-centered. It's all about your pleasure. It's about you. A selfish, self-centered emotion created by a selfish moment for you."[38] In fact, the very affective conditions ideologically dispose the satisfied person towards "adjustment to his society" and therefore to "a euphoria in [real] unhappiness."[39] For instance, the act of consumption is a meaningless activity, a "compulsive, irrational" one that simply functions as "an end in itself, with little relation to the use of, or pleasure in the things bought and consumed."[40] What is subsequently produced is a listless and lifeless subject. In the end, these instrumentalized lives are ultimately disposable, what Bauman calls the "collateral damage inflicted on the 'collateral victim' of capital."[41] It is even more significant that while the lives of all citizens are diminished and discardable, black people appear to be denied existence altogether since they are holographic rather than real. An important marker of heterogeneity is denied its very reality, and this racially marks social hibernization so that blackness becomes entirely a means instrumentalized for white entertainment.

As the image of the "happy" THX who is literally alienated from the product of his labor suggests, the values of the system have been internalized. SEN exemplifies this when his attempted escape from the city produces anxiety sufficient to make him return and even to confess to the picture of OMM.

"Religion" is located within this social disciplinary process as, consequently, one of several mystifying and disciplinary forces inimical to human flourishing and healthy desire. A scene depicts THX entering a glass-doored confession booth. The transparency of the booth suggests a lack of privacy and state-monitoring, and the booth contains a looming electronic icon of Jesus in the confessional, based on Hans Memling's painting *Christ Giving His Blessing* (1478). Despite this, and a form of monastically performed Gregorian chant, the movie offers several gestures towards including Eastern traditions through the name for the system as OMM, and home worship being conducted with Tibetan symbols clanging. Even if the form that the critique of Christianity takes is largely dependent upon nineteenth-century accounts, the Eastern references do something unexpected, albeit linking up with the state-sanctioned narcotics: it ironizes the hippie ransacking of Buddhist traditions to develop a post-Christian self-help spirituality. The Jesus-formed depiction of OMM utilizes a characteristically calming tone, yet, despite claiming that "My time is yours" and "I understand," it is clear that the confessor is not listening. A later scene, with the same timing and content of OMM's "responses," and this one's cut-away shot revealing tape-reels as OMM's "responses" are given, acknowledge that this a prerecorded and generic confession-hearing. The e-confessor reels off an array of banal generalities that explicitly connect the religiosity, the state-provision and control, production, and consumption of the "technological society."[42] Accordingly, THX is declared to be "a true believer . . . a subject of the divine, created in the image of man by the masses for the masses," a reference reflecting the movie's Marcusian concern with massification. The confessor subsequently offers the "blessings of the state, blessings of the masses," and enjoins "let us be thankful we have an occupation to fill." The penitential requirement is consequential in this production/consumption dynamic. THX is required to "Work hard. Increase production. Prevent accidents. And be happy," with the second screened confession shifting to "Let us be thankful we have commerce. Buy more. Buy more now. Buy. And be happy." The mechanical reproduction of religious catharsis here presents the kind of personal therapy that maintains the atomized subject's socialization within the dominant social arrangements, thereby mitigating any capacity for prophetic protest.

IS IT TOO LATE? RESISTING THE ATOMIZATION OF HOPE

Marx and Engels argue that subjects are formed by their "material conditions" and realities, and the conditioning on view in *THX 1138* produces docile subjects who are diminished to the point of possessing only the most trivial forms of agency.[43] According to Bauman, "all societies are factories of meanings. They are more than that, in fact: nothing less than the nurseries of *meaningful life*."[44]

There are, however, two particularly clear and significant moments of nontrivial agency in the movie. The first is that of LUH. She is instrumental in helping the titular protagonist awake from his slumbers, and it is this that results in the pair's discovery of each other. A tender scene, supported by a distinctively gentle flute-driven harmony, depicts the consequential noncommodifying mutual recognition by the pair, "the symbiotic nature of relatedness."[45] The visceral display of flesh-tones disrupts the otherwise sterile aesthetic metaphor for social hygienic homogeneity. They materially expose themselves to each other in an unexpected and illegal way, in contradistinction to the atomizing subject-formations of the state system. The pleasure they gain from each other is markedly different from that of hedonism since it is relationally mutual and equitable, demanding intensive vulnerability of one to another and the enjoyment of the other as ends and not self-interested means or commodities. They attentively recognize each other's material existence, as each other comes into view without the distorting narcotic self-intensification.[46] Therein, as Linda Ruth Hamilton argues about both *Brazil* and *1984*, this focuses the moment "of explicitly utopian hesitation and contemplation—[so that it is] figured . . . as the spectacle of a woman's body."[47]

With the state's separation of the couple from each other, and on learning of LUH's liquidation, THX's instinct is to flee. Lucas's commentary on this suggests it is a moment of flight when THX uses his agency to "to step out . . . rather than being stuck in . . . [a] little rut . . . in cages with open doors."[48] However, this is a complacently trivializing interpretation for at least three reasons. Firstly, ideologically, it fails to acknowledge the significance of "our inescapable situatedness; situatedness in class, race, and gender in nationality, in history—in short, in all kinds of determinations, which no biological individual can evade."[49] Pye and Myles rightly have little patience for this type of privileged claim by Lucas. "If he had not been the white, middle-class son of a California businessman, he might well have found it hard to escape his 'cage.' Many others are not as fortunate. Brute economics keeps them trapped."[50] The writer-director's reflections sound like bourgeois self-help therapy, and the implication is of an imagination bound to capitalism's endless capacity for renewing and reinvigorating itself. Secondly, it is not evident that THX's escape attempt is in any way premeditated rather than purely instinctive. In fact, it is the fear that comes with a consciousness of the situation that provokes SEN to return to the city, anxiously disoriented by his isolation when at the end of his journey on the expressway. Thirdly, and crucially, with the failure of the hologram SRT 5752 to operate a vehicle for getaway THX's running leaves him on his own. After the suggestions of the discovery of the erotics of a recovered sociality, something odd would occur should this final act reinforce the culture's solipsism. The vital role in the third act played by the hologram suggests a distinctive moment of alterity, of an other who offers challenge to assumptions and perspectives and therefore orientation in the journey of THX's self-realization. After all, Horkheimer admits, "the emancipation of the individual is not an emancipation from society, but the deliverance of society from atomization, an atomization that may reach its peak in periods of collectivization and mass culture."[51]

The genius of the final scene, nonetheless, is that it is *ambiguous*. On the one hand, THX has successfully evaded the pursuing security androids and reached the surface. Now he is free from the stultifying and commodifying massification. The visualization of two birds in flight offer a sense of hope since not all life on the surface had been destroyed after all. On the other hand, the filmmaker's aesthetic choices for the scene are significant. For instance, while the score is less somber than in the city scenes, it can hardly be described as bombastically triumphant; while the color scheme distinctively contrasts with the severe visual tones of the city, there is an oddly barren quality about the image; the sun is setting rather than rising; the protagonist is immobilized; and as silhouetted he possesses even fewer differentiating features than when melting into the city's monochromatic background. Moreover, it is unclear that the warnings about the inhabitability of the surface are mistaken. It is "a precarious success at best."[52]

Consequently, the movie ends with a distinctive moment of *irresolution*, a refusal to wrap the critical struggle up cheaply in the sentimental cinematic convention of a consoling image. As Horkheimer argues, "the belief that all will be well cannot reconcile us to the bad things that have happened."[53] In this regard, THX himself cannot serve as a heroically emancipatory subject. The spectacle of escape is itself contained and framed to erase collective resistance. On saying that, however, the movie's critique of the socio-economic processes of dehumanization is intensified. Otherwise put, this less than hopeful ending highlights the importance of preventing matters from having to get this far. This, then, would fit Gordon Browning's claim that anti-utopian fiction is not reducible to "a prophecy of doom or a warning that we must brace ourselves for a certain disaster."[54] Such fiction, Browning continues, "instead [offers] a warning accompanied by faith or at least a hope that the situation will be improved if man will only accomplish a certain series of necessary reforms."[55]

CONCLUSION: THE "SORT OF REALITY WE BUY INTO"

According to Douglas Kellner, Marcuse's "*One-Dimensional Man* showed that the problems confronting the emerging radical movement were not simply the Vietnam war, racism or inequality, but the system itself, and that solving a wide range of social problems required fundamental social restructuring."[56] This work endeavored to reveal "what the contemporary world really is behind the ideological and material veil."[57]

Marcuse's work was well-known in the 1960s, and Lucas's *THX 1138* appears to follow the general shape of this social analysis.[58] The result is the imaginative construction of a superficially satisfied society that has succumbed to multiple ways of dehumanizing its citizens by instrumentally reducing them to their productive and consumptive capacity and adjusting them to these conditions through a range of disciplinary means, including religion. For this society of atomized individuals, there appears to be no capacity for imagining and collectively provoking social change at all. While for them it is evidently too late to flourish, confronting the contemporary values and choices that maintain such conditions is the critical challenge the movie radically provokes for its audience. According to Telotte, *THX 1138* "lays bare some of the more disturbing elements of American cultural ideology—particularly an inherent racism, a deadening disjunction between the individual and his or her work, and a capitalist reduction of everything and everyone to bottom-line budgetary numbers. . . . Lucas's film seems intent on cautioning about the sort of reality we buy into."[59] Even if it now seems culturally impossible to imagine a utopian alternative to capitalism, and while *THX 1138* does not help in this regard, it at least cautions against "the paralysis of criticism" by demonstrating what Erika Gottlieb calls the "morality play" function of critical dystopian fiction.[60]

NOTES

1. This process is what Rahime Çokay Nebioğlu describes as the construction of an "immanent dystopia." Rahime Çokay Nebioğlu, *Deleuze and the Schizoanalysis of Dystopia* (New York: Palgrave Macmillan, 2020), 38.

2. George Lucas, in Dale Pollock, *Skywalking: The Life and Films of George Lucas* (Hollywood: Samuel French, 1990), 93; George Lucas, cited by Judy Stone, "George Lucas," in *George Lucas: Interviews*, ed. Sally Kline (Jackson, MS: University Press of Mississippi, 1999), 4. The other two dystopian studio movies of 1971 were Stanley Kubrick's *A Clockwork Orange* and Robert Wise's *The Andromeda Strain* (1971).

3. Lucas, cited by Stone, "George Lucas," 5.

4. Herbert Marcuse, *One-Dimensional Man: Studies in the Ideology of Advanced Industrial Society*, 2nd ed. (London: Routledge, 2002), 52, xlv.

5. Pollock, *Skywalking*, 93.

6. M. Keith Booker, *The Dystopian Impulse in Modern Literature: Fiction as Social Criticism* (Westport, CT: Greenwood Press, 1994), 19.

7. Raffaella Baccolini and Tom Moylan, "Introduction: Dystopia and Histories," in *Dark Horizons: Science Fiction and the Dystopian Imagination*, ed. Raffaella Baccolini and Tom Moylan (New York: Routledge, 2003), 1–2.

8. Marcuse, *One-Dimenional Man*, xl.

9. Constance Penley, "Time Travel, Prime Scene and the Critical Dystopia," in *Fantasy and the Cinema*, ed. James McDonald (London: BFI Publishing, 1989), 197. An *aesthetic dystopia* is a piece of fiction in which the dystopianism is an element of a larger plot as, for instance, in romance stories set against a dystopian backdrop. A *negative utopia* can have a more nihilistic outcome in that the fiction challenges the possibility of utopian imaginations of any better future. A *critical dystopia* still holds out hope that the fiction's critique can have an emancipatory benefit.

10. George Orwell, "Letter to Francis A. Henson," in *Collected Essays, Journalism and Letters of George Orwell*, ed. Sonia Orwell and Ian Angus (Harmondsworth: Penguin, 1970), 564.

11. Erika Gottlieb, *Dystopian Fiction East and West: Universe of Terror and Trial* (McGill: Queen's University Press, 2001), 4.

12. Lucas, cited by Stephen Farber, "George Lucas: The Stinky Kid Hits the Big Time," in Kline, 39.

13. Lucas, cited in Brian Jay Jones, *George Lucas: A Life* (London: Headline, 2017), 119; Marcuse, *One-Dimensional Man*.

14. Vincent Canby, "Wanda's a Wow, So's THX," *New York Times* (March 21, 1971), cited in Jones, *George Lucas: A Life*, 125.

15. J.P. Telotte, *Science Fiction Film* (Cambridge: Cambridge University Press, 2001), 130.

16. Michael Pye and Lynda Myles, "George Lucas," in Kline, 64–86 (68).

17. *Buck Rogers, Chapter Two: Tragedy on Saturn*, directed by Ford Beebe and Saul A. Goodkind (1939), https://www.youtube.com/watch?v=F3P9IOBFrOw.

18. All citations from the movie are taken from *THX 1138 Director's Cut*, directed by George Lucas (Lucasfilm, 2004), DVD.

19. Lucas, cited by Stone, "George Lucas," 5.

20. Terry Eagleton, *Why Marx was Right* (New Haven, CT: Yale University Press, 2011), 104–5. Cf. Wendy Brown, "We Are All Democrats Now . . . ," in *Democracy in What State?*, by Giorgio Agamben et al. (New York: Columbia University Press, 2011), 55.

21. Theodor W. Adorno and Max Horkheimer, *Dialectic of Enlightenment: Philosophical Fragments*, trans. Edmund Jephcott (Stanford: Stanford University Press, 2002), xvii.

22. Zygmunt Bauman, *Liquid Modernity* (Cambridge: Polity, 2000), 87.

23. Marcuse, *One-Dimensional Man*, 64.

24. Karl Marx and Friedrich Engels, "The Communist Manifesto," in *Karl Marx: Selected Writings*, ed. David McLellan (Oxford: Oxford University Press, 1977), 224.

25. Aldous Huxley, *Brave New World* (London: Vintage, 2007).

26. Adorno and Horkheimer, *Dialectic of Enlightenment*, xiv.

27. Slavoj Žižek, *The Courage of Hopelessness: Chronicles of a Year Acting Dangerously* (London: Allen Lane, 2017), 23.

28. Telotte, *Science Fiction Film*, 137.

29. Henry A. Giroux, *Zombie Politics and Culture in the Age of Casino Capitalism* (New York: Peter Lang, 2014), xix.

30. Henry A. Giroux, *America's Addiction to Terrorism* (New York: Monthly Review Press, 2016), 63.

31. Walter Benjamin, *Illuminations*, trans. Harry Zohn (New York: Schocken Books, 1968), 224, 234.

32. Slavoj Žižek, *Welcome to the Desert of the Real: Five Chapters on September 11 and Related Dates* (London: Verso, 2002), 2.

33. Adorno and Horkheimer, *Dialectic of Enlightenment*, xv.

34. Marcuse, *One-Dimensional Man*, 5.

35. Christopher Lasch, *The Culture of Narcissism: American Life in an Age of Diminishing Expectations* (New York: W.W. Norton & Company, 1979), 218; Theodor Adorno, in Theodor Adorno and Max Horkheimer, *Towards a New Manifesto*, trans. Rodney Livingstone (London: Verso, 2011), 46.

36. Judith Butler, "Rethinking Vulnerability and Resistance," in *Vulnerability in Resistance*, ed. Judith Butler, Zeynep Gambetti, and Leticia Sabsay (Durham, NC: Duke University Press, 2016), 12.

37. Lucas, cited by Stone, "George Lucas," 5.

38. Lucas, cited in Chris Taylor, *How Star Wars Conquered the Universe: The Past, Present, and Future of a Multibillion Dollar Franchise* (New York: Basic Books, 2014), 72.

39. Marcuse, *One-Dimensional Man*, 110, 7.

40. Erich Fromm, *The Sane Society* (London: Routledge & Kegan Paul, 1956), 135.

41. Zygmunt Bauman, *Consuming Life* (Cambridge: Polity, 2007), 92.

42. Marcuse, *One-Dimensional Man*, 28.

43. Karl Marx and Friedrich Engels, "The German Ideology," in McLellan, 160.

44. Zygmunt Bauman, *The Individualized Society* (Cambridge: Polity, 2001), 2.

45. Fromm, *The Sane Society*, 31.

46. Murch suggests that with SEN's desire for a relationship with THX, there are homosexual overtones, while Lucas denies that the desire is sexual. Either way, the movie reinforces a heteronormativity. *THX 1138 Director's Cut: Commentary*, directed by George Lucas and Walter Murch (Lucasfilm, 2004), DVD.

47. Linda Ruth Hamilton, "Dream Girls and Mechanic Panic: Dystopia and its Others in *Brazil* and *Nineteen Eighty-Four*," in *Liquid Metal: The Science Fiction Film Reader*, ed. Sean Redmond (London: Wallflower Press, 2004), 70.

48. Lucas, cited by Stone, "George Lucas," 4.

49. Frederic Jameson, *Archaeologies of the Future: The Desire Called Utopia and Other Science Fictions* (London: Verso, 2005), 170.

50. Pye and Myles, "George Lucas," 69.
51. Max Horkheimer, *Eclipse of Reason* (Mansfield Centre: Martino Publishing, 2013), 135.
52. Telotte, *Science Fiction Film*, 137.
53. Horkheimer, in Adorno and Horkheimer, *Towards a New Manifesto*, 91.
54. Gordon Browning, "Toward a Set of Standards for Everlasting Anti-Utopian Fiction," *Cithara* 10, no. 1 (1970): 18.
55. Browning, "Toward a Set of Standards," 18.
56. Douglas Kellner, "Introduction," in Marcuse, *One-Dimensional Man*, xxxv.
57. Marcuse, *One-Dimensional Man*, 70.
58. Mark T. Decker argues that the influence was one that was indirect, occurring as a consequence of the incorporation of Marcuse's theories "into a critical and oppositional zeitgeist." Mark T. Decker, *Industrial Society and the Science Fiction Blockbuster: Social Critique in the Films of Lucas, Scott and Cameron* (Jefferson, NC: McFarland, 2016), 2.
59. Telotte, *Science Fiction Film*, 128–9.
60. Marcuse, *One-Dimensional Man*, xlii; Gottlieb, *Dystopian Fiction East and West*, 4.

BIBLIOGRAPHY

Adorno, Theodor W. and Horkheimer, Max. *Dialectic of Enlightenment: Philosophical Fragments*. Translated by Edmund Jephcott. Stanford: Stanford University Press, 2002.
Adorno, Theodor and Max Horkheimer. *Towards a New Manifesto*. Translated by Rodney Livingstone. London: Verso, 2011.
Baccolini, Raffaella and Tom Moylan. "Introduction: Dystopia and Histories." In *Dark Horizons: Science Fiction and the Dystopian Imagination*, edited by Raffaella Baccolini and Tom Moylan, 1–12. New York: Routledge, 2003.
Bauman, Zygmunt. *Consuming Life*. Cambridge: Polity, 2007.
———. *The Individualized Society*. Cambridge: Polity, 2001.
———. *Liquid Modernity*. Cambridge: Polity, 2000.
Benjamin, Walter. *Illuminations*. Translated by Harry Zohn. New York: Schocken Books, 1968.
Booker, M. Keith. *The Dystopian Impulse in Modern Literature: Fiction as Social Criticism*. Westport, CT: Greenwood Press, 1994.
Brown, Wendy. "We Are All Democrats Now . . . " In *Democracy in What State?*, by Giorgio Agamben, Alain Badiou, Daniel Bensaid, Wendy Brown, Jean-Luc Nancy, Jacques Rancière, Kristin Ross, and Slavoj Žižek, 44–57. Translated by William McCuaig. New York: Columbia University Press, 2011.
Browning, Gordon. "Toward a Set of Standards for Everlasting Anti-Utopian Fiction." *Cithara* 10, no. 1 (1970): 18–32.
Buck Rogers. Chapter Two: Tragedy on Saturn. Directed by Ford Beebe and Saul A. Goodkind (1939), https://www.youtube.com/watch?v=F3P9IOBFrOw.

Butler, Judith. "Rethinking Vulnerability and Resistance." In *Vulnerability in Resistance*, edited by Judith Butler, Zeynep Gambetti, and Leticia Sabsay, 12–27. Durham, NC: Duke University Press, 2016.

Decker, Mark T. *Industrial Society and the Science Fiction Blockbuster: Social Critique in the Films of Lucas, Scott and Cameron*. Jefferson, NC: McFarland, 2016.

Eagleton, Terry. *Why Marx was Right*. New Haven, CT: Yale University Press, 2011.

Farber, Stephen. "George Lucas: The Stinky Kid Hits the Big Time." In *George Lucas: Interviews*, edited by Sally Kline, 33–44. Jackson, MS: University Press of Mississippi, 1999.

Fromm, Erich. *The Sane Society*. London: Routledge & Kegan Paul, 1956.

Giroux, Henry A. *America's Addiction to Terrorism*. New York: Monthly Review Press, 2016.

———. *Zombie Politics and Culture in the Age of Casino Capitalism*. New York: Peter Lang, 2014.

Gottlieb, Erika. *Dystopian Fiction East and West: Universe of Terror and Trial*. Montreal: McGill Queen's University Press, 2001.

Hamilton, Linda Ruth. "Dream Girls and Mechanic Panic: Dystopia and its Others in *Brazil* and *Nineteen Eighty-Four*." In *Liquid Metal: The Science Fiction Film Reader*, edited by Sean Redmond, 64–73. London: Wallflower Press, 2004.

Horkheimer, Max. *Eclipse of Reason*. Mansfield Centre: Martino Publishing, 2013.

Huxley, Aldous. *Brave New World*. London: Vintage, 2007.

Jameson, Frederic. *Archaeologies of the Future: The Desire Called Utopia and Other Science Fictions*. London: Verso, 2005.

Jones, Brian Jay. *George Lucas: A Life*. London: Headline, 2017.

Kellner, Douglas. Introduction to *One-Dimensional Man: Studies in the Ideology of Advanced Industrial Society*, by Herbert Marcuse, xi-xxxviii. 2nd edition. London: Routledge, 2002.

Kline, Sally, ed. *George Lucas: Interviews*. Jackson, MS: University Press of Mississippi, 1999.

Lasch, Christopher. *The Culture of Narcissism: American Life in an Age of Diminishing Expectations*. New York: W.W. Norton & Company, 1979.

Marcuse, Herbert. *One-Dimensional Man: Studies in the Ideology of Advanced Industrial Society*, 2nd edition. London: Routledge, 2002.

Marx, Karl and Friedrich Engels. "The Communist Manifesto." In *Karl Marx: Selected Writings*, edited by David McLellan, 221–47. Oxford: Oxford University Press, 1977.

———. "The German Ideology." In *Karl Marx: Selected Writings*, edited by David McLellan, 159–91. Oxford: Oxford University Press, 1977.

Nebioğlu, Rahime Çokay. *Deleuze and the Schizoanalysis of Dystopia*. New York: Palgrave Macmillan, 2020.

Orwell, George. "Letter to Francis A. Henson." In *Collected Essays, Journalism and Letters of George Orwell*, edited by Sonia Orwell and Ian Angus, 564. Harmondsworth: Penguin, 1970.

Penley, Constance. "Time Travel, Prime Scene and the Critical Dystopia." In *Fantasy and the Cinema*, edited by James McDonald, 197–212. London: BFI Publishing, 1989.

Pollock, Dale. *Skywalking: The Life and Films of George Lucas*. Hollywood: Samuel French, 1990.

Pye, Michael and Lynda Myles. "George Lucas." In *George Lucas: Interviews*, edited by Sally Kline, 64–86. Jackson, MS: University Press of Mississippi, 1999.

Stone, Judy. "George Lucas." In *George Lucas: Interviews*, edited by Sally Kline, 3–7. Jackson, MS: University Press of Mississippi, 1999.

Taylor, Chris. *How Star Wars Conquered the Universe: The Past, Present, and Future of a Multibillion Dollar Franchise*. New York: Basic Books, 2014.

Telotte, J.P. *Science Fiction Film*. Cambridge: Cambridge University Press, 2001.

THX 1138 Director's Cut. Directed by George Lucas. Lucasfilm, 2004. DVD.

THX 1138 Director's Cut: Commentary. Directed by George Lucas and Walter Murch. Lucasfilm, 2004. DVD.

Žižek, Slavoj. *The Courage of Hopelessness: Chronicles of a Year Acting Dangerously*. London: Allen Lane, 2017.

———. *Welcome to the Desert of the Real: Five Chapters on September 11 and Related Dates*. London: Verso, 2002.

Epilogue

We know that our world will one day come to an end. According to *The Hitchhiker's Guide to the Galaxy*, the end of the world comes about after a particularly dull and bureaucratic species known as the Vogons were charged with building a bypass for an interstellar highway through the vicinity of the Sol system.[1] Unfortunately for Earth's inhabitants, their mostly harmless planet was destroyed to make way for the bypass, allowing people living at point A to reach point B (and vice versa) as quickly as possible. Only the Earth's dolphins and a single human man survived the Vogons' work on that day.[2] Similarly, situated in a time bubble that extends beyond the temporal end of the universe, *The Restaurant at the End of the Universe* allowed its guests to eat "sumptuous meals whilst watching . . . the whole of creation explode around them."[3] Throughout history, the end of world and the end of the universe have been foretold over and over again.

Outside of fictitious and otherwise ambitiously prophetic accounts of the end of the world, however, consensus amongst astrophysicists tells us that the end of the universe will happen in one of a number of spectacular scenarios. Theoretical astrophysicist Katie Mack writes:

> Each scenario presents a very different style of apocalypse, with a different physical process governing it, but they all agree on one thing: there will be an end. In all my readings, I have not yet found a serious suggestion in the current cosmological literature that the universe could persist, unchanged, forever . . . A few of the scenarios carry with them a hint of possibility that the cosmos might renew itself, or even repeat, in one way or another, but whether some tenuous memory of previous iterations can persist in any way is a matter of rather intense ongoing debate . . . What seems most likely is that the end for our little island of existence known as the observable universe is, truly, the end.[4]

She presents five of these theories about the end of the cosmos: the Big Crunch, Heat Death, Big Rip, Vacuum Death, and the Bounce.[5] While all of these scenarios feature whimsical names, their results are nothing but the total and complete end of the universe as we know it. Similar to Asimov's Hari Seldon, some scholars in recent decades have attempted to preserve the sum of human knowledge through eternity, safeguarding it from a collapse of society or universe, but that process has often proven for naught.[6] However, a seed vault on the remote Norwegian island of Svalbard has successfully served as a backup for more than 1 million samples, with a capacity of up to 4.5 million samples, of the world's crop diversity since 2008.[7] Mack's epilogue speaks of human legacy and the lasting impact human knowledge in the greater life of the universe, and interviews with experts all come to a similar, pithy conclusion: life is all about the journey.[8]

But imagining what happens to humankind prior to and as a result of transitions like the end of societies, worlds, and universes is deeply ingrained in human fascination about all things eschatological, a term that refers to the study of the end times. Many of the chapters in this volume covered works of popular culture that envision human reality after that transition—after the end of one era and at the beginning of another. Human anxiety rises in anticipation of transitions, and likewise human fascination with those transitions gives the dystopia genre a greater purpose. Knowing that the cosmos cannot endure unchanged fosters the sense that dystopia may be unavoidable. The metaphorical Doomsday Clock ticks ever closer to midnight providing a countdown to an end.[9] While ultimately the end of the world and universe may be outside of human control, human responsibility should avoid the apathetic stance that human action is therefore insignificant. Dystopia fails when it becomes a tool of inaction or harmful human action. Dystopia thrives when it invites good and responsible action even in the face of insurmountable odds. What follows are some of the general connections between the chapters in this volume as they relate to the status of humankind in dystopian conditions and amidst transition.

CONNECTIONS

The chapters in this volume indeed represent a diverse set of approaches, methodologies, and perspectives concerning the study of dystopia and its intersections with theology and religion. As a matter of principle, the editors did not set out a single definition of dystopia for all of the contributors; rather, the editors asked each contributor to form their own concise definition of the term based on their own social locations and academic fields. What resulted was not ten separate definitions of dystopia guided by sources antithetical or converse to one another. Rather, several common themes and concepts connect each chapter together into an interconnected web of critical and academic discourse on the academic study of dystopia as viewed through the lenses of the academic fields of theology and religious studies. What follows are a few of those connections as understood by the editors of the volume. As stated in the preface, we invite the reader to make their own connections between the various chapters before reviewing the connections that we perceive in the material.

Intertextuality was a common connection between many chapters in this volume, especially those that approached a mix of ancient and modern texts. In their analysis of *Ghost in the Shell*, Amanda Pumphrey and Nicholaus Pumphrey explored the series as inherently intertextual, each volume or issue shaping the way that other volumes and, indeed, the entire series is perceived. Likewise, C.J. McCrary linked the biblical Jubilee with *The Purge*, providing a reading where one text influenced a reading of the other. Additionally, the editors mentioned the intertextual quality of some dystopian works, such as George Orwell's *1984*, in the first chapter. The intertextual nature of many of the chapters with ancient and modern texts underscore that dystopian themes are common across generations and cultures. While we want to avoid being anachronistic, intertextual work allows for critical correlation to take place in manners which mutually inform ancient and modern media. As suggested in chapter 1, demythologization and existentialism provide one avenue for religious and theological intertextual work.

Dealing with the concepts of apocalyptic, apocalypticism, and the apocalypse was also readily present in many chapters. In addition to the first chapter by the editors that argued dystopia is a demythologized apocalyptic, both Shayna Sheinfeld and Brandon Simonson explored early Jewish apocalyptic literature and how it related to dystopian themes in modern works. Reading the *Foundation* novels as a work of apocalyptic literature, Simonson found that dystopian themes led to the creation (and preservation) of sectarian communities in ancient and modern literature alike. Bound together by common experience, and in the case of *Foundation* the "religious" experience of psychohistory, communities become more cohesive in the face of dystopian tribulation. Seldon's regular otherworldly appearances share secret information have a revelatory function similar to examples of early Jewish apocalyptic literature. Exploring young adult dystopian works *The Hunger Games* and *Divergent*, Sheinfeld read sacrifice in an ancient, apocalyptic setting as inherently dystopian in nature. With Sheinfeld, we find it significant that young adult dystopian literature in particular draws from ancient understandings of sacrifice. While young adult literature has a wider popular readership, its intended audience is especially impressionable to the formation that occurs through reading and watching dystopian works.

Sacrifice was primarily found in the works of Shayna Sheinfeld and C.J. McCrary, both of whom found links between ancient and modern material. Sheinfeld explored the notion of self-sacrifice in early Jewish apocalyptic literature as a counterpart to young adult dystopian fiction. McCrary found sacrifice in *The Purge* and the biblical Jubilee as related to and justifying sovereign power. While sacrifice does not belong to the realm of religion and theology alone, it is a rich topic for comparative work with dystopia which often asks questions concerning the value of human action or basic needs. In this way, sacrifice reveals what humans prioritize with regard to well-being, freedom, and social relating, as well as religious and theological undertones that increasingly "none" readerships might miss. By nature of social living and engaging in community, human life requires certain sacrifices. Dystopia can assist in considering the purposes and functions of sacrifice.

Catharsis, or even the lack of catharsis, was readily apparent in many chapters in this volume. Questions of catharsis were evident in the chapters by Beáta Gombkötő and John McDowell. Because dystopia is a malleable genre and topic overall, questions about the role of catharsis in dystopian studies and dystopian literature is crucial. For some scholars, there is a risk that dystopia presents a worldview absent of catharsis and the possibility of change. Engaging these types of dystopian works from this approach would produce a vicious cycle of dystopian anxiety. Dystopian anxiety exists, dystopian anxiety produces dystopian work, and those works only reinforce, or even exacerbate, dystopian anxiety. Such a cycle is impossible to break. However, even the most despair-laden dystopian works do not have to be devoid of catharsis or a critical possibility of change. Gombkötő took a literary approach that looked at the possibility of intratextual catharsis before turning to the response of readers. However, the intratextual resolution of conflict, which can lead to catharsis, is not a guarantee of catharsis in the reader. McDowell warns against the dystopian danger of apathy or even paralysis which presents situations so dire the possibility of change is denied, or change is unimaginable apart from confining dystopian systems. Here, catharsis, even that achieved by reading or watching dystopian works, can be a means of inaction rather than action when the reader or viewer leave with emotions purged but no desire to change material conditions in the real world. The irresolution presented in dystopian works should lead readers to actualized resolution in the real world.

The actualization of change to prevent further erosion into dystopian possibilities was a common theme throughout the volume. The task of literary dystopia, Gregory Claeys concludes, is "to warn us against and educate us about real-life dystopias."[10] Many of our contributors saw the same purpose in the works of popular culture that they reviewed, but this was especially evident in the chapters by Thomas Hermans-Webster and Scott Donahue-Martens. Many dystopian works present gruesome realities that are violent. Because of the violence, some contributors questioned whether certain dystopian works have positive formative function. Justin Martin encouraged readers to engage dystopian works by intentionally considering the moral complexities dystopia presents. David Penn invites readers to allow *The Walking Dead* to haunt with religious and theological questions about ultimate reality.

CONCLUSION

Orson Scott Card's *Ender's Game* has many dystopian elements. The book describes Earth's military counter-response after repelling an alien invasion. Population control, large powerful governments, and child soldiers are some of the explicit dystopian elements. The main character, Ender, was born with the hopes that he would become one of the leading military children. He was taken from his family at six years old to attend battle school in space. Throughout the book, Ender was made into a weapon to fight an alien species, called "the buggers," as the narrative convinced humankind that it was this alien species that attacked humanity. Toward the end of the book, at eleven years old, Ender trains to be the commander of Earth's fleet. Ender faces many significant decisions in the book and has decisions forced upon him. He, unknowingly, destroys an entire civilization when his military superiors told him he was playing a game. The realization that he committed genocide of an entire species overwhelms Ender. Earlier in the book he told his sister: "In the moment when I truly understand my enemy, understand him well enough to defeat him, then in that very moment I also love him. I think it's impossible to really understand somebody, what they want, what they believe, and not love them the way they love themselves."[11] Ender's understanding of the enemy allowed him to defeat them militarily, but his superiors had to trick Ender into killing the aliens because of the way Ender's understanding stems from love.

The conclusion reveals that the aliens had been communicating with Ender throughout the story, without anyone's knowledge. In the end, Ender came to see that the aliens were sentient, just like human beings, and that they were unaware human beings were also sentient. Ender learned that the aliens had no intention of attacking further after this realization took place. It was only when a way of communicating across differences that understanding of intentions could take place. Ender walked into a place the aliens built for him prior to their deaths. Just as Ender understood them, they understood that Ender would come. The aliens understood Ender, too, and they trusted him with their most precious gift. "In the agony of my tortured dreams they came to know me, even as I spent my days destroying them; they found my fear of them, found also that I had no knowledge I was killing them. In the few weeks they had, they built this place for me."[12] Speaking mind to mind, Ender "hears" the queen leader of the aliens say,

We are like you: We did not mean to murder and when we understood, we never came back again. We thought we were the only thinking beings in the universe, until we met you, but never did we dream that thought could arise from the lonely animals who cannot dream each other's dreams. How were we to know? We could live with you in peace. Believe us, believe us, believe us.[13]

Ender takes the cocoon containing the last of the species and is faced with the choice he was forced to make unknowingly before. Ender could choose to kill the species forever or allow them to live, understanding that he must be the one the make peace. The book ends with Ender searching for a place where the cocoon can thrive. He chooses life.

Toward the end of the book, Ender asks the man in charge of the battle school about the aliens. Graff tells him what he knows, which is not much. They do know that the aliens can communicate with each other across space faster than the speed of light. Toward the end of that chapter, "Ender asked Graff one last question. 'Why are we fighting the buggers?'"[14] Graff lists several reasons that people assume the aliens attempted their invasion against humanity, including religion, resources, and violence. Pushed by Ender to respond with his beliefs, Graff speaks of the significance of language, communication, and understanding. Ender replies, "So the whole war is because we can't talk to each other."[15] Graff responds, "If the other fellow can't tell you his story, you can never be sure he isn't trying to kill you."[16] Language, understanding, and story are powerful means of communicating across differences and communicating change.[17] Perhaps dystopia is a way of communicating through language and story so that mutual understanding can lead to better ways of relating.

NOTES

1. Douglas Adams, *The Hitchhiker's Guide to the Galaxy* (New York: Del Ray, 2009).

2. Adams, *The Hitchhiker's Guide to the Galaxy*; Douglas Adams, *So Long and Thanks for All the Fish* (New York: Del Ray, 2009).

3. Douglas Adams, *The Restaurant at the End of the Universe* (New York: Pocket Books, 1982), 102. Future Perfect tense omitted with apologies to Dr. Dan Streetmentioner. (Adams, *The Restaurant at the End of the Universe*, 101).

4. Katie Mack, *The End of Everything (Astrophysically Speaking)* (New York: Scribner, 2020), 12–13.

5. Mack, *The End of Everything*, 12–14.

6. Several examples come to mind, but Mack's epilogue mentions Freeman Dyson's attempt in 1979. Mack, *The End of Everything*, 207–8.

7. Svalbard Global Seed Vault, accessed May 28, 2022, https://www.seedvault.no.

8. Mack, *The End of Everything*, 209.
9. Bulletin of the Atomic Sciences, "Doomsday Clock," accessed May 28, 2022, https://thebulletin.org/doomsday-clock/current-time/.
10. Gregory Claeys, *Dystopia: A Natural History* (Oxford: Oxford University Press, 2017), 501.
11. Orson Scott Card, *Ender's Game* (New York: Tor Books, 1994), 238.
12. Card, *Ender's Game*, 321.
13. Card, *Ender's Game*, 321.
14. Card, *Ender's Game*, 252.
15. Card, *Ender's Game*, 253.
16. Card, *Ender's Game*, 253.
17. Another parallel that bears mention is Ted Chiang's novella "Story of Your Life" and later film adaptation *Arrival*. In the story, linguist Dr. Louise Banks is called upon by the US Government to make first contact with an alien species (who are known as the "heptapods") that has established a presence across the world. Tension arises in the film adaptation when the linguist does not make sufficient enough progress to satisfy the military leaders, who are concerned that the aliens are a threat to global safety. Only by learning and experiencing the language of the alien visitors is Dr. Banks able to defuse other tensions on Earth and, consequently, the heptapods depart the planet peacefully. Ted Chiang, "Story of Your Life," in *Stories of Your Life and Others* (New York: TOR, 2002), 91–146; *Arrival*, directed by Denis Villeneuve (Paramount Pictures, 2016), Blu-ray.

BIBLIOGRAPHY

Adams, Douglas. *The Hitchhiker's Guide to the Galaxy*. New York: Del Ray, 2009.
———. *The Restaurant at the End of the Universe*. New York: Pocket Books, 1982.
———. *So Long and Thanks for All the Fish*. New York: Del Ray, 2009.
Arrival. Directed by Denis Villeneuve. Paramount Pictures, 2016. Blu-ray.
Bulletin of the Atomic Sciences. "Doomsday Clock." Accessed May 28, 2022. https://thebulletin.org/doomsday-clock/current-time/.
Card, Orson Scott. *Ender's Game*. New York: Tor Books, 1994.
Chiang, Ted. "Story of Your Life." In *Stories of Your Life and Others*, 91–146. New York: TOR, 2002.
Claeys, Gregory. *Dystopia: A Natural History*. Oxford: Oxford University Press, 2017.
Mack, Katie. *The End of Everything (Astrophysically Speaking)*. New York: Scribner, 2020.
Svalbard Global Seed Vault. Accessed May 28, 2022. https://www.seedvault.no.

Index

1 Corinthians, 13:11, 66
2 Maccabees, 16, 118, 121
4 Ezra, 17–18, 103
1984, 2, 135, 150, 162, 167, 170, 181
2001: A Space Odyssey, 162

Adorno, Theodor, 164–65
Agamben, Giorgio, 135–36
AI. *See* artificial intelligence
Altered Carbon, 87
Althaus-Reid, Marcella, 67
anthropic exceptionalism, 34
Antiochus IV Epiphanes, 16
apocalypse, 2, 12, 20, 74, 77, 80–82, 101–11, 179, 181; definition of, 15–16, 112n15
apocalyptic, ix, x, xi, xiin1, 1–2, 28, 33, 38, 181; definition of, 15–16, 112n3, 112n15; genre, 12–20, 101–11; post-, 60, 124
apocalypticism, 103, 181; definition of, 15–16, 112n15
Aristotle, 7, 10, 83n9, 147
artificial intelligence (AI), 6, 60–62, 87
Asimov, Isaac, x–xi, 68n4, 101–11, 111n1, 113n23, 113n26, 113n32, 114n45, 180
Asimov's Guide to the Bible, 105
astrophysics, 179–80

Attack of the Clones, 165
Augustine, Saint, viii
Avatar, 59

Beelzebub, 20
Bonilla-Silva, Eduardo, 43, 48–50, 53
Bourdieu, Pierre, 42
Buck Rogers, 163–64
Bultmann, Rudolf, 1, 13–15, 20–21
Burns, Ken, 29
Butler, Judith, 69n26, 168
Butler, Octavia, 9–10, 91

Cain and Abel, x, 51–55, 57n49
capitalism, 20, 37n25, 51, 94, 164, 166–72
Caputo, John, 89–92, 95–96, 97n12
Carnival, 133–34
catharsis, xi, 11–12, 137, 147–51, 154–58, 166–69, 182
change, 8–13, 18–19, 33, 46, 48, 75, 80, 82, 104–8, 147–58, 172, 180, 182, 184
Claeys, Gregory, xiin4, 2–5, 11–12, 30, 36n2, 104, 122, 182
class, 51, 62, 88, 119, 124, 138, 153–54, 158, 170
Collins, John J., 16, 112n12

COVID-19 pandemic, vii, xiin1, 22n34, 113n18, 114n45
Critical Race Theory (CRT), 42–44, 52–53
CRT. *See* Critical Race Theory
cyberpunk, x, 61, 67
cyborg, 59–67, 68n5, 69n26, 69n27, 70n41

Dead Sea Scrolls, 110–11, 127n18
demythologization, ix, 1, 12–20, 21
Descartes, Rene, 62
Deus ex Machina, xi, 147–58
Dick, Philip K., 61, 134–35
Dickens, Charles, 95–96, 135
Divergent, xi, 117, 123–24, 181
Doomsday Clock, 180
Dragomán, György, xi, 148–52, 157–58
Dust Bowl, 29
dystopia: critical, viii, ix, xi, 4–5, 7–8, 12, 20, 47, 51–52, 55, 91, 113n19, 162, 172, 173n9; definition of, viii, xiin4, xiin5, 1–8, 11–13, 15, 19, 29, 33, 35n2, 48, 60–61, 74, 89, 91, 100–105, 122–123, 134–135, 147, 158, 162, 173n9

ecocatastrophe, 30–35
ecotheology, 27–36, 37n20
Ender's Game, 183–84
Enoch, 17, 25nn86–87, 103, 112n8
ER, 88
eschatology, 88, 95, 103–4, 109; apocalyptic, 104, 109; prophetic, 103–4, 109
eucharist, x, 35
eutopia, 3–7, 30, 36n2
Ex Machina, 65, 87

Fahrenheit 451, 11
Feast of Fools, 134
feminist theology, 65–67, 155
Fokkema, Douwe, 4, 6–7, 22n36

Foundation, x–xi, 101–11, 113n23, 113n26, 113n28, 113n30 113n32, 114n35, 114n45, 181
Fromm, Erich, 164

gender, 59–67, 68n5, 69n26, 69n30, 88, 128n25, 170
Genesis, The Book of: 1:26, 77; 1:26–28, 31, 37n20; 2–3, 65; 4:9b, 51; 4:10, 52; 4:15, 54
Ghost in the Shell, x, 59–67, 67n1, 68nn4–5, 181
Gibson, William, 61
GITS. *See Ghost in the Shell*
The Giver, x, 41–55, 56n12
The Good Place, 2–3
Gottlieb, Erika, 11, 12, 15, 83n7, 172
Gutierrez, Gustavo, 51–52

habitus, x, 41–55
Halberstam, Jack, 62, 65–66
The Handmaid's Tale, viii, 135
Hansen, Carter, 43–44, 50
Hanson, Paul, 103–4
Haraway, Donna, 37n25, 60, 62, 65, 67, 68n4, 68n5
Hebrews, xi, 117, 121–22, 123, 124, 127nn16–18
The Hitchhiker's Guide to the Galaxy, 179
Horkheimer, Max, 164, 165, 171
The Hunger Games, viii, xi, 117, 123–26
Hurricane Katrina, vii, xiin1, 22n34, 113n18

I, Robot, 87
imagination, 2, 6, 89–93, 97n19, 133–35, 170,
interactionism, 76–77
Interstellar, ix–x, 27–36
intertextuality, 60, 66–67, 181
Ishikawa, Noboru, 37n25

Jesus, 77, 94, 118, 121–24,
  148, 157, 169
John, 14:1–2, 79
John Paul II (pope), 66
Jubilee, xi, 90, 133–43, 181–82
justice, 12–20, 23n41, 28, 35, 53–55,
  74–77, 102–5, 117, 135

Kearney, Richard, 7–8
Keller, Catherine, 34, 97n12

Lord of the Flies, 11, 19–20
Lowry, Lois, x, 41, 43, 45,
  47, 49, 56n12
Lucas, George, xi, 161–72
Luke, 15:11–32, 77

Malinowski, Bronislaw, 109–10
Malm, Andreas, 37n25
Marcuse, Herbert, 161, 162, 167, 172
The Matrix, 9, 59
Matthew: 20:13–16, 77; 25:31–46, 77
mechanization, 30
Metropolis, 168
mind-body dualism, x, 59, 62–63,
  65, 67n3, 89
minimization, 42–43, 53–54
More, Sir Thomas, 4, 7, 22n21, 104,
Moylan, Tom, 5, 7, 11, 22n27,
  104, 161–62

Nietzsche, Friedrich, 90

Orwell, George, 2, 134–35,
  150, 162, 181

Parable of the Sower, 9
Pittenger, Norman, 34–35
psychohistory, 106–11, 181
The Purge, xi, 133–43, 181–82

queer theory, 62, 65–67

race, 32, 41–43, 48–55, 66,
  67n1, 88, 170

Ready Player One, viii, 135
Ready Player Two, 8
redemption, 92, 102–5
Ricoeur, Paul, x, 7, 23n41, 41–55, 55n5
Rubenstein, Mary-Jane, 92

Sabbatical, xi, 134–43
sacrifice, xi, 16, 48, 128n19, 129n31,
  133–43, 148, 157, 181–82;
  self-sacrifice, 63, 95, 117–26,
  128n25, 128n27
salvation, ix, xi, 12–13, 15, 28, 31–35,
  64, 101–5, 107, 108, 117–26, 156
SCDT. *See* Social Cognitive
  Domain Theory
Seinfeld, 88
Shirow, Masamune, 59–60, 62,
  67n3, 68n17
The Shortest Ice Age, xi, 148–58
sin, 34, 65, 94
Social Cognitive Domain Theory
  (SCDT), 73
Soelle, Dorothee, 150, 153–58
sovereign, xi, 104, 133–43, 182
State of Exception, 135, 143

technology, vii–viii, 5–9 29–32, 60–64,
  67, 93, 108–111, 135, 166–169
Tembo, Kwasu, 62, 64
Térey, János, xi, 148–58
Testament of Moses, xi, 117–24,
  127n15, 127n18
Thatamanil, John, 89
THX 1138, xi, 161–72, 174n46
Tirosh-Samuelson, Hava, 140–41
totalitarianism, 6–7, 45, 150, 157
Tracy, David, 10

Upload, 8
utopia: anti-, 4, 6, 36n2, 172; critical,
  4–5, 91; definition of, 1–6, 30, 74,
  104; failed, 3, 41, 43, 50, 52, 61;
  satire, 4; utopianism, 4

van der Ven, Johannes, x, 73–82

The Walking Dead, x, 73–82, 87–96, 182–83
Weber, Max, 165
The White King, xi, 148–58

wonder, x, 89–92, 93, 95–96

zombie, x, 73–82, 87–96

About the Editors and Contributors

Rev. Scott Donahue-Martens is a Ph.D. candidate in homiletics at Boston University School of Theology. His research explores intersections between homiletics and hermeneutics, especially through the work of Paul Ricoeur. Many of the practical implications of his research address matters of difference regarding identity, especially racialized identities. A preview of this research was published in his article "Beneath the Veneer: Critical Race Theory's Challenge to White Color-Blind Preaching." He has also contributed to the *Theology, Religion, and Pop Culture* series with a chapter titled, *Imaginative Hermeneutical Theology: Paul Ricoeur and Dungeons & Dragons* in *Fantasy, Theology, and the Imagination*.

Brandon Simonson, Ph.D. (Boston University) is an Instructor of Biblical Studies at Boston University School of Theology and Adjunct Lecturer in the Department of Religious and Theological Studies at Merrimack College. Dr. Simonson is an Aramaist and linguist with an interest in onomastics and the history of religion in the Aramaic speaking worlds of Syria, Mesopotamia, and Egypt during the first millennium BCE. He frequently employs popular culture, music, and literature in his undergraduate Religious Studies pedagogy. His work can be found in the Oxford Handbook series, *Names: A Journal of Onomastics*, and other journals in the fields of ancient languages and religions.

* * *

Beáta Gombkötő was born in Hungary. She received a Master's in Theology from The Evangelical-Lutheran Theological University, Budapest, and a Bachelor's in English language and literature, communication (journalism) from Kodolányi János University. She lives in an eternal love triangle between literature and theology. She considers herself a progressive mystical theologian, who is researching and experiencing *Deux ex Machina* in everything and everywhere. As a PhD candidate, she is studying how in contemporary Hungarian literature suffering in itself can be a mode of *Deus ex Machina*.

Rev. Dr. Thomas G. Hermans-Webster is the Assistant Professor of United Methodist Studies at the Pacific School of Religion in Berkeley, California. He teaches and researches in the fields of Christian process and relational theology, ecological theology, ecclesiology, and United Methodist theology. He is currently developing a process theology of the eucharist that advances the work of Norman Pittenger and Theodore Walker, Jr., for planetary well-being.

Justin F. Martin, Ph.D., is currently Assistant Professor of Psychology at Whitworth University. His research explores the development of sociomoral concepts and the ways these concepts are portrayed in superhero and dystopian media. His recent journal publications examine the viewpoint diversity in Wakanda and parent-child co-viewing of superhero media. He also writes for various popular press outlets such as *Modern Treatise*, *PopMatters*, the *Center for Scholars and Storytellers*, *Popular Culture and Theology*, and *Think Christian*.

C.J. McCrary possesses a Masters in Theological Studies from Boston University (2019) and is currently pursuing a Ph.D. in Religion, Literature, and Culture at the University of Virginia. Her research addresses a constellation of issues surrounding the historical role of horror fiction(s) in the Protestant tradition, ranging from the grotesque political cartoons of the Reformation to the anti-Catholic propagandizing of nineteenth-century Gothic fiction. More of her essays regarding the modern horror film, theology, and the religious imagination can be found in Fortress Press and Lexington Books' forthcoming volume *Theology, Religion, and Wes Craven*.

John C. McDowell is Associate Dean at Yarra Theological Union in the University of Divinity, and Professor of Philosophy, Theology, and Ethics. Among his publications are several studies in popular culture: *The Politics of Big Fantasy: Studies in Cultural Suspicion* (Jefferson, NC: McFarland Press, 2014); *The Ideology of Identity Politics in George Lucas* (Jefferson, NC: McFarland Press, 2016); and *The Gospel According to Star Wars: Faith, Hope and the Force*, 2nd ed. (Louisville, KY: Westminster John Knox Press, 1st ed. 2007, 2nd ed. 2017). He has also contributed to a number of volumes in the *Theology, Religion, & Pop Culture* and to other popular culture series.

Dr. David Penn is Assistant Professor of Religious Studies at Rivier University. He is a practical theologian whose research interests include adolescent development, pedagogy in higher education, popular culture, and theopoetics. His work has appeared in *The Journal of Religious Education, The Journal of Youth Ministry,* and *The World Christian Encyclopedia.*

Amanda L. Pumphrey, Ph.D., has a degree in Women's & Gender Studies in Religion from Claremont Graduate University and teaches courses on Transnational Feminisms, Sexual Ethics, and Queering Christianity. Amanda's current scholarship focuses on (re)defining submission within evangelicalism through BDSM and their essay entitled "Confessions of a Pentecostal Queer" appears in the *Bible Belt Queers* anthology.

Nicholaus B. Pumphrey, Ph.D., is the Associate Professor of Religious Studies and Curator of the Quayle Bible Collection at Baker University. Pumphrey has published several works on pop culture and religion, including three articles on Muslims in Marvel Comics. He has also written articles on the intersection of comic books and the Bible including a book titled *Superman and the Bible: How the Idea of Superheroes Affects the Reading of Scripture.*

Shayna Sheinfeld is Assistant Professor of Religion at Augsburg University. Her research focuses on ancient Jewish and Christian scriptures and their afterlives. Along with numerous articles, Sheinfeld is the author of *Jewish and Christian Women in the Ancient Mediterranean* (with Sara Parks and Meredith JC Warren), editor of *Gender and Second-Temple Judaism* (with Kathy Ehrensperger), and editor of *Theology and Westworld* (with Juli L. Gittinger).

www.ingramcontent.com/pod-product-compliance
Lightning Source LLC
Chambersburg PA
CBHW021815020526
44115CB00042B/913